THE
IRISH COMIC
TRADITION

THE
IRISH COMIC
TRADITION

BY

VIVIAN MERCIER

OXFORD UNIVERSITY PRESS

LONDON   OXFORD   NEW YORK

OXFORD UNIVERSITY PRESS

Oxford London New York
Glasgow Toronto Melbourne Wellington
Cape Town Salisbury Ibadan Nairobi Lusaka Addis Ababa
Bombay Calcutta Madras Karachi Lahore Dacca
Kuala Lumpur Hong Kong Tokyo

TO
GINA

PREFACE

THIS book makes no claim to be the last word on its subject; it is much closer to being the first one. So far as I know, mine is the first sustained attempt to show that an unbroken comic tradition may be traced in Irish literature from approximately the ninth century down to the present day.

The prevalence of the comic spirit in Anglo-Irish literature of the twentieth century needs no demonstration. One has only to start listing the names of writers—Joyce, Synge, O'Casey, George Moore, James Stephens, Lady Gregory, Frank O'Connor—and at once the point is made. Even W. B. Yeats or Samuel Beckett has his own special vein of defiant or despairing humour.

During the nineteenth century Irish wit and humour were already proverbial in the English-speaking countries. Indeed, it has often been remarked that most of the masters of English stage comedy since the Restoration—Congreve, Farquhar, Goldsmith, Sheridan, Wilde, Shaw—either grew up in Ireland or came of Irish stock.

All sorts of theories have been advanced to explain these indisputable facts. Shaw actually gave the credit to the Irish climate, as if wit or a sense of humour were a disease like rheumatism or tuberculosis, both of which are often blamed on the prevailing dampness in Ireland. It seems more reasonable, however, to attribute cultural phenomena in the first place to cultural causes. If it can be demonstrated that Gaelic literature has from the earliest times shown a bent for wild humour, a delight in witty word play, and a tendency to regard satire as one of the indispensable functions of the literary man, then the prevalence of these traits in Anglo-Irish literature is most probably due to cultural continuity.

Gaelic literature is notorious for its conservatism: the use of archaic diction and orthography, of archaic allusions, of an archaic subject matter recurs throughout its long history—no doubt primarily because for many centuries most of the literature was produced by a professional caste or class of poets, inheritors of the druids and most familiar to English-speaking readers under the name of 'bards'. As a result, it is easy to trace a continuous comic tradition in Gaelic. The chief problem which confronted me in writing this book was how to prove the existence of a continuity between Anglo-Irish literature and Gaelic literature. I do not wish to exaggerate this problem, however: cultural interchange at the oral level, in idioms, metaphors, proverbs, folk tales, folk beliefs, has been continuous from the first English invasion down to the present moment.

Direct *literary* influence before the Anglo-Irish Literary Revival, which began in the 1880's, is harder—and often impossible—to prove, for two reasons: first, few earlier writers of English could read Gaelic; secondly, most Gaelic speakers were illiterate in their own language. But when we notice striking similarities between literary works in the two languages, where direct influence was clearly impossible, the resemblance can often be explained by the fact that both works were drawing upon a common stock of themes and attitudes, and even, at times, of techniques: Gaelic metres were sometimes employed in English by bilingual song writers and then borrowed by those who knew no Gaelic.

Although a glance at the Table of Contents should reveal much of the plan and scope of this book, perhaps the chapter headings require some explanation and amplification. I have divided a vast subject into a few basic rhetorical categories: humour, wit (including word play), satire, and parody. These categories are neither numerous enough to include every aspect of the comic nor, in certain respects, mutually exclusive. Satire in particular employs wit, humour, parody, and even word play besides the irony which is often regarded as its most characteristic device. On the other hand, I have given no separate treatment to the best known and most easily identifiable branch of the comic, stage comedy. Gaelic civilization never developed a theatre, although some of the mumming and miming at weddings and wakes contained the rudiments of drama. Since my subject is the continuity of Gaelic and Anglo-Irish tradition, it seemed pointless to increase the size of this book by a chapter which dealt with Anglo-Irish stage comedy in isolation. As a matter of fact, I wrote such a chapter and then omitted it at the suggestion of my wife.

Obviously an entire book could be devoted to Irish humour alone. My two chapters on this subject deal with what I regard as its most characteristic aspects: fantasy, the macabre, and the grotesque. The so-called 'rollicking' type of Irish humour—emphasizing drunkenness, pugnacity, clumsy amorousness, superstition, boasting, hyperbole, malapropisms, and Irish bulls—I have chosen to ignore, for two good reasons. On the one hand, it is already excessively familiar to most people; on the other, it is largely an Anglo-Irish phenomenon, resulting from the observation of Gaelic folk ways through the lenses of a different culture. A similar type of humour can be found in Gaelic, but it is a relatively late development that originates in social satire: the behaviour of uncultured Gaelic speakers is viewed contemptuously by an educated class after the unity of Gaelic civilization disintegrated in the seventeenth century. (See the section 'Social Satire' in Chapter 6.)

The inclusion of three separate chapters on satire is a matter of mere expediency. Satire proliferates so enormously in Gaelic literature that a single chapter on the subject would have taken up almost half the book. Even now, the chapter 'Satire in Modern Irish' is by far the longest. I hope the reader will agree with me that it would have been a pity to shorten it further.

As regards method, it will be seen that this book is descriptive rather than critical or historical. I am less concerned with evaluating Irish comic literature than with establishing its outlook, characteristic methods, and favourite subject matter. Nor have I attempted a complete literary history of the subject. The recurrence of an identical comic pattern in widely separated periods might be too readily overlooked if I followed a purely chronological plan. The progress of each chapter is roughly chronological, but where a certain vein of wit, say, has remained virtually unchanged through the centuries, I follow it to the end before turning back to another type which emerged later. In general, I have given more space to the Gaelic material, as being less familiar to the English-speaking reader, than I have to the Anglo-Irish.

Where a comic trend in Gaelic literature seemed unparalleled in Anglo-Irish literature, or vice versa, I have sometimes omitted it altogether; the reader should therefore be wary of assuming a greater homogeneity between the two literatures than actually exists. Still, I have tried not to act the special pleader too much: although I have omitted a number of writers and works that I consider insignificant, I might well have omitted more and included fewer quotations had I not wanted to give the reader sufficient evidence on which to base his own conclusions. The whole subject of the relationship between Gaelic and Anglo-Irish literature has been bedeviled by so many intemperate generalizations on both sides of the argument that I was determined not to force my own views upon the reader.

One further self-imposed limitation will become evident in the course of this book: except in my last chapter, I have virtually ignored many of the Anglo-Irish writers who neither lived most of their lives in Ireland nor continued to write much about Ireland after they had left her. Thus I have a great deal to say about Swift and Joyce, but very little about Shaw and Wilde, though I have made an exception in favour of Samuel Beckett. Also, in the absence of a chapter on stage comedy, I have said less than I should have liked to about Synge and O'Casey. Both studied Gaelic, and the work of both shows a general affinity with the Gaelic tradition, but their very originality has made it difficult to link them with any one specific branch of that highly conservative heritage. In any case, I think it is fair to say that a framework has been established into which the alert reader can fit those writers who, he feels, have been unjustly neglected: for instance, Brendan Behan, whose meteoric career began when this book was already well under way.

Some of the limitations imposed on this book can hardly be described as voluntary: I am not a Gaelic scholar but rather a student of Gaelic, and my reading knowledge of Modern Irish has been acquired in the most desultory fashion. After I first began to think about this book eight years ago—and indeed after one chapter had been written—I spent a year studying Old and Middle Irish at Trinity and University Colleges in Dublin. In dealing with the Gaelic material, I have made use wherever possible of translations by reputable scholars, sometimes consulting the Gaelic only where a difficulty or omission was apparent in the translation. If no translation of an important text was available, I grappled with the original; as one might expect, texts which have never been translated are either very easy or fiendishly difficult. I have made no use of manuscript or oral sources.

Clearly my task would have been far easier if a comprehensive account of the Gaelic comic tradition were already in existence, but even the available histories of Gaelic literature give the subject sketchy, almost grudging treatment. Fred Norris Robinson's 'Satirists and Enchanters in Early Irish Literature' is the only adequate handling known to me of any substantial part of the tradition. In his vast *Motif-Index of Early Irish Literature* Tom Peete Cross allots little more than half a page to humour and refers to one short article on the topic. I was therefore compelled to attempt almost single-handed a synoptic view of a subject matter ranging over eleven centuries and two languages: that is, if we agree to call Old, Middle, and Modern Irish—which differ at least as much as Old, Middle, and Modern English—one language. Let me add humbly that I could never have made the attempt at all but for the work which countless scholars and literary men have been doing piecemeal for over a century. Detailed acknowledgements of my debts will be found in the notes to the individual chapters. I can only hope that those who investigate this fascinating subject in the future will find much in my pages to agree with while profiting by my mistakes.

V.M.

Great Neck, New York
17 March 1961

PREFACE TO
THE PAPERBACK EDITION

The present paperback edition is almost identical with the original hardbound one. A few printer's errors have been corrected, as well as a few errors of fact on the part of the author. Some important works in related fields that were overlooked in the first edition or have been published since 1962 are listed below. The reader should also note that Austin Clarke, now in his seventies, continues to publish satirical poems, while more books by the late Brian O'Nolan ('Flann O'Brien') are now in print on both sides of the Atlantic than at any time before his death in 1966.

Two important books on the grotesque—translated respectively from the Russian and the German—are Mikhail Bakhtin's *Rabelais and His World* (Cambridge, Mass., 1968) and Wolfgang Kayser's *The Grotesque in Art and Literature* (Bloomington, Ind., 1963). Seán Ó Súilleabháin has translated his *Caitheamh Aimsire ar Thórraimh* as *Irish Wake Amusements* (Cork, 1967). 'Mac Lavy's Advice' was edited in full, with a translation, by Seosamh Ó Dufaigh in the *Clogher Record* for 1965 and reprinted, with corrections, as a pamphlet for Cumann Seanchais Chlochair under the title *Comhairle Mhic Clamha ó Achadh na Muilleann* (n.p., 1966). Seán Ó Tuama's *An Grá in Amhráin na nDaoine* (Dublin, 1960) illustrates and sometimes corrects what is said about Gaelic love poetry and satires on marriage on Chapters 4 and 6.

I should perhaps have explained in the preface to the original edition my reasons for not including a bibliography. In the first place, I wanted to keep the price of this book as low as possible. In the second place, a complete bibliography would necessarily have been a monstrosity, jumbling together the weighty and the lighter-than-air, scholarly editions and the most ephemeral of squibs. The device of using bold-face numerals in the carefully compiled index to draw attention to the bibliographical footnotes should smooth the path of even the laziest scholar.

V.M.

Boulder, Colorado
23 February 1969

CONTENTS

ACKNOWLEDGEMENTS

A BOOK that has been so long in the making necessarily owes a debt to many persons and institutions. I was planning a more general book on the comic when Stanley Kunitz suggested that I concentrate on the Irish tradition. Blessings on him. A sabbatical leave from the City College of New York and a fellowship from the (Ford) Fund for the Advancement of Education made possible my year of study in Dublin. My teachers there were Father Francis Shaw, S.J., and the late Gerard Murphy, both of University College, and Gordon Quin and David Greene of Trinity College; the last-named devoted many hours of his spare time to giving me a priceless initiation into Early Irish literature. In New York I studied Early Irish with Mrs. Alexander Kerns and Charles Dunn. These six people taught me all I know of the older language and would have taught me more if I had had the time or the capacity. A grant-in-aid from the American Council of Learned Societies freed me from summer teaching at a crucial period of the book's progress. I am grateful too for research funds granted by the Research Committee of the City College of New York and the Department of English at the University of California, Berkeley.

My warm thanks go also to John H. Raleigh and Mark Schorer for criticism which helped me to prune and unify the manuscript; to Stanley Edgar Hyman and Arthur Waldhorn for nourishing my interest in anthropology and related fields of study; to Whitney Blake, Elizabeth Cameron, Padraic Colum, Dan Davin, Robert C. Dickson, Richard Ellmann, David H. Greene, Arthur Hutson, Edgar Johnson, Hugh Kenner, David McDowell, Máire MacEntee, Conor Cruise O'Brien, Thomas Parkinson, and Henry Nash Smith for helpful suggestions or general encouragement; to Patrick Henchy of the National Library of Ireland for his prompt response to my requests for information or photostats; to Micheál Ó hAodha of Radio Éireann for drawing my attention to Padraic Fallon's dramatization of *The Vision of Mac Conglinne*; to Anita (Mrs. Henry) Lynn and Janet Mathiesen for their skilled typing; to the technical staff of the Clarendon Press for their patience and skill; and to the anonymous scholar who read my typescript at the request of the Press for helping me to avoid several pitfalls. I owe especial gratitude to Tomás de Bhaldraithe of University College, Dublin, for his careful reading of the proofs.

Not having found an opportunity to acknowledge it elsewhere, I should like to record my general indebtedness to an unpublished lecture by Daniel A. Binchy, 'Some Mediaeval Irish Precursors of *Finnegans Wake*'. Howard Meroney's published studies in Early Irish satire and David Greene's unpublished translations, though given credit at the appropriate points, also demand special acknowledgement here.

Portions of this book have appeared in somewhat different form in *Studies*, *The Kenyon Review*, and *English Institute Essays 1955*. My thanks for permission to reprint this material are due to Father Roland Burke Savage, S.J., Editor of *Studies*; to Kenyon College and Robie Macauley, Editor of *The Kenyon Review*; and to the English Institute and the Columbia University Press.

Grateful acknowledgements of permission to reprint copyright material are also rendered to the following organizations and individuals in Great Britain and Ireland: Irish Texts Society for extracts from *The Bardic Poems of Tadhg Dall Ó Huiginn*, edited and translated by Eleanor Knott; Kenneth Hurlstone Jackson for extracts from *A Celtic Miscellany: Translations from the Celtic Literatures*; Francis MacManus for extracts from his translation of *The Parliament of Clan Thomas*, originally published in *The Bell*; Macmillan & Co., Ltd., and Frank O'Connor for extracts from the latter's *Kings, Lords and Commons*; the Editor of *Studies* for the translation by the late Osborn Bergin reprinted in full on p. 143 of this book; Mr. M. B. Yeats and Macmillan & Co., Ltd., per A. P. Watt & Son, for extracts from three poems and a play by the late W. B. Yeats.

In the United States of America grateful acknowledgements of permission to reprint are rendered to the following: Grove Press, Inc., for extracts from *Watt* by Samuel Beckett and from *Malone Dies* by Samuel Beckett, translated from the French by the author, copyright 1956 by Grove Press; Harvard University Press for extracts from *A Celtic Miscellany* by Kenneth Hurlstone Jackson, copyright 1951 by Kenneth Hurlstone Jackson;

Alfred A. Knopf, Inc., for extracts from *Kings, Lords and Commons* by Frank O'Connor, copyright 1959 by Frank O'Connor; The Macmillan Company for extracts from *Collected Poems* by W. B. Yeats, copyright 1903, 1933 by The Macmillan Company, copyright 1931 by W. B. Yeats, copyright 1940, 1961 by Bertha Georgie Yeats; The Macmillan Company for extracts from *Collected Plays* by W. B. Yeats, copyright 1934, 1952 by The Macmillan Company; Carey McWilliams, Editor of *The Nation*, for extracts from an article by Frank O'Connor; Random House, Inc., for extracts from *The Collected Works of John M. Synge*, copyright 1935 by The Modern Library, Inc.; Random House, Inc., for extracts from *Ulysses* by James Joyce, copyright 1934 and renewed 1961 by Lucia Joyce and George Joyce; The Viking Press, Inc., for numerous brief extracts from *Finnegans Wake* by James Joyce, copyright 1939 by James Joyce.

A NOTE ON TERMINOLOGY,
BOOK TITLES, AND PROPER NAMES

THE noun 'Gaelic' is used throughout this book to refer to the Irish language, whether Old, Middle, or Modern. The adjective 'Gaelic' is applied to anything spoken or written in that language or forming part of the culture of habitual speakers of Gaelic. I employ this rather suspect word— which has, however, good standing in American usage—to avoid the ambiguity of such expressions as 'Irish literature', 'Irish culture', hoping that the Gaels of Scotland will forgive me for ignoring the equal ambiguity inherent in the use of 'Gaelic'. When referring to the writings of Irishmen in the English language, I employ the phrase 'Anglo-Irish literature'. 'Irish literature' therefore refers to literature by Irishmen in *both* Gaelic and English.

Scholars find it hard to agree on the respective initial dates of Old, Middle, and Modern Irish, for the very good reason that the written language changed much more slowly than the spoken; most people are aware of such a tendency even in Modern English, but it was much stronger among the highly conservative Gaelic scribes. The late Gerard Murphy, in his *Early Irish Lyrics* (Oxford, 1956), dates Old Irish from *c.* 650 to *c.* 900, Middle Irish from *c.* 900 to *c.* 1200, and Modern Irish from *c.* 1200 onwards. This represents a somewhat extreme view. While some scholars would date the beginning of Old Irish as early as *c.* 600, the beginning of Middle Irish is sometimes dated *c.* 950, and that of Modern Irish often *c.* 1300 or even later. The description hereinafter of a work as being in Modern rather than Middle Irish or vice versa should be regarded as a statement about its linguistic garb rather than its date. Old and Middle Irish, by the way, are known collectively as Early Irish.

When a Gaelic work is mentioned for the first time, I give its best-known Gaelic title in italics, followed in parentheses by an English translation of that title. Thereafter I generally refer to the work by its English title except when the Gaelic title is much the neater. If the work has been published separately or is long enough to be so published, its English title is italicized; otherwise the English title is given in quotation marks.

When a Gaelic author is mentioned for the first time, his name is given its commonest Gaelic spelling, followed in parentheses by its usual Anglo-Irish form (if any), which is employed thereafter as a compassionate gesture to those unfamiliar with Gaelic pronunciation. I say 'Anglo-Irish form' rather than 'English form', meaning that the name of Eoghan Ruadh Ó Súilleabháin is anglicized as Owen Roe O'Sullivan rather than Redhaired Owen O'Sullivan. Where a name is clearly of Norman-French rather than Gaelic origin, I have sometimes omitted the Gaelic version altogether. The common Gaelic first name 'Tadhg' is sometimes anglicized as 'Teigue' and sometimes left alone, since Anglo-Irish usage is quite inconsistent on the point. Whatever the spelling, please pronounce the name as the English word 'thigh' followed by a hard 'g'.

I

The Archaism of Gaelic Comic Literature

IN my preface I have indicated that the plan of this book has a rhetorical basis: the chapters which follow are arranged primarily in terms of the increasing complexity or sophistication of the techniques employed by the various branches of comic literature. Humour, though it sometimes achieves considerable subtlety, is intellectually the simplest form of the comic. It springs from the absurd, that which is laughable because it is untrue or irrational or, at the very least, exaggerated. Of the types of humour dealt with in this book, the fantastic demonstrates the truth of this assertion most easily, but macabre and grotesque humour can be shown to have a similar origin. It is true that life is cruel and ugly, but the macabre and grotesque do not become humorous until they have portrayed life as even more cruel and ugly than it is; we laugh at their absurd exaggeration, simultaneously expressing our relief that life is, after all, not *quite* so unpleasant as it might be.

Wit has traditionally been regarded as intellectually superior to, and also more complex than, humour; in fact 'wit' and 'intellect' were once synonymous in English, while *esprit* still retains both these meanings in French. In spite of the irrational element of word play, particularly common in Irish wit, a witty remark is both absurd and true: in other words, paradox, I believe, lies at the bottom of all wit; it is paradoxical truth which distinguishes a witty remark from the mere absurdity of a humorous one. For instance, when a Wilde character defines a cynic as 'a man who knows the price of everything and the value of nothing', the words 'price' and 'value' are so nearly identical in meaning that the remark seems self-contradictory at first sight; only when we discriminate between the two apparent synonyms do we see its truth. A witty pun normally seems even more absurd: the definition of an Irish bull as 'a male animal which is always pregnant' lacks wit until one realizes that the word 'pregnant' is being used in a metaphorical rather than a literal sense; not all Irish bulls are in fact pregnant, but enough of them are, including the remark itself, to make it an acceptable half-truth.

Satire represents a further stage of complexity, both quantitatively and qualitatively, for, besides employing a great variety of other comic devices—wit and humour among them—it usually depends in some degree upon the fundamental satiric device, irony. I expect most of my readers will agree that irony, in the basic sense of saying one thing and meaning the exact opposite, demands a more complex intellectual response than wit does: wit confronts us with a patent absurdity and asks that we make sense of it, whereas really subtle irony may be mistaken for the literal truth. Sustained irony, such as that in Swift's *A Modest Proposal*, will be taken literally unless the reader accepts certain norms of behaviour and realizes that the ironist shares them. The careful reader of *A Modest Proposal* feels that nobody in his right mind could discuss cannibalism so cold-bloodedly; therefore Swift must be joking. Even the most direct denunciations of ugliness, filth, stinginess, and the like, which are very common in Irish satire, depend for their effect upon the reader's conceiving of beauty, cleanliness, generosity, and so on as norms. Three elements, then, are necessary for a satisfactory response to irony: the reader's possession of norms, his ability to compare ironic statements with these norms, and his realization, based on certain hints let fall by the ironist, that the latter shares his norms.

Parody makes even greater demands on the reader: first of all, he must recognize the work or the genre parodied; then he must see the absurdity of the parody by comparison with the original; finally, this absurdity must be reflected back from the parody on to the original, so that he can see in the latter the inherent tendency to absurdity which made the parody feasible to begin with.

It is, then, possible to justify the arrangement of chapters in this book on rhetorical grounds alone. But that is far from being the whole story. Because Gaelic literature and Gaelic society retained archaic traits until a late period, and because, also, this archaic society borrowed the Roman alphabet relatively early, it is possible in Gaelic literature to trace these various comic devices back closer to their origins than one can in almost any other literature except the ancient Greek.

Viewed in this light, the order of our chapters takes on a new significance. It may be fallacious to assume that in literature, as in biology, more complex organisms are evolved later than the simpler ones, but an examination of the sources of the Irish comic tradition does seem to confirm this assumption. For instance, the types of humour examined in the two chapters immediately following this one originate in non-verbal magic and in myth. Next, word play originates in verbal magic and becomes wit as the magical elements gradually wither away. Satire develops out of injurious spells as the druidic wizard evolves into a poet or bard. Parody finally appears as the poets cast off their earlier magic pretensions entirely and become skilled verbal craftsmen, fully aware that literary effects are attributable to technique rather than to occult powers, and aware, too, that technique can be imitated and ridiculed.

Parody and the more subtle types of satire demonstrably appear at a later date than humour, word play, wit, and the cruder forms of satire. All these simpler forms of the comic occur simultaneously in texts traceable to originals of approximately the ninth century, but this fact does not prove that they evolved simultaneously—only that they first appeared in written form about that time. My suggestion of an evolutionary sequence is based upon the relative archaism of the *sources* which apparently underlie these early manifestations of the comic. To make my argument clearer, I shall now examine these sources in more detail, chapter by chapter.

After considerable inner debate, I decided that the chapter on fantastic humour should precede that on macabre and grotesque humour, in the belief that non-verbal magic is more primitive than myth. It is true that I could not have written the fantasy chapter without introducing the notions of gods and mythology, but the divine and semi-divine figures which appear there are always viewed in the context of their magical powers. A. G. van Hamel has suggested the term 'divine magicians' as a more suitable description than 'gods' for many of the figures in Celtic mythology,[1] and it is as magicians that Manannán

---

[1] A. G. van Hamel, *Aspects of Celtic Mythology*, reprinted from the *Proceedings of the British Academy*, xx (London, 1934), 7.

and Óengus (Angus) appear in the humorous tales of the Irish Mythological Cycle. Similarly, the humorous *bruidhean* tales of the Finn Cycle depend for their basic situations upon the magic powers of a series of more-or-less anonymous enchanters. To believe that a king may be changed into a goat or a hero glued immobile on a bench in a magic dwelling does not require the prior development of a concept of divinity. On the contrary, the notion that certain human beings possess a *mana* which enables them to impose their will on others in this way possibly gave rise to the deification of wielders of this occult power. It may be objected that the two stories about Cuchulain which I have included as examples of fantastic humour do not involve magic but rather the hero's possession of abnormal strength and fierceness; one does not have to read very widely in the Ulster Cycle, however, to realize that Cuchulain is at least in part a magician, by virtue of his magic weapon, the *gae Bulga*, and his strange power of distortion, which comes upon him before his more superhuman feats; his strength is also contingent on the observance of a number of taboos. Cuchulain's feat at Bricriu's feast and his boyhood encounter with the vats of water seem to me similar manifestations of his magic powers. The humorous tales of giants and leprechauns bring us to more debatable ground: I have yet to hear of a leprechaun without magic powers, but giants often seem to possess no superhuman qualities except their size and strength—a truly colossal exception. Perhaps this size and strength are but outward signs of *mana*. This much we can say: neither leprechauns nor giants are gods, and the wonders they accomplish are no greater than those credited to human beings with magical gifts; indeed, giants are frequently worsted by the superior magic of human beings. At any rate, Irish fantastic humour, though overlaid with accretions of myth, legend, and folklore, can be shown to depend ultimately upon magic, which is older than these, as action is older than speech.

Macabre and grotesque humour, as I define them, elude the category of magic; the latter deals with forces which man believes he can control, but the macabre and grotesque are concerned with forces which in the long run are uncontrollable: reproduction and death. Here we pass into the realm of myth: the 'Sheela-na-gig', with her ferocious mouth, skeleton ribs, and grotesquely exaggerated sex organ, is essentially a goddess of creation-and-destruction, known by many different names in Celtic mythology. Her effigy has miraculously survived in scores of places in Ireland, whereas her male counterpart, a phallic god with similar powers and also known by many names, seems to be represented only by 'standing stones'. The myths of both have found their way into print only in fragmentary or disguised form, but their rituals, presumably older than the myths, survived in the Irish wake games or mimes until very recently.; similar miming at weddings appears to have died out considerably earlier. Again the question of precedence between the two chapters on humour is placed in doubt, since mimed ritual, like non-verbal magic, can antedate speech. However, short of printing both chapters on facing pages, there is no way of escaping this dilemma. The point to hold fast to is this: the origins of humour are pre-verbal, whereas wit, satire, and—*a fortiori*—parody depend on words for their very existence. To speak of 'mimed satire' or 'mimed parody' would involve too great an abuse of linguistic tradition: the word 'mimicry' comprehends both these ideas, whereas 'parody' from Greek times and 'satire' from Roman times have always been employed in a verbal context. Similarly '*áer*', the oldest Irish word for 'satire', seems always to have reference to a verbal activity.

The notion that wit, so closely related to intellect, should ultimately derive from the irrationality of verbal magic is one that the reader may find particularly hard to accept. However, the irrational element in wit, together with the similar techniques at work in the creation of both wit and dreams, was long ago discussed by Freud in *Wit and Its Relation to the Unconscious*, a book indispensable to the full understanding of *Finnegans Wake*. No wide gap separates the two forms of irrationality; indeed, analogies between magic and dreams are fairly commonplace in the writings of both anthropologists and psychoanalysts. Ideally, I ought to establish that wit was derived from word play, which in turn was derived from magic spells. In my chapter on the subject, although I have not settled the question of priority, I have at least shown that wit and word play—in the sense of play *on* words—can be separated from one another only with the greatest difficulty; in the Irish tradition of wit they have, in fact, defied separation.

Now, although it is hard to find satisfactory examples of
the process, it seems likely that plays on words were given
magical significance before they were thought of as comic: a
similarity in the names of two objects would suggest other
analogies between them; using certain rituals in connexion
with one object might then be supposed to influence the other.
Esoteric lore is often preserved by primitive societies in the
form of riddles, but the most instructive Gaelic example that
I have found happens to be Christian, and thus far from
primitive:

> What son eats the body of his father in the womb of his mother?
> —The body of the Lord which the priest eats in the Holy Church.

Here is a witty paradox, in part dependent on word play
('Mother Church') for its truth, but ultimately dependent on
something greater, the miracle which turns bread into the body
of the Lord. In a pagan context one would use the word 'magic'
in place of 'miracle' and thus recognize the fusion of wit, word
play, and magic in one sacred jest.

Furthermore, word play in its other sense—play *with* words
rather than *on* words—is an important element in the Old
Irish spells and incantations given by Whitley Stokes and John
Strachan in *Thesaurus Palaeohibernicus*, ii (Cambridge, 1903),
248-50. Indeed, word play is so prevalent in all verbal magic
that it is summed up in the popular expression 'hocus-pocus',
which reproduces neatly the kind of jingle common in spells
and in the modern nursery rhymes apparently derived from
them. It is not necessary to know Old Irish in order to recognize
the alliterations, jingles, and repetitions in a largely untrans-
latable passage like the following from an incantation against
a thorn (Stokes and Strachan, p. 248): *díuscart dím andelg delg
díuscoilt crú ceiti méim méinni bé ái béim nand dodath scenn toscen
todaig rogarg fiss goibnen aird goibnenn renaird goibnenn ceingeth ass.*
Similar characteristics are to be found in the spells for a thorn
and for disease of urine on page 250 of the same work. I am
convinced that the evolutionary sequence from word magic to
word play to wit holds good in all languages; it is merely a
little easier to follow in Gaelic because of that Irish conservatism
and archaism which I have already been at pains to stress.
Irish wit, in English as well as Gaelic, has never broken its ties

with word play: as Joyce so vividly exemplifies, the favourite form of witticism in Ireland is still the pun.

About the origin of Gaelic satire in verbal magic there can be no doubt at all: it is a well-attested fact that a superstitious fear of the power of satire, which was believed capable of causing physical injury or even death, persisted in Ireland down to at least the beginning of the nineteenth century and may not be entirely extinct today. Fred Norris Robinson, in 'Satirists and Enchanters in Early Irish Literature', has dealt with the matter of origins so thoroughly and so convincingly that he has left little for anyone else to say. In spite of my belief that they have very similar origins, I have placed satire later than wit because of what one may call its institutional nature. Satire, unlike wit or humour, is an official function of the trained poet, though one which he soon begins to exercise for his own power and prestige rather than for those of his patrons or his tribe. There is evidence in the sagas of its having been used as a weapon of war to hamper the enemy's strength by its magical operation; however, the earliest examples which survive suggest that satire was in fact chiefly used to punish niggardly patrons and other enemies of the individual poets. Satire was also institutional in the sense that regulations for its proper use and punishments for its improper use occur frequently in the Early Irish laws. Early Irish satire as we know it, then, is associated with a fairly complex society.

On the other hand, because it forms an old-established, integral part of the professional poets' activities, Gaelic satire, both early and late, retains the stamp of its origins. For one thing, it abounds in word play: the quantity of synonyms and nonce-words which it employs makes it the despair of editors and translators; I also get the impression that alliteration is an ornament particularly prized in satiric verse. Verbal virtuosity, always greatly cultivated in Gaelic prose and verse, reaches its peak in satire. Furthermore, as I shall often have occasion to note, lampoon is by far the commonest type of Gaelic satire; just as the old spells were naturally directed against individuals or specific groups, the newer satires name names and attack individuals rather than universal vices or follies. The fact that poetry was a profession and an institution helped to preserve the archaic quality of Gaelic satire; at the same time, the layman's fear of satire must have helped poetic institutions to survive so long with undiminished prestige. Satire ensured for the poet the same respect that his supposed occult power had obtained for the druid.

The institutionalizing of poetry, which required a trained poet to have had from seven to twelve years of schooling, favoured the development of parody by its preoccupation with technique. I know of no comparable example of parody in Western European vernacular literature which antedates *Aislinge Meic Conglinne* (*The Vision of Mac Conglinne*), written not later than 1200. Men parody first works that they have studied in school; hence Latin parodies occur earlier than vernacular ones in Western Europe generally. The Irish, however, had employed the written vernacular for scholarly purposes since at least the eighth century; hence vernacular parody might conceivably have appeared much sooner even than it did in Ireland. The two outstanding early works of parody in Gaelic ridicule the two major learned traditions of Gaelic Ireland: the clerical and the bardic. In Robin Flower's words, *The Vision of Mac Conglinne* 'is one long parody of the literary methods used by the clerical scholars. At every turn we recognize a motive or a phrase from the theological, the historical, and the grammatical literature.' Its later counterpart, *Imtheacht na Tromdháimhe* (*The Proceedings of the Burdensome Bardic Company*), is, to employ Flower's words again, 'one long riotous attack on the poets and their ways'. If the two great institutions of the Church and professional poetry had not cultivated vernacular learning, these two great works of parody could not possibly have been written. This is not to say that the two parodies do not exploit myth, magic, and folklore; on the contrary, they exploit them with tremendous gusto, but at second hand, by ridiculing literature which is based on such archaic sources.

Here we meet one of the two factors which make Gaelic archaism crucial to the Gaelic comic genius: namely, the ambivalence with which the Gaelic writer views his archaic heritage; like Homer or Aristophanes, he seems to believe in myth and magic with one half of his being, while with the other half he delights in their absurdity. We shall see in the next chapter how the same basic *bruidhean* material may become a fierce and noble hero-tale or an uproarious burlesque; similarly, an edifying saint's legend may become an anti-clerical satire through quite small alterations and amplifications.

The other factor is simply this: his archaism keeps the Gaelic writer in touch with the play-spirit of a more primitive society. As a matter of fact, the play-spirit may also underlie the ambivalence which I have just been discussing. Johan Huizinga maintains that primitive man is not nearly so implicit a believer in his own rituals as civilized man tends to think him. Summing up an anthropologist's account of the 'unstable nature of religious feeling among the Loango negroes', Huizinga writes, 'Their belief in the sanctities is a sort of half-belief, and goes with scoffing and pretended indifference.'[1] It would be hard to frame a sentence which more accurately defines the ambivalence toward myth and magic—and sometimes toward Christian rites and accounts of miracles—shown by comic literature in Gaelic.

What I have said above concerning the primitive sources of Gaelic comic writing is much more fully documented in the pages which follow, especially Chapters 2, 3, 4, and 5. The reader who is sceptical now may come round to my point of view as he reads on. For me, at any rate, the vitality and gaiety of Irish comic literature are inseparable from its archaism. I do not say this in any myth-mongering spirit nor claim that literary archaism puts the reader in touch with occult forces. On the other hand, I do agree with Huizinga that, after a certain stage of civilization has been reached, the play-spirit begins to atrophy. Far from regarding wit and humour as the flower of a highly complex civilization, I have found them much more prevalent and more highly valued where life is relatively simple.

Though I have spoken only of Gaelic literature in this chapter, this book of course deals with Anglo-Irish literature also; my conclusions about Anglo-Irish comic writing will be found in the final chapter. This much I would say now on the subject: the continuity of Anglo-Irish and Gaelic culture can be more easily proved in this area than in almost any other; even before the deliberate and self-conscious archaizing of the Irish Literary Revival began, Anglo-Irish literature had

[1] Johan Huizinga, *Homo Ludens: A Study of the Play-Element in Culture* (Boston, 1955), p. 23.

absorbed much of the archaic outlook of Gaelic literature, and it is precisely because of this archaism that many of Anglo-Irish literature's finest achievements lie in the realm of the comic. Its contact with the play-spirit of an archaic civilization has enabled it to play with words, with ideas, with taboos, in a mood of abandon which has won the fascinated if somewhat apprehensive admiration of most of the literate world.

2

Fantasy in Irish Humour and Ribaldry

Introductory

RATHER than write a long, amorphous chapter on Irish humour in general, I have decided to focus on two aspects of that many-headed monster in two companion chapters. At best, humour is hard to define and to classify; also, a great deal of so-called Irish humour is indistinguishable from its British counterpart. Inductively, I have reached the conclusion that Irish humour shows two distinctive emphases—one on fantasy, the other on the grotesque and the macabre. The humour of other cultures besides the Irish displays one or other of these emphases, but I doubt whether both types of humour have been simultaneously fostered to the same degree by any other people.

I begin with fantasy partly because Anglo-Saxon culture associates Irish humour pre-eminently with leprechauns and other fairy folk: witness the musical comedy *Finian's Rainbow*, the Disney film *Darby O'Gill and the Little People*, and the continued appeal of James Stephens's *The Crock of Gold*, literary ancestor of the popular entertainments just mentioned.

Except for its overemphasis on the leprechaun, the Anglo-Saxon mind has not been deceived about the predominance of fantasy in Irish humour, which stems from the abundance of magic and marvel in more serious Irish literature. This in turn possibly stems from the peculiar character of pre-Christian Celtic—and particularly Irish—religion. A. G. van Hamel's controversial lecture, *Aspects of Celtic Mythology*,[1] makes one doubtful whether the word 'religion' is applicable at all, so steeped in magic were pagan Celtic beliefs and practices. Without discussing the druids specifically, van Hamel encourages me in my belief that they were never priests in any true sense, but

[1] A. G. van Hamel, *Aspects of Celtic Mythology*, reprinted from the *Proceedings of the British Academy*, vol. xx (London, 1934).

rather wizards or magi. He doubts the applicability of the term 'gods' to most of the mythological figures in Early Irish literature (though, *faute de mieux*, I shall often employ it in this book), and suggests instead the phrase 'divine magicians'.

This ancient belief in magic, which notoriously has never died out in Ireland, pervades every form of Early Irish literature, corrupting the realism of the sagas and completely overwhelming the saints' lives. Not a single Irish saint, from St. Patrick onwards and downwards, has escaped the flood of magical folklore which obliterates all but the most immovable landmarks of a saint's actual life on earth.

However, if the Irish have a highly developed appetite for the magical and the marvellous, their sense of the ludicrous has reached an equally high pitch of development. Behind the bards and the hagiographers, who endlessly strive to outdo each other in their accounts of heroic deeds and saintly miracles, there lurks the figure of the sceptic and/or parodist. Anyone who knows the contradictions of the Irish mind may come to suspect that the sceptical parodist is but the bard or the hagiographer himself in a different mood. I refer the reader to a later chapter on parody for an extreme example of either fantastic exaggeration or brilliant parody, the life of St. Findchua of Brigown.

The marvellous, then, is but one stage in the development of many an Irish tale; in a later version, the same story may appear as parody or burlesque or humorous fantasy. In his study *The Ossianic Lore and Romantic Tales of Medieval Ireland*, Professor Gerard Murphy has suggested that certain cycles of Early Irish tales lend themselves to this development better than others.[1] Thus two of the four early cycles, the Ulster and the Kingly, fell into disuse, whereas the Finn and Mythological Cycles flourished—or became decadent, if you like—accumulating folklore and magical motifs to the point where they grew first unintentionally and then deliberately ludicrous.

Professor Murphy speaks of 'the kingly grandeur, the genuine picture of ancient barbarism, and the unity of structure which mark so many Old Irish tales',[2] but it would be hard to prove that some of the earliest tales we know, even in the noble Ulster Cycle, do not contain fantastic humour that

[1] Gerard Murphy, *The Ossianic Lore and Romantic Tales of Medieval Ireland* (Dublin, 1955), pp. 30–31.   [2] Murphy, p. 31.

was deliberately intended as such. It would of course be almost equally hard to prove that they do. In his *Motif-Index of Early Irish Literature*, Professor Tom Peete Cross expressed himself very cautiously on the subject, under the heading 'Humour of lies and exaggeration':

> Early Irish sagas abound in examples of epic exaggeration, some of which may have been intended as humorous.[1]

As with the humour which Samuel Butler detected in Homer, we cannot be sure that what seems funny to us now was always intended to be so.

I am going to set before the reader one doubtful example of such humour from the Ulster Cycle; the text comes from *Lebor na Huidre* (*The Book of the Dun Cow*), a manuscript not older than 1100, though the linguistic forms of the tale suggest a ninth-century original. I must go on to explain that the boy hero Cuchulain is returning home in his chariot, elated by his first successful raid into enemy territory; he comes in sight of the Ulster stronghold, Emain Macha:

> . . . and Cuchulain said: 'I swear by the god by whom the Ulstermen swear, unless a man is found to fight with me, I will shed the blood of every one who is in the fort.'
> 'Naked women to meet him!' said Conchobar.
> Then the women of Emain go to meet him with Mugain, the wife of Conchobar Mac Nessa, and bare their breasts before him. 'These are the warriors who will meet you today,' said Mugain.
> He covers his face; then the heroes of Emain seize him and throw him into a vessel of cold water. That vessel bursts round him. The second vessel into which he was thrown boiled with bubbles as big as the fist therefrom. The third vessel into which he went, he warmed it so that its heat and its cold were rightly tempered.[2]

Given the dating, we cannot say that this is a truly primitive version of the story; even the ninth century was four hundred years removed from paganism. We *can* say, however, that Mugain's ironical remark is intentionally humorous; few readers, too, will feel that the marvellous story of the three vessels was intended to be heard with a perfectly straight face.

[1] See Tom Peete Cross, *Motif-Index of Early Irish Literature* (Bloomington, Indiana, 1952), p. 528.
[2] L. Winifred Faraday, tr., *The Cattle-Raid of Cualnge* (London, 1904), p. 34.

On the other hand, Cuchulain's confusion before the bare breasts of the women was probably *not* intended to be humorous, though the modern reader might think it a sly reference to Cuchulain's age, which is supposed to be only seven at the time. However, Cross's *Motif-Index* shows that the taboo against a man's looking at a woman's breasts was exploited elsewhere in the sagas as a means of outwitting an opponent and capturing him while his face was averted.[1]

In the story of Cuchulain and the vessels, then, we may have an authentic and early example of fantastic humour. The well-known story of *Fled Bricrend (Bricriu's Feast)* from the same cycle offers us a far less doubtful example of the same kind of humour, derived from an eighth-century original.[2]

Bricriu, a notorious satirist, stirs up contention among the three chief heroes of Ulster at his feast. Later, when the heroes' wives go outside with their women-servants to relieve themselves, Bricriu suggests to each that she should take precedence of the other two in re-entering the banquet hall:

> The three companies thereupon went out until they met at a spot three ridges from the hall. None of them knew that Bricriu had incited them one against the other. To the hall they straightway return. Even and easy and graceful their carriage on the first ridge; scarcely did one of them raise one foot before the other. But on the ridge following, their steps were shorter and quicker. On the ridge next to the house it was with difficulty each kept up with the other; so they raised their robes to the rounds of their hips to complete the attempt to go first into the hall. For what Bricriu had said to each of them with regard to the other was that whosoever entered first should be queen of the whole province. The amount of confusion then occasioned by the competition was as it were the noise of fifty chariots approaching.[3]

The humour rapidly reaches the level of fantasy as the alarmed warriors shut the doors against the thundering horde of women. The three heroes then want to fight for the privilege of opening the doors. Instead, a 'war of words' among the wives is decided on. When their boasting of their respective

[1] Cross, p. 371.

[2] Myles Dillon, *Early Irish Literature* (Chicago, 1948), p. 18.

[3] Tom Peete Cross and Clark Harris Slover, eds., *Ancient Irish Tales* (New York, 1936), pp. 259–60. Translation by George Henderson.

husbands' deeds proves inconclusive, two of the heroes break holes in the wall to admit their wives. Cuchulain, however, lifts up the entire wall of the house to admit his wife, Emer, her fifty women-servants, and the fifty women belonging to each of the other two wives.

When Cuchulain drops the wall of wattles, it sinks seven feet into the ground, shaking the whole house and making the balcony from which Bricriu had been watching the quarrel fall into the courtyard; Bricriu and his wife are tossed from it into the dunghill among the dogs.

As this saga continues, it incorporates a great deal of more serious material, including an early version of the story now known to English literature as *Sir Gawain and the Green Knight*. In the anecdote of the women's rivalry, however, we can see that the fantasy and the humour are inseparable. If the women had not raced each other so comically, nobody would have needed to shut the door against them. If the doors had not been closed, Cuchulain's marvellous feat, with its comic sequel, would not have been necessary. Furthermore, a comic intention is implicit throughout by virtue of Bricriu's characterization as a satirist and his nickname of 'Poison-tongue'.

I need hardly labour the point further. Fantastic humour may have appeared in the Irish hero-tales as early as the eighth century.

Otherworld tales

In the preceding section I mentioned the Mythological Cycle. Properly speaking, this cycle is concerned only with the adventures of the *Tuatha Dé Danann* ('The Tribes of the God— or Goddess—Danu').[1] We learn how these mysterious 'tribes' with their many magical powers conquered Ireland and held it against their enemies until at last they were defeated by the Milesians or Gaels. Thereupon they took refuge in 'fairy mounds', some of which were prehistoric burial sites, where they remain 'to this very day'.

The Early Irish term for a fairy mound is *síd*, while the plural of the same word, *síde*, identifies the supernatural inhabitants of the mound, who can be loosely termed 'fairies', so long as we do not expect them to possess all—or only—the

---

[1] The translation suggested by van Hamel, p. 11.

attributes of J. M. Barrie's Tinker Bell.[1] Sometimes they behave like gods, sometimes like the spirits of the dead, sometimes like nothing but themselves.

A very common motif in the Mythological Cycle and elsewhere concerns the mortal who loves and/or is loved by a fairy being and who goes voluntarily or is carried off into a fairy mound. This is perhaps the original type of Irish Otherworld story. But the Otherworld may also be located outside Ireland; its inhabitants then are not true members of the Tuatha Dé Danann. Professor Myles Dillon makes the distinction very clear in the following passage:

> Manannán, while being lord over the Tuatha Dé Danann, is not one of them. He is, however, a foster-son of their erstwhile king, the Dagda. He dwells outside Ireland, as always in the cycle . . . and belongs to the nobles of the Land of Promise. These people . . . appear to be higher in the order of supernatural beings than are the Tuatha Dé. . . .[2]

This 'Land of Promise' (*Tír Tairngire*) is also known as 'The Land of the Young' (*Tír na nÓg*), 'Delightful Plain' (*Mag Meld* or *Mell*), and 'The Many-Coloured' (*Int Ildathach*). The best and earliest description of this Celtic Elysium is to be found in *Immram Brain Maic Febail* (*The Voyage of Bran, Son of Febal*), which 'may go back in its written form to the seventh century'.[3] Hunger, cold, ugliness, unsatisfied desire, death, and decay are unknown there.

Visits to this happy land do not, strictly speaking, belong to the Mythological Cycle. Professor Dillon prefers to classify them as 'Adventures' or 'Voyages', following the usual terminology of their Irish titles. *Echtrae* (Modern Irish *Eachtra*) is the Early Irish term for a supernatural adventure and *Immram* that for a voyage. Secular voyages to the Land of Promise pave the way for accounts of saints' voyages—motivated supposedly by the search for a hermitage, the desire to do penance, or the urge to seek exile as an equivalent of the martyrdom that eluded most Irish saints. Most famous of these voyage tales is the Latin *Navigatio Brendani*, which gave rise to the legend that St. Brendan of Clonfert discovered America.[4]

---

[1] For the Modern Irish equivalents of *síde* and *síd*, see the entries *sídhe* and *síodh* in Patrick S. Dinneen, *Foclóir Gaedhilge agus Béarla, An Irish–English Dictionary*, rev. ed. (Dublin, 1927). *Sídhe* equals Anglo-Irish 'Shee'.

[2] Dillon, p. 67.   [3] Dillon, p. 104.

[4] On the voyage and vision literature, see C. S. Boswell, *An Irish Precursor of*

The later voyage literature often includes visions of Heaven and Hell. There is also a separate category of tales devoted exclusively to such visions, the most notable of which is *Fís Adamnáin* (*The Vision of Adamnan*), found in *The Book of the Dun Cow*. There are visions, too, of the pagan Otherworld. The two virtually interchangeable words for 'vision' in Irish are *fís* and *aisling(e)*.

Most of the Otherworld literature, whether *echtrae*, *immram*, *fís*, or *aislinge*, is summed up and annihilated in a single devastating work of parody, *Aislinge Meic Conglinne* (*The Vision of Mac Conglinne*), dating from the twelfth century. In Chapter 8 below I analyse some of the parodistic elements contained in it. I purposely omit any detailed consideration there of the actual vision which gives the work its name, preferring to discuss it here.

In the *Lebor Brecc* (*Speckled Book*) version of the *Vision*, Mac Conglinne gives three preliminary summaries in verse of what he has seen. Then he embarks on 'the fable', a longer, more connected account, mainly in prose. As the fable unfolds it recalls this or that feature of the vision literature. In a characteristic opening, a phantom (*scál*) from the Otherworld warns Mac Conglinne against death by drowning—in gravy! The prophetic phantom's prophetic name is Buarannach ('Fluxy' or 'Squittery'), and he is from the fairy mound of Eating. Since Mac Conglinne's digestion is not powerful enough to cope with the orgy of eating promised him by Buarannach, the latter advises him to seek out the hermitage of the Wizard Doctor.

In answer to Mac Conglinne's further questions, the phantom gives a different version of his name and lists the names of his relatives, servants, and domestic animals:

> 'Wheatlet, son of Milklet,
> Son of juicy Bacon,
>   Is mine own name.
> Honeyed Butter-roll
> Is the man's name
>   That bears my bag.'[1]

Dante (London, 1908), and Howard Rollin Patch, *The Other World According to Descriptions in Medieval Literature* (Cambridge, Mass., 1950).

[1] *Aislinge Meic Conglinne, The Vision of MacConglinne*, ed. and tr. Kuno Meyer (London, 1892), p. 78.

And so on. The phantom then sends Mac Conglinne off to what the Germans call *Schlaraffenland* and the French *Le Pays de cocagne;* here, it is called 'the country of O'Early-Eating'. Mac Conglinne soon embarks upon a marvellous voyage or *immram* in a small boat made of beef fat:

Then we rowed across the wide expanse of New-Milk Lake, through seas of broth, past river-mouths of mead, over swelling, boisterous waves of butter-milk, by perpetual pools of gravy, past woods dewy with meat-juice, past springs of savoury lard, by islands of cheeses, by hard rocks of rich tallow, by headlands of old curds, along strands of dry cheese; until we reached the firm, level beach between Butter-mount and Milk-lake and Curd-point at the mouth of the pass to the country of O'Early-eating, in front of the hermitage of the Wizard Doctor.[1]

A description of this hermitage, surrounded by 'seven score hundred smooth stakes of old bacon' and replete with other edible marvels, follows. Then we hear of the doorkeeper, of the Wizard Doctor, and of the latter's son. Mac Conglinne, after recounting his symptoms at great length, obtains from the Doctor an interminably long prescription; this will magically cure his immense hunger and his small powers of digestion. Mac Conglinne's 'fable' ends with these words from the Wizard Doctor:

'Whatever disease may seize thee from it, Mac Conglinne, 'tis I that will cure thee, excepting one disease, I mean the disease of sages and of gentlemen, the best of all diseases, the disease that is worth perpetual health—loose bowels.'[2]

The Vision of Mac Conglinne as a whole represents one of the highest points ever attained by the Irish comic genius. Of recent years it has been adapted twice for public performance in Ireland: first in Austin Clarke's verse play *The Son of Learning*[3] (also known as *The Hunger Demon*) and then in Padraic Fallon's radio version, *The Vision of Mac Conglinne*, first broadcast by Radio Éireann in 1953.

Bruidhean tales

One particular Otherworld theme lends itself easily to comic treatment. In the words of Professor Murphy,

[1] *Aislinge*, p. 84.   [2] *Aislinge*, p. 100.
[3] *The Collected Poems of Austin Clarke* (London, 1936), pp. 157–213.

The *bruidhean* theme, which is a feature of Early Modern Fionn lore, seems to be . . . in origin . . . mythological, but has been preserved in Ireland mainly by folk tradition. It relates how Fionn was enticed to a magic dwelling (*bruidhean*) and how he suffered ill-treatment there. Folklore preserves it in a form in which its original mythological connections are evident and which makes it almost certain that the original *bruidhean* was an otherworld dwelling equivalent to the Greek Hades.[1]

In Part III of *Duanaire Finn* (*The Poem-Book of Finn*) Professor Murphy analyses side-by-side a folk-tale with a comic ending and a serious literary tale of the *bruidhean* type, *Bruidhean Chaorthainn* ('The Rowan-tree Dwelling'), which probably dates from the sixteenth century.[2] It seems clear from his analysis that the literary tale is derived from the folk-tale, rather than vice versa. Professor Murphy believes that the heroic tale has bowdlerized one motif in the folk-tale for the sake of preserving the dignity of Finn and his warriors.

In both tales, Finn and his heroes are glued to their seats by magic in the fairy dwelling. All are safely released in the end by magic balm or blood except Conán *Maol* ('The Bald'), who is traditionally both mocker and butt in the Finn Cycle. Conan (his name is usually Anglicized without the accent) is represented in *Bruidhean Chaorthainn* as so greedy that he has to be fed by the rescuers before being released. Perhaps in punishment for his greed, the magic fluid runs short when his turn comes, so that part of his skin remains sticking to the couch. In various versions of the folk-tale Conan loses the skin of his buttocks. A sheepskin is used to supply the place of the human skin; as a result, Conan grows enough wool on his *derrière* to supply the Fianna with stockings. In the more dignified version of *Bruidhean Chaorthainn*, Conan loses only the skin of his heels, his shoulders, and the back of his head—whence his baldness.

In the course of this chapter and the next we shall grow accustomed to the idea of 'comic gods'. Perhaps the greedy, lecherous Conan, with his sheep-like (or goat-like) lower half, belongs to an older tradition than the rude, fierce, sadistic 'iron man' who bears his name in the heroic tales and poems of

[1] Murphy, p. 52.
[2] *Duanaire Finn*, Part III, ed. Gerard Murphy, Irish Texts Society XLIII (Dublin, 1953), pp. xxiv–xxix.

the Finn Cycle.[1] The taste of literary men and that of the folk must coincide before certain folk-motifs find their way into the written word, but that is no guide to the age of the motifs. I have already quoted Professor Murphy as believing that the folk-tales are closer to the mythological origins of the *bruidhean* theme than the literary tales, although these folk-tales are known only from transcriptions or recordings made in the last century and a half.

Whatever his original character, Conan is always the butt in the humorous *bruidhean* tales of the Finn Cycle. In the serious tales of this type, Finn and his other warriors undergo painful or frightening experiences which are not at all illusory; Finn's sufferings, to the best of my knowledge, never humiliate him or make him look ridiculous. It is far otherwise with Conan, as we have seen, and many of his most ridiculous plights involve dreams or hallucinations.

One such tale exists in several folk versions—some involving Conan, some not—and also in a variety of literary adaptations.[2] The folk-tale is perhaps best represented by Patrick Kennedy's version, 'Conan's Delusions in Ceash', in his *Legendary Fictions of the Irish Celts*[3]—that is, if his unacknowledged source there be in fact a folk-tale at all. 'Conan's Delusions' seems to resemble rather closely a manuscript poem, *Laoidh Chab a Dosan* ('The Lay of Cab-a-Dosan'), which is thus described by Robin Flower:

a pseudo-Ossianic lay . . . of late and indecent character, relating a farcical adventure of Conán Maol in the Bruidhean of Céis Corann co. Sligo. . . .[4]

According to Kennedy, a dwarf invited Finn and some of the Fianna to a *bruidhean*. After eating and drinking what the dwarf offered them, the warriors went to bed. Soon, a surpassingly beautiful woman appeared in Finn's room and invited him to come home with her in her chariot. Fortunately, Finn chewed his 'thumb of knowledge' and saw that she was in reality a withered hag. He warned the others, and each of

---

[1] For the latter aspect of Conan see *Duanaire Finn*, Part I, ed. Eoin MacNeill, Irish Texts Society VII (London, 1908), p. l (i.e. p. 50 of introduction).

[2] Gerard Murphy in *Siabhradh Mhic na Míochomhairle*, ed. Séamus Ó Ceithearnaigh (Dublin, 1955), pp. xix–xx.

[3] Patrick Kennedy, *Legendary Fictions of the Irish Celts* (London, 1866), pp. 232–5.

[4] Robin Flower, *Catalogue of Irish Manuscripts in the British Museum*, ii (London, 1926), 139.

the heroes except Conan resisted temptation. The lecherous Conan, however, jumped into the chariot at once. In a moment he felt himself falling into a deep well of scalding water; he just saved himself by clutching a beam. When his cries for help summoned the heroes, they found him astride 'a flesh-fork that lay across the caldron in which their supper had been cooked'.

The next time the woman appeared, Conan hesitated, but only momentarily. He soon found himself in a wood, with a gigantic beast swallowing his head. When the heroes arrived once more, the beast turned out to be nothing but a cat licking his face.

The third time Conan yielded to temptation, his yells were terrifying to hear. His comrades found him lying with his hair fastened to the floor, writhing in all the pangs of childbirth. Finn eventually, by his magic, compelled the dwarf to release Conan, but not before the top of the jester's head had become bald.

Kennedy records another, very late version (apparently told to him in English) of this story under the title 'The Misfortunes of Barrett the Piper'.[1] Barrett has 'bad thoughts' three times in the night, although no woman is mentioned; each time he gets up and meets with some misfortune. The first time he is found on the hen roost in the kitchen; the second time, 'there was Jack sthraddle-legs on the pot-rack' over the fire; the third time, he gets into a bed in the next room and is promptly attacked by labour pains. At his son's suggestion, Jack Barrett makes the sign of the cross: his pains and his mysterious host both disappear at once. As in most such stories, the house in which they spent the night has gone the next morning, and they find themselves in the dry moat of a *ráth* or 'fairy fort' by the roadside.

The most consciously literary version of this story—and the most consciously humorous, too—is attributed to Brian Dubh Ó Raghallaigh (Brian Duff O'Reilly), who was living in County Cavan about 1725.[2] It has recently been edited by James Carney under the title *Siabhradh Mhic na Míochomhairle* (*The Delusion of the Son of Evil Counsel*). Patrick Kennedy gives a lengthy summary of this story in his *Legendary Fictions*.[3]

[1] Kennedy, pp. 177–9.   [2] *Siabhradh Mhic na Míochomhairle*, pp. vii–ix.
[3] Kennedy, pp. 132–42.

The humorous intent of this fantastic tale shows itself in many ways besides the ridiculous nature of the adventures. The character of the 'hero' (supposedly the author himself) is a compound of cowardice and lust. In its style the prose narrative—which is interspersed with lyrical passages of verse—seems a deliberate parody of the bombast prevalent in Modern Irish romantic tales and traceable ultimately to the *Lebor Laigen* (*The Book of Leinster*) redaction of *Táin Bó Cualnge* (*The Cattle Raid of Cooley*). Furthermore, one must be alert for plays on words, at least in the passage describing the Son of Evil Counsel's game of backgammon.[1]

The basic plot is simple enough. The Son of Evil Counsel—the author—finds himself in a mysterious castle belonging to a *gruagach* or enchanter who has a very beautiful daughter. If the Son will take part next day in a fairy battle, he may marry the daughter—that is, if he survives the battle. After the game of backgammon between the Son and the Enchanter, everybody goes to bed. The Son, overcome with desire for the fairy maiden, thinks a bird in the hand is worth two in the bush. He goes looking for the girl and soon finds himself in a haunted spot, from which he escapes to a boat on a stormy sea. When the Gruagach answers his cries for help, he finds the Son in the cellar 'seated on a cullender that was covering a vat of strongly-working new beer'.

Later in the night the Son weakens and goes in search of the maiden again. This time,

his heart turned into water when he saw a beast, black, devilish, hideous-coloured, heavy-headed, dull-buzzing, approaching him. A great plum or a small apple would fit on every one of his coarse hairs [a favourite detail in the hero-tales].[2]

Running away from this monster, he comes to 'a stormy, dangerous, coarse-waved, light-leaping, strongly-diffused, streamy, troublesome river . . .', into which he jumps although he cannot swim. This time the Gruagach finds him wallowing in the trough of pigs' food; the monster, of course, was a pig—a pet pig.

The Enchanter sends the Son off to bed with a lecture which fills him with shame. When the Son awakens in the morning,

[1] David Greene, '*Un Joc Grossier* in Irish and Provençal', *Ériu*, xvii (1955), 12 (text), 13–14 (glossary).   [2] Kennedy, pp. 139–40.

the castle is gone and he is alone on the wall of an old *lios* or fort. He wanders through the length and breadth of Ireland seeking the fairy maiden, but eventually she comes to him in a dream at the very spot where he had awakened from his adventure and tells him that she is married. He thereupon becomes a reformed character where women are concerned.

Some manuscripts of the tale contain a third arising in the night, during which the erring Son flees a monster and climbs a tree, only to have the tree set on fire below and around him. When the Enchanter arrives this time, the Son finds himself atop a huge candle-holder in the middle of the floor; the hideous monster he has fled from is a puppy.[1]

Surprisingly, the Son of Evil Counsel does not have to suffer the pains of childbirth, though that would be a fairly appropriate penalty for attempted seduction. Perhaps O'Reilly felt that this harsh folklore motif was out of keeping with the sentimental and chivalrous ending of his tale.[2]

The gods go a-begging

The power to change one's own or another's shape or to assume impenetrable disguises has always lent itself to comic exploitation. Whether all the Tuatha Dé Danann had the power of shape-changing I cannot say with confidence, but 'the nobles of the Land of Promise' had it, and above all Manannán. Manannán Mac Lir ('Son of the Sea'), who gives his name to the Isle of Man, is the Irish Proteus, a sea-god whose disguises are infinite. He loves to play pranks and confer benefits while in disguise.

By far the most delightful story of Manannán's disguises that I know is *Ceatharnach Uí Dhomhnaill* ('O'Donnell's Kern'), a sixteenth-century tale edited and translated by Standish Hayes O'Grady in *Silva Gadelica*.[3] The Kern dressed in narrow stripes, who appears so uncouth, leaves little doubt of his identity when he says, 'I am in Islay one day, in Cantyre another; [a day in Man and] a day in Rathlin, and another on the white cairn in Slievefuad; for I am a poor rambling rakish fellow'. All or

[1] *Siabhradh Mhic na Míochomhairle*, pp. 61–66.
[2] See Flower, ii. 128, for references to two other burlesque tales influenced by O'Reilly's.
[3] Standish Hayes O'Grady, ed. and tr., *Silva Gadelica*, ii (London, 1892), 311–24.

most of these places appear to be sacred to Manannán. One manuscript of the tale ends by explicitly stating that the Kern was Manannán.[1]

The Kern travels from chieftain to chieftain playing his pranks, but the cleverest are those he plays at the court of Teigue O'Kelly. The first trick is bogus: he places three rushes on his hand and says he will blow away the middle one without disturbing the other two if he is given five marks; Teigue promises the money, so the rogue holds the two outside rushes down with two fingers of his other hand and blows away the middle rush easily. One of O'Kelly's followers who undertakes to do the same thing finds that he has pushed his finger-tips right through the palm of his hand. The Kern heals him.

Then the Kern undertakes to wag one ear while keeping the other motionless. This he does by seizing the ear in his hand and waggling it. When O'Kelly's follower tries this trick, he pulls his ear off and has to be healed again by the Kern.

Finally the Kern accomplishes a real trick far outshining the famous Indian rope trick. He tosses up a silken thread so that it catches on a cloud. Along the thread he sends a hare, a dog, and a boy—a regular little hunting scene. They disappear in the cloud; then he sends a beautiful girl up after them to see that the hare does not get hurt.

After a while the Kern becomes suspicious and starts reeling in the thread. Sure enough, the boy is between the girl's legs, and the dog is picking the hare's bones. In a fury the Kern cuts off the boy's head. When O'Kelly chides him, the Kern puts the boy's head on again—back to front! Seeing his mistake, he twists the head the right way round. 'For one instant O'Kelly looked aside, and of all earthly airts he never knew into which one the conjuror was vanished from him.'

The motif of the head put on back to front recurs in *Bodach an Chóta Lachtna* ('The Churl with the Grey Coat'), another story of Manannán in disguise.[2] Like this tale, *Eachtra an Ghiolla Dheacair* ('The Adventure of the Tiresome Fellow') is connected with the Finn Cycle.[3] Here Manannán appears

---

[1] O'Grady, ii. 323 n.

[2] 'Bodach an Chota-Lachtna, or the Clown with the Grey Coat', *Irish Penny Journal*, i (24 Oct. 1840), 132. This story is also translated in O'Grady, ii. 324–31.

[3] For a translation see O'Grady, ii. 292–311.

again as a churl, this time an astonishingly lazy one, with an almost equally sluggish horse.

Older than any of the above stories is *Compert Mongáin ocus Serc Duibe Lacha do Mongán* ('The Conception of Mongán and His Love for Dubh Lacha'), a richly humorous story of shifting identities. On this fifteenth-century story are based part of 'Mongan's Frenzy' in James Stephens's *Irish Fairy Tales* and Austin Clarke's verse comedy, *The Plot Succeeds*.

Mongán, an historical king of Ulster, forms the centre of a small cycle of tales.[1] One account makes him the son of Manannán, though his earthly father was his predecessor in the kingship, Fiachna; the latter is alleged to have knowingly extended to Manannán, in exchange for a victory in battle, the same kind of hospitality unwittingly accorded to Zeus by Amphitryon.

Another story in the cycle asserts that Mongán was a reincarnation of Finn. At any rate, the powers of shape-changing which Mongán puts to such humorous use are similar to those possessed by Manannán, who is supposed to have taught them to the king during the latter's twelve- or sixteen-year education in the Land of Promise.

Eager to possess a herd of white cows with red ears, Mongán promises Brandubh, King of Leinster, literally anything in exchange for them. Brandubh, having delivered the cows, demands Dubh Lacha, Mongán's wife. She urges Mongán to keep his word, but then makes Brandubh promise not to marry her for a year.

During the year Mongán pines for Dubh Lacha, and his servant Mac an Daimh pines for *his* wife, Dubh Lacha's maid. The two chief magical episodes in the story concern, first, how the two husbands gain access to their wives during the year and, second, how Mongán regains his wife.

Setting off for the Leinster capital, Mongán and Mac an Daimh meet the monk Tibraide and one of his fellow monks. Mongán's magic causes a river and a bridge to appear before the monks in the middle of the plain. While crossing this bridge, the monks fall into the river and are carried downstream. Mongán and his servant proceed to impersonate them. They meet Brandubh, who is away from home; he encourages them to go to his fort and hear the confessions of Dubh Lacha and

[1] Myles Dillon, *The Cycles of the Kings* (London and New York, 1946), p. 49.

her maid. Once alone with their wives, the two 'monks' hurry them to bed.

Meanwhile, Tibraide at last arrives at the royal fort:

> The doorkeepers said: 'We never saw a year in which Tibraides were more plentiful than this year. You have a Tibraide within and a Tibraide without.'[1]

Mongán insists that he himself is the real Tibraide and that the Tibraide outside is Mongán in disguise. As a result there is a great slaughter of Tibraide's followers and a serious breach between Brandubh and the holy man.

After other erotic but not magical episodes, the year comes to an end. By his magic Mongán succeeds in transforming a hideous hag into a very beautiful princess, supposedly the daughter of the King of Munster. Brandubh falls in love with the disguised hag and finally agrees to allow Mongán, himself disguised as the King of Connacht's son, to take Dubh Lacha in exchange for the hag. When everybody else is drunk, Mongán, Mac an Daimh, and their two wives slip away to Ulster. In the morning Brandubh awakes to find the hag in his bed:

> 'Are you Greyhaired Cuimne of the Mill?' he said. 'Ay,' said she. 'Pity that I should have slept with thee, Cuimne.'[2]

Eachtra Chléirigh na gCroiceann ('The Adventure of the Skin-Clad Cleric') is another of the god-in-disguise stories which has become attached to the legend of an historical king. In this tale the disguised god is a member of the Tuatha Dé Danann: Angus *Óg* ('the Young') or *na nÉn* ('of the Birds') son of the Dagda and often associated with Brugh na Bóinne, the prehistoric burial site at Newgrange on the Boyne, whence he is known as *an Bhrogha* ('of the Brugh', *brugh* being roughly a synonym for *síd*).

As I have no direct knowledge of this manuscript tale, I shall quote Robin Flower's summary:

> Aonghus an Bhrogha comes to the court of Congal Cindmagair (king of Ireland 705–710) in hideous guise as a cleric of S. Patrick's company to demonstrate to the king that his boast of his wife's excelling chastity is premature. He transforms the king into a goat which he sells to the queen, and the king, thus transformed, wit-

---

[1] Dillon, *Cycles*, p. 53.   [2] Ibid., p. 55.

nesses his wife's lightness. Afterwards the king is brought back to his natural shape on the hill of Howth and is taken overseas to a fairy island. From the island he brings a magic cup by means of which his wife, her lover, the prior of a monastery, and various other characters are caught in a compromising situation, the hands of the queen and her lover adhering to the cup and the other characters adhering to them.[1]

As we shall see, Austin Clarke took Congal's transformation and elaborated it lovingly to form one episode of his novel *The Sun Dances at Easter*.

We are familiar with divine prankishness from Greek and Roman literature; it has even been said that Homer introduces the gods mainly as comic relief. However, after Homer—and especially after Aristophanes—the gods are treated with greater respect, so that even the amours of Zeus-Jupiter are taken seriously and a story like that of Philemon and Baucis is given a moralistic flavour. Irish literature has preserved the primitive attitude with typically Irish conservatism; furthermore, as the myths only began to be written down after the Christianization of Ireland, no deference to what were regarded as pagan idols or evil spirits inhibited Irish treatment of the old gods. We shall find other examples later of a happy Irish reluctance to narrow the legitimate field open to humour.

The humour of leprechauns

I have great sympathy with the remarks of Patrick Kennedy upon the subject of leprechauns:

> Our notice of the Cluricawn, Leprechaun, or Lurikeen, shall be brief, as he is one of the best known of all the fairy tribe. [Thomas] Keightley and [T. Crofton] Croker have given us a surfeit of the deceitful old rogue.[2]

One could now add many many more names to those of the two early-nineteenth-century folklorists mentioned by Kennedy, and the surfeit has become correspondingly more nauseating.

The tradition of the *leipreachán* as a fairy shoemaker with a pot of gold seems to be of quite recent origin. The word itself is derived from Old Irish *lucorpan* (*lu-chorpán*) meaning 'tiny little body', which later became, by metathesis, *luprachán*,

---

[1] Flower, ii. 367–8.　　　　　　　　[2] Kennedy, p. 129.

whence *leipreachán*. The first literary reference to *lucorpain* (the plural of *lucorpan*) occurs in an eighth-century saga about Fergus Mac Léti, King of Ulster, which was cited as an authority in the *Senchas Már*, a compendium of Early Irish law.

According to this tale, Fergus fell asleep by the seashore one day. A number of *lucorpain* or water-sprites tried to carry him off to their home under the sea, but he awoke when his feet touched the waves. He managed to grab three of the little people and made a bargain with them: if he spared their lives, they must grant him a wish. The *abac* ('dwarf') who acted as spokesman gave him 'a charm for passing under seas and pools and lakes', but warned him not to enter Loch Rudraige in Ulster. With magic herbs in his ears, Fergus used to travel underseas in company with the *lucorpain*, but eventually he broke the taboo and ventured into Loch Rudraige, where a sea monster ultimately killed him.[1]

There is not a glimmer of humour to be seen in this tale, which incorporates other tragic elements omitted from my summary. One must assume, therefore, that a whole body of folklore about the *lucorpain* or *Tuath Luchra* ('People of Luchra') already existed separately in the eighth century or grew up independently later. This lore exploited the comic possibilities of what are essentially, in spite of their magic powers, miniature human beings.

Why very small and very large anthropomorphic creatures should be thought comic is probably a matter for the psychoanalyst. Perhaps the idea of becoming very small is associated with a regressive desire to re-enter the womb, that first and only completely blissful environment; similarly, the idea of very great size may suggest to our unconscious minds superhuman capacities for physical (including sexual) gratification. King Fergus's abnormal sexual endowment in the story summarized just below is a case in point.

At any rate, the Early Modern Irish version of *Aidheadh Fhearghusa* (*The Death of Fergus*) edited and translated by Standish Hayes O'Grady in *Silva Gadelica*[2] gives an impression of the utmost incongruity, since the wealth of comic detail about

---

[1] D. A. Binchy, 'The Saga of Fergus Mac Léti', *Ériu*, xvi (1952), 33–48,

[2] O'Grady, ii. 269–85. O'Grady does not translate the indelicate or obscene passages, which will be found in the Gaelic text, vol. i, pp. 238–52.

leprechauns leaves us quite unprepared for the tragic ending. Although the leprechauns are no longer water-sprites, their king gives Fergus, as something between a ransom and a farewell gift, a pair of shoes which enable the wearer to travel just as easily by sea as by land. The tragic denouement in Loch Rudraige, against which Fergus now receives no warning, is one of the few similarities between this version and the eighth-century tale. O'Grady's source was the British Museum MS. Egerton 1782, 'written at various periods from 1419 to 1517',[1] but the language of the extravaganza suggests a date as early as the fourteenth or even thirteenth century.

Aodh de Blacam, Gerard Murphy, and doubtless other writers too have suggested that the leprechaun material in the later version of *The Death of Fergus* was made available to Swift in some form, supplying him with hints for Gulliver's adventures in Lilliput and Brobdingnag.[2]

A comparison of particular details from both works does not present a true picture of their affinity, so I shall first give a brief summary of the text published by O'Grady. One day at a feast Iubdán, the king of the leprechauns, grows very boastful about the invincibility of his army. His chief poet, Eisirt, son of Bec ('Little'), bursts out laughing and asserts that one Ulsterman would take hostages from all the king's four battalions. Naturally Iubdán is furious, but he grants Eisirt three days in which to prove his story true if he can. Eisirt goes to Ulster and wins the approval of King Fergus by his poetic skill and his keen eye for the love intrigues at the Ulster court. He brings back to Iubdán the Ulster dwarf, Aedh, who 'could stand on a full-sized man's hand'. Eisirt, in turn, could stand on Aedh's hand. Iubdán is abashed when he sees the 'giant' Aedh.

As a punishment for his incredulity, Iubdán must go to Ulster and be the first to taste King Fergus's porridge the next morning. Iubdán's wife, Bébó, accompanies him. Unfortunately, Iubdán gets stuck in the porridge and is captured. The episodes which follow are an odd mixture of lyrical poetry and obscene anecdote. For instance, Fergus and Bébó have sexual inter-course, although she is only three fists tall, whereas his male

---

[1] O'Grady, ii, pp. viii, xi.
[2] Aodh de Blacam, 'An Anglo-Irish Reading Programme: The 18th Century', *Irish Monthly*, xlvii (1919), 669; Murphy, *Ossianic Lore*, pp. 31–32.

member is seven fists long. Fergus places his hand on the crown of her head—for a reason which the reader can probably guess and which is made all too explicit in the ensuing dialogue between the amorous pair. Iubdán then reveals a talent for obscene witticism, but he also proves to be a seer and poet of great gifts.

The battalions of the leprechauns come in search of their king. When they fail to ransom him with promises of magic crops, they proceed to annoy the Ulstermen with four petty plagues. Finally they make their biggest threat: they will put the men and women of Ulster to shame by shaving the hair off everyone in the kingdom. Iubdán, however, sends them away in peace. After a year's stay, Iubdán offers Fergus the choice of any one of his magic possessions. Fergus chooses the shoes. Before this gift has had the tragic consequences already indicated, Aedh returns to Ulster with a poem full of praise for the leprechauns and their land. Iubdán goes home safely with Bébó, but Fergus meets his death fighting the *sinech* of Loch Rudraige.

Among the detailed similarities to *Gulliver's Travels* we may note the following. Iubdán shows the same overweening pride as the king of Lilliput. Aedh, like Gulliver, admires the flawless complexions of the tiny folk, who are very similar in size to the Lilliputians: seventeen pretty girls could lie in his bosom, four men in his belt, and 'all unknown to me, among my beard would be another'. The dwarf reminds us also of the Brobdingnagian dwarf, though he plays no pranks on Eisirt. It is Fergus who orders Eisirt to be dropped into a tankard of ale when he spurns human food and drink, recalling Gulliver's adventure in the bowl of cream. Eisirt and Iubdán both object to the 'infected breaths' of humans, just as Gulliver objected to the body odour of the Brobdingnagians—and as a Lilliputian objected to his.

When I related the loves of Bébó and Fergus to Professor Henry Popkin, he suggested a parallel between that passage and the one where Gulliver feels

obliged to vindicate the Reputation of an excellent Lady, who was an innocent sufferer upon my Account. The Treasurer took a Fancy to be jealous of his Wife, from the Malice of some evil Tongues, who informed him that her Grace had taken a violent Affection for my

Person; and the Court-Scandal ran for some Time that she once came privately to my Lodging. This I solemnly declare to be a most infamous Falshood. . . .[1]

Gulliver's fierce defence of the Lilliputian lady's honour implies the possibility of some such fantastic connexion as that between Bébó and Fergus, which the Irish tale attributes to a feminine capacity that the misogynistic Swift might well profess to believe in.

I cannot claim any or all of these parallels as more than coincidences, especially as the Gaelic story has no evident satiric purpose. However, it is conceivable that some folk or literary version of the tale was translated for Swift's benefit. We know that his 'Description of an Irish Feast', dating from 1720, was based upon a literal translation from the Gaelic; what had happened once *could* happen again. At the very least we can say that Gulliver's first two voyages, if translated into Modern Irish, would not be thought incompatible with Gaelic tradition.

It is worth noting that, apart from the depredations of the leprechaun battalions, the Puckish tricks in the above story are perpetrated mainly by humans upon leprechauns. In more recent tradition it is usually the leprechaun who is the prankster. Recalling the attempted abduction of Fergus in the eighth-century tale, we may choose to regard the modern trend as a return to an early tradition.

Finn and the humour of giants

In examining the *bruidhean* tales, we have already seen the tendency of humorous tales to evolve out of—or rather, to merge *into*—the Finn Cycle. There may be a number of reasons for this tendency. Gerard Murphy suggests two primary ones.

First of all, the literary tradition may have been affected by a change in its audience from noblemen to farmers.[2] In the second place, says Professor Murphy,

though the tendency to give prominence to buffoonery in Fenian poetry is late, the roots of that tendency may be ancient.[3]

[1] Jonathan Swift, *Gulliver's Travels*, With an Introduction by Harold Williams (Oxford, 1941), p. 49.   [2] *Duanaire Finn*, Part III, p. xcviii.
[3] Ibid.

He endorses the Chadwicks' observation in *The Growth of Literature* that gods were often handled

in a rough humorous way markedly different from the respectful way in which nobles were treated.[1]

We shall find some curious examples of this in the next chapter. Professor Murphy also notes the occasional treatment of the Fianna as giants in the earlier literature and the humorous tone of the eighth-century tale, 'The Quarrel Between Finn and Oisín'.

Combining these hints of the antiquity of giant-motifs and amusing motifs in Fionn tradition with the fact that Fionn was probably originally a god, and therefore liable to humorous treatment, we may conclude that burlesque treatment had been associated with Fionn and his companions from very remote times by unlearned story-tellers, and that what is new is merely the transference of those themes, under folk influence, from oral tradition to the literature, the way for the transference having been gradually prepared by the decay of the heroic tradition. . . .[2]

Finn becomes, in late tradition, almost as much of a butt for humour as Conan.

A third reason for this humorous trend—and one which has not been put forward previously, to my knowledge—is of psychological origin. The father-aspect of Finn is present almost from the earliest records of the Finn tradition. In 'The Quarrel Between Finn and Oisín' most of the tale consists of a verse 'lampoon' (*oblirach*) in which Finn's son mocks his father's age, while in the alternate couplets Finn mocks his son's youth and inexperience.[3] As early as the tenth century,[4] the elopement of the youthful Diarmaid with Gráinne, the young bride of the ageing Finn, introduces an Oedipus-like theme, though Finn causes the death of Diarmaid in the legend rather than vice-versa. Now, while Oedipus is always tragic, his father Laius or any equivalent figure tends to become comic. Comedy, in fact, could not exist without the stereotype of the old man who refuses to 'act his age'. Some psychoanalysts have concluded that even the circus clown, in the words of Martin Grotjahn,

---

[1] *Duanaire Finn*, Part III, p. xcix.　　　　　　　　　[2] Ibid.
[3] Kuno Meyer, ed. and tr., *Fianaigecht*, Royal Irish Academy Todd Lecture Series XVI (Dublin, 1910), pp. 22–27.　　　　[4] Ibid., p. xxiv.

'represents a depreciated father figure'.[1] The clownish Finn of late folklore vividly illustrates this depreciation.

One could push this train of thought even farther and claim that the third reason includes the other two. Depreciation of the father figure, as the circus clown shows, has an appeal which, though universal, particularly attracts an unsophisticated audience. Also, disrespect for the father includes disrespect for the father-god and for the giant—who towers over the average man as the average father towers over his young son.

I should now like to summarize very briefly the comic-giant aspects of the Finn tradition. First of all, the gods in disguise who appear in the cycle often do so in the form of giants. This is true both of the *Giolla Deacair* and of the Churl with the Grey Coat, already mentioned above. Secondly, Finn and his followers are themselves represented as giants on many occasions, usually with somewhat comic results. The oral tradition often depicts them as changing the Irish landscape: building the famous basalt formation in County Antrim known as the Giant's Causeway or tearing out a piece of earth to make Lough Neagh and hurling it into the Irish Sea to form the Isle of Man.[2] The folk tradition about Oisín after he returns from the Land of Youth to find his companions dead and St. Patrick triumphant often represents Finn's son as a giant with an enormous appetite. Professor Murphy groups a number of such traditions and tales under the general title 'Oisín and Patrick's Housekeeper'. Oisín always complains that the saint's housekeeper isn't giving him enough to eat.[3] Finally, there are tales which resemble

an international group of folk tales whose theme is the tricking of a stupid Ogre by a human hero (Aarne-Thompson 1060 sq.).[4]

A well-known example of this last type of tale shows Finn himself as a cowardly giant: if he does trick the stupid Ogre, it is only by humiliating himself at the same time. A summary of the late Anglo-Irish version given by Patrick Kennedy in his

[1] Martin Grotjahn, *Beyond Laughter* (New York, 1957), pp. 91–97; see also the reference to Sidney Tarachow's work, p. 119.

[2] *Duanaire Finn*, Part III, pp. xvi–xviii, combined with personal knowledge of widely current Irish folklore.

[3] *Duanaire Finn*, Part III, pp. xix–xx.

[4] Ibid., p. xvi.

Legendary Fictions will sufficiently illustrate the comic exploitation of giants.[1]

Kennedy entitles his story 'Fann (*sic*) Mac Cuil and the Scotch Giant'. The Scottish giant comes to Ireland via the Giant's Causeway in search of Finn. The latter, seeing that the Scotsman is three feet taller than he, gets into his child's cradle and pretends to be a baby, though Finn is three feet taller than the tallest man in Ireland.

When the Scottish giant arrives, Finn's wife makes him welcome, insincerely expressing regret that Finn himself is not at home. She gives the Scotsman a griddle cake with the iron griddle baked inside. The visiting giant breaks his teeth on the iron. Then she offers the cake to the 'baby', who bites off the bread and leaves the iron. When the Scottish giant sees the baby chewing happily, he is as amazed at the infant's vigour as he was before at its size.

After his meal, the Scotsman is given gateposts to play at 'fingerstones' with, and a huge boulder to use as a ball. When the 'ball' hits him on the head, he decides to hurry home to Scotland without waiting for the supposedly colossal Finn to return home.

I think we have now seen enough of the rudimentary humour associated with Irish giants—the more so as many other peoples besides the Irish tell similar folk-tales. In the next two sections I want to show how twentieth-century Irish writers have used the various themes of humorous fantasy already enumerated in this chapter. On the whole, modern adaptations of these themes are considerably more subtle than those examined in this section and the preceding one.

The fantastic tradition in Modern Anglo-Irish humour

Nineteenth-century Irish literature in English made considerable use of Irish folklore for comic purposes. Indeed, there seems to have been a widely held view that any fantastic Irish tale recounted in dialect was *ipso facto* comic. I still have a vivid memory of a roomful of Irish schoolboys writhing in boredom and embarrassment while a master read aloud to us as a treat 'Daniel O'Rourke's Dream' by William Maginn. This drunkard's dream of being carried up to the moon by an eagle was

[1] Kennedy, pp. 203–5.

reprinted in an anthology of Irish humour as recently as 1915, but I cannot believe that anybody would find it funny today.[1] Perhaps it is symptomatic of the decay of imagination among Victorian middle-class readers that literally *any* fantasy not drenched in pathos was regarded as humorous.

Gradually, however, the Irish Literary Revival, through such plays as Yeats's *Land of Heart's Desire*, revealed once more the tragic and symbolic potential of fantasy. There followed from this the realization that comic fantasy might have its symbolic values too. Synge's *The Well of the Saints*, which explored the ironic consequences of a miracle commonplace enough in the Irish saints' lives, was apparently the first fantastic comedy with symbolic overtones. Lady Gregory, George Fitzmaurice, Yeats, and others were to follow Synge's lead.

Years after Synge's death, Yeats dramatized a similar miracle in *The Cat and the Moon*. His blind beggar chose sight at the holy well and—like Synge's pair of blind beggars—lost his illusions, for he found that his lame companion had been robbing him. After beating the lame beggar, the blind one departs in bitterness. But the lame man, who chose to become blessed rather than to be cured, leaves the stage happy in spite of his beating—and he goes off dancing, too, for his lameness has been cured without his asking.[2]

More purely entertaining than either of the above plays, Austin Clarke's 'poetic farce' *Black Fast*[3] centres on a contest in dialectic and miracle-working between two Early Irish saints, Cummian and Romanus. Each is anxious to prove by a miracle that the method of calculating the date of Easter which he favours is the correct one. Cummian, upholding Celtic custom, maintains that Lent is over. Romanus, upholding Rome, contends that Lent is still going on. When a banquet disappears from King Connal's table, Romanus claims the miracle as a proof of his correctness. But the feast sails through the air to Cummian's monastery, where the monks proceed to devour it. Lent must be over!

Mervyn Wall's humorous novel of witchcraft and demonic

[1] See Charles L. Graves, ed., *Humours of Irish Life* (London, n.d.), pp. 1-8.
[2] *The Collected Plays of W. B. Yeats*, 2nd ed. (London, 1952), pp. 459-72.
[3] Austin Clarke, *Black Fast* (Dublin, 1941).

possession, *The Unfortunate Fursey*,[1] opens with some stirring examples of the resistance offered to the Devil by the tenth-century monks of Clonmacnois. Unfortunately, Mr. Wall does not show a real familiarity with the Irish saints' lives, so that much of the magic lore he exploits for comic purposes is British or Continental rather than Irish. The same may be said of Paul Vincent Carroll's *The Wayward Saint* and Sean O'Casey's *Cock-a-Doodle Dandy*, both set in modern Ireland. O'Casey's play has a stronger satiric purpose than the other two works just mentioned, but every comic novel or play which deals with ecclesiastical miracles or with exorcism is bound to have satiric overtones in Catholic Ireland.

There will be more to say about the satiric potential of fantasy in my chapters on satire. For instance, Eimar O'Duffy, in *King Goshawk and the Birds* and its sequel *Asses in Clover*, made satiric use of elements from the Ulster Cycle. He had earlier dramatized *Bricriu's Feast*.[2]

No matter how purely farcical it seems, Irish comic fantasy in this century is always carefully shaping its raw material: sharpening it for satire, patterning it for symbol and allegory, always giving it direction of one kind or another. At least some of the results of this shaping have proved to be unified works of art, more coherent, if less rich, than the great touchstone, *The Vision of Mac Conglinne*.

Otherworld visions have played little part in this new comic literature, however. Gerald Macnamara's little play, *Thompson in Tir-na-n-Og*,[3] promises far more than it achieves. The basic conceit is brilliant: a present-day Ulster Orangeman is transported to the Land of Youth, where he finds all the legendary and mythical heroes of Ireland—and especially of Ulster. Except for thirst and belligerence, he has nothing in common with them. The Orangeman's determined ignorance of Irish culture and tradition is thus satirized, but the basic situation is never developed as drama.

This is the only example I can recall in contemporary Irish writing of a comic Otherworld visit. Perhaps the theme became

[1] Mervyn Wall, *The Unfortunate Fursey* (London, 1946). There is also a sequel, *The Return of Fursey* (London, 1948).

[2] Eimar O'Duffy, *King Goshawk and the Birds* (London, 1926); *Asses in Clover* (London, 1933); *Bricriu's Feast* (Dublin, 1919).

[3] Gerald Macnamara, *Thompson in Tir-na-n-Og* (Dublin and Cork, n.d.).

too closely associated with the *avant-garde* during the early part of the literary revival for a comic treatment to seem anything other than Philistine burlesque.

There are comic possibilities for a modern writer in the *bruidhean* theme. A modern version of the *Adventures of the Son of Evil Counsel* might give a new dimension to the 'sentimental education' type of novel. The fact remains that I do not know of any such work.

The god-in-disguise theme, however, has appealed strongly to recent writers, especially the late James Stephens. His novel *The Demi-Gods*[1] is a story of three 'guardian angels' who come to live in disguise with a tinker family—father, daughter, and donkey. The names of these angels—Finaun, Caeltia, and Art —are suggestive. Finaun is an old, old man, like Finn in some of his manifestations, and his name is but a diminutive of 'Finn'. Caeltia obviously bears the name of Caoilte, next to Oisín the most famous survivor of the Fianna, whose legend is as much involved with St. Patrick's as is Oisín's. Art's is the only name not immediately identifiable with the Finn Cycle.

The alleged angels show few Christian characteristics. They seem as amoral as Patsy Mac Cann, the thieving, amorous tinker—and even fonder than he of a good fight. The 'seraph' Cuchulain also appears on earth in the course of the book. Neither *The Demi-Gods* nor *The Crock of Gold* is entirely comic, but much of the humour in the former arises from the angels' difficulties in learning human ways.

The Crock of Gold[2] combines a number of folk motifs with a good deal of other material, grave and gay. The gods return to earth in this book too, but not in disguise. Greek Pan appears in Ireland, only to be ousted by Angus Óg. In Anglo-Irish literature Angus is usually characterized, as here, in the role of a Celtic god of love, resembling both Apollo and Eros.

Among the bewildering cast of characters to be found in *The Crock of Gold* are two fairy hags married to two philosophers, and a tribe of leprechauns from Gort na Cloca Mora. The leprechauns' attempt to rescue one of the philosophers from a group of policemen forms one of the funniest scenes in the book. If one must have books devoted entirely to leprechauns,

[1] James Stephens, *The Demi-Gods* (London, 1914).
[2] James Stephens, *The Crock of Gold* (London, 1912).

perhaps the most satisfying reworking of latterday traditions about these little people is Seumas O'Kelly's short novel *The Leprechaun of Killmeen*.[1] Here a realistic farming community is shown trying to cope with both a leprechaun and the greed his crock of gold inspires in many of them.

The Pooka, possibly a late intruder from Teutonic folk-lore, described in this case as a tiny fairy horse, appears in Austin Clarke's one-act verse comedy, *The Viscount of Blarney*.[2] Using the plot of Patrick Kennedy's 'Cauth Morrisy Looking for Service'[3] as a framework, Mr. Clarke introduces us to other folk-lore figures besides the Pooka: the Night-Hag, disguised as Cauth's fostermother; Jack o'Lantern; a Gallant who serves the Viscount of Blarney; and the Viscount himself, who comes to wed Cauth but reveals himself as the Devil.

The folk-lore of the Devil—whatever some prejudiced persons may think—is not distinctively Irish enough to concern us here. I shall just mention in passing Myles na gCopaleen's Abbey Theatre comedy, *Faustus Kelly*, about an Irish politician who sells his soul to the Devil. Adaptations of universal fairy tales, such as Lady Gregory's 'wonder play' *The Dragon*,[4] hardly concern us here either. Still, I cannot easily forget the hero's substituting a squirrel's heart for that of the defeated dragon, so that the monster becomes a vegetarian!

To conclude this section appropriately, I must endeavour to give an account of the most fantastic novel written by an Irishman in the twentieth century—with the doubtful exception of *Finnegans Wake*. I mean *At Swim-Two-Birds* by Flann O'Brien.[5] (Both 'Myles na gCopaleen' and 'Flann O'Brien' are pseudonyms of Brian O'Nolan.)

Here is a novel about an undergraduate, not unlike Stephen Dedalus, at University College, Dublin, who is writing a novel about a Dublin novelist named Dermot Trellis. Trellis has perfected the technique of 'aestho-autogamy' first developed by his brother novelist William Tracy, and 'creates' his characters so literally that they come to life and have to be accommodated

[1] Seumas O'Kelly, *The Leprechaun of Killmeen* (Dublin, n.d.).
[2] Austin Clarke, *The Viscount of Blarney and Other Plays* (Dublin, 1944).
[3] Kennedy, pp. 158–63.
[4] Lady Gregory, *Three Wonder Plays* (New York and London, 1922). *The Jester* in this volume dramatizes some of Manannán's pranks.
[5] Flann O'Brien, *At Swim-Two-Birds* (London, 1939).

in his hotel. He has absolute power over these characters, except when he is asleep.

The characters in Trellis's current novel include some Dublin cowboys left over from a Western novel by the late Mr. Tracy and some personages of Trellis's own manufacture. Among the latter is a girl so beautiful that he rapes her and begets a son, Orlick Trellis.

More to our present purpose, the characters in this extraordinary novel of Trellis's—which must, incidentally, resemble the books of James Stephens already mentioned—include the Pooka Fergus Mac Phellimey ('a species of human Irish devil endowed with magical powers'), the Good Fairy, and Finn Mac Cool.

The last-named is described very much in the comic-giant vein of late Finn tradition:

> Finn Mac Cool was a legendary hero of old Ireland. Though not mentally robust, he was a man of superb physique and development. Each of his thighs was as thick as a horse's belly, narrowing to a calf as thick as the belly of a foal. Three fifties of fosterlings could engage with handball against the wideness of his backside, which was large enough to halt the march of men through a mountain-pass.[1]

In the course of the book, Finn relates a goodly portion of the fantastic—but not at all humorous—Middle Irish tale *Buile Shuibne* (*The Madness of Sweeny*) about an historical Irish king who becomes insane through a saint's curse and lives in trees like a wild man of the woods. Eventually the cowboys and others in Trellis's novel meet Mad Sweeny in person.

All these various characters lead lives of their own while Trellis is asleep, and they eventually manage to keep their creator drugged most of the time. Not only the conversations but the poker games of this incongruous group are related in humorous detail.

Prompted by the Pooka and seeking to avenge his wronged mother, Orlick, who has inherited some of his father's literary ability, starts writing a novel about Dermot Trellis. In the course of Orlick's novel Dermot is put on trial for his life before a court and jury made up of his own characters. As all this novelist's nightmare 'really' happens, Dermot's life is not worth

[1] O'Brien, p. 10.

a pin. Just then, fortunately, Dermot's servant burns the pages
of manuscript which give life to all these vindictive characters.
Dermot escapes, very shaken. Thus ends the novel-within-the-
novel. The undergraduate novelist, identified only as 'I',
having earned his B.A., ends his own Joycean autobiography
happily. As we have seen, fire has put an end to Dermot
Trellis's novel-within-the-novel-within-the-novel. The extinction of Orlick Trellis, meanwhile, has abruptly terminated *his*
novel-within-the-novel-within-the-novel-within-the-novel!

What is the shaping principle of this fantasy? What does it
endeavour to symbolize or satirize? I would say that it is an
example of what we have since learned to call 'the anti-novel'
—an assault on the conventions of all fiction, but especially on
those of the so-called 'realistic' novel. The 'I' of *At Swim-Two-
Birds* actually puts forward a manifesto for the anti-novel in the
following (not wholly serious nor wholly jesting) terms:

a satisfactory novel should be a self-evident sham to which the
reader could regulate at will the degree of his credulity. It was
undemocratic to compel characters to be uniformly good or bad or
poor or rich. Each should be allowed a private life, self-determina-
tion and a decent standard of living. . . . Characters should be interchangeable as between one book and another. The entire corpus
of existing literature should be regarded as a limbo from which
discerning authors could draw their characters as required, creating
only when they failed to find a suitable existing puppet.[1]

Whether he believed in these principles or not, Mr. O'Nolan
certainly acted upon them and made Dermot Trellis put them
into practice also. By doing so, Mr. O'Nolan contrived a
method of demonstrating that the realistic novel, the moralizing
novel spiced with sin, the Western cowboy yarn, the hero-tale,
the myth, the folk or fairy tale, each has its own equally valid
or invalid convention, its own formula. Each formula in turn
is illustrated and then parodied. It is hardly possible to conceive
a more purely *literary* use of oral and traditional material than
that made by the author of *At Swim-Two-Birds*.

Fantasy as a pretext for ribaldry

Purely erotic writing does not come naturally to the modern
Irish. (Some readers will say that this is the greatest single

[1] O'Brien, p. 33.

understatement in my entire book!) In the next chapter I seek out some of the reasons for their grotesque and macabre treatment of sexual humour. Even in the few modern Irish writers who have treated the erotic with frank pleasure, we find a tendency to lighten the burden of passion with humour and fantasy. This is particularly noticeable in the work of George Moore and Austin Clarke, more so even than in the work of Joyce.

We have already encountered a blend of erotic humour with fantasy in *The Delusion of the Son of Evil Counsel*, the activities of the king of the leprechauns and his queen, and the story of 'O'Donnell's Kern', to name only three examples. One curious Gaelic story, *The Romance of Mis and Dubh Ruis*, has clearly undergone some erotic rehandling in the earliest manuscript now known, dated 1769.[1]

Mis, who gave her name to the mountain of Slieve Mish in County Kerry, must originally have been a goddess and belongs to the Mythological Cycle. In this story, however, she is the daughter of a human king; she goes mad with grief when she sees her father's dead body, and drinks his blood. Fleeing to Slieve Mish, she terrorizes the countryside round about. Fur and hair grow all over her body, her nails become claws, and she gains superhuman strength—reminding one both of Swift's Yahoos and of Mad Sweeny.

Eventually, the harper Dubh Ruis wins her back to sanity, primarily by having sexual intercourse with her, though he first attracts her by the sound of his harp. Brian Ó Cuív, editor of the text, regards the intercourse as 'presumably part of the early tradition',[2] and the humanization of Mis would be much less convincing without it, but the original motif has doubtless been gleefully elaborated.

Mis first recognized the harp as something her father had owned; then she recognized the silver and gold which Dubh Ruis had spread around him. He had also 'opened his trousers or his breeches and bared himself, for he thought that if he could lie with her and know her, it would be a good means and device for bringing her to her sense or her natural reason'. The story continues as follows:

As she looked at him, she caught sight of his nakedness and his

[1] Brian Ó Cuív, 'The Romance of Mis and Dubh Ruis', *Celtica*, ii (1954), 325–33.   [2] *Celtica*, ii. 327 n.

members of pleasure. 'What are those?' she said, pointing to his bag or his eggs—and he told her. 'What is this?' said she about the other thing which she saw. 'That is the wand of the feat,' said he. 'I do not remember that,' said she, 'my father hadn't anything like that. The wand of the feat; what is the feat?' 'Sit beside me,' said he, 'and I will do the feat of the wand for you.' 'I will,' said she, 'and stay you with me.' 'I will,' said he, and lay with her and knew her, and she said, 'Ha, ba, ba, that was a good feat; do it again.' 'I will,' said he; 'however, I will play the harp for you first.' 'Don't mind the harp,' said she, 'but do the feat.'[1]

Dubh Ruis, however, pleaded that he was hungry, so she caught a stag for him. Although she wanted to eat it raw, he insisted on cooking it for them both and gave her bread also. She remembered then that her father had eaten cooked meat and bread. After the meal the harper massaged and scoured her with the broth of the stag and cleaned her a great deal. They slept together, but he could not waken her in the morning, so he built a hut around her. When she awoke at last, toward evening, and did not see him,

she began to lament (and he was secretly listening to her) and to say, among other things:

It is not the gold I weep for, the sweet harp or the eggs,
But the wand of the feat which Dubh Ruis, son of Raghnall, had.[2]

After two months of the same treatment—music-therapy, baths, massage, and 'tender, loving care'—Mis was completely restored to her former self. She returned home with Dubh Ruis, married him, bore him four children, and lived happily with him until his violent death; she then composed an elegy on him, which also survives.

This delightful, rather Freudian story is not far removed in spirit from some of the tales in George Moore's *A Story-Teller's Holiday*. The main source of Moore's tales was Kuno Meyer's conviction that the *virgo subintroducta* was one of the methods used to mortify the flesh in the early Irish Church. The chief evidence for Meyer's belief, the poem about *Crínóc*, has unfortunately since been exploded by a younger scholar, Professor James Carney. *Crínóc* means 'old-young', and seems to be the

---

[1] I am indebted for this translation to my friend David Greene, Fellow of Trinity College, Dublin, and Professor of Irish in the University of Dublin.

[2] David Greene's translation.

joking name given by the monkish poet to his boyhood's psalm-book, which he has found again in his old age. It is a book, not a woman, which has 'slept with four men' since he owned it, and now returns to him a virgin or, as we would say, 'intact'.[1]

The only one of Moore's humorous stories—for his book contains pathetic tales of love also—which seems to have a firm basis in Irish tradition is that which deals with the temptations of Father Scothine.[2] I do not know whether the Gaelic original was humorously intended, but it certainly deserves to be quoted in full from the notes to *The Martyrology of Oengus the Culdee*:

Now two maidens with pointed breasts used to lie with him every night, that the battle with the Devil might be the greater for him. And it was proposed to accuse him on that account. So Brénainn came to test him, and Scothín said: 'Let the cleric lie in my bed tonight,' saith he. So when he reached the hour of resting the girls came into the house wherein was Brénainn, with their lapfuls of glowing embers in their chasubles; and the fire burnt them not, and they spill (the embers) in front of Brénainn, and go into the bed to him. 'What is this?' asks Brénainn. 'Thus it is that we do every night,' say the girls. They lie down with Brénainn, and nowise could he sleep with longing. 'That is imperfect, O cleric,' say the girls: 'he who is here every night feels nothing at all. Why goest thou not, O cleric, into the tub (of cold water) if it be easier for thee? 'Tis often that the cleric, even Scothín, visits it.' 'Well,' says Brénainn, 'it is wrong for us to make this test, for he is better than we are.' Thereafter they make their union and their covenant, and they part *feliciter*.[3]

Obviously this little anecdote is full of humour, intentional or not. In retelling it at more than twenty pages' length, Moore adds nothing to its ironical treatment of the 'imperfect' Brénainn. On the other hand, Moore makes fun of Scothín, inventing a story about how the holy man chose his two temptresses after seeing the better-developed one cavorting naked in the river. The girls' mother, in at first refusing to

[1] See James F. Kenney, *The Sources for the Early History of Ireland*, i (New York, 1929), 735, for bibliography, and Frank O'Connor, *Kings, Lords and Commons* (New York, 1959), p. 12, for comment. See also James Carney, '*A Chrínóg, Cubaid do Cheól*', *Éigse*, iv (1943–4), 280–3; Myles Dillon, ed., *Early Irish Society* (Dublin, 1954), pp. 75–76.

[2] George Moore, *A Story-Teller's Holiday*, i (New York, 1929), 145–68.

[3] *Félire Óengusso Céli Dé*, ed. and tr. Whitley Stokes (London, 1905), p. 41.

accept Scothín's suggestion, makes a remark that Moore must have chuckled over as it came from his pen:

> You're a great saint, Father Scothine, said the woman; you are so, and high enough will you be perched in the kingdom of heaven without making a step-ladder of my daughter's two breasts.[1]

But, aside from this one remark, I much prefer the dialogue in the original—understated, but full of overtones.

Austin Clarke's three fine erotic novels of medieval Ireland —*The Bright Temptation*, reminiscent of *Daphnis and Chloe*; *The Singing-Men at Cashel*, a sombre tale of repression and obsession; and *The Sun Dances at Easter*—all owe something to Moore, but Mr. Clarke's knowledge of Gaelic and understanding of the medieval mind far surpass his predecessor's. *The Bright Temptation* makes use of various motifs from folk-lore and mythology: a clumsy demon called the Prumpolaun; Glen Bolcain, the valley where all the madmen of Ireland, including King Sweeny, are said to resort; and the 'Sheela-na-gig', of which I shall have much to say in the next chapter.[2]

However, it is *The Sun Dances at Easter* which blends erotic and mythological themes into the most charming comic-romantic fantasy written by a modern Irishman. More adult and more genuinely Irish than *The Crock of Gold*, it does not match the Anglo-Saxon stereotype of Irish humour and fantasy; it therefore passed almost unnoticed at its publication in 1952.[3]

The Sun Dances at Easter consists of five parts: Parts One, Three, and Five carry the main narrative, while Parts Two and Four are versions of traditional stories, told by the cleric Enda. These interpolated stories dovetail into the main narrative with exquisite precision.

Part One begins with a plump, jolly, and ragged 'hermit'— actually Angus of the Birds wearing the same disguise as in 'The Adventure of the Skin-Clad Cleric' above—advising Orla, wife of Flann, to make a pilgrimage to the holy well of St. Naal if she wishes to end her barrenness. Orla gets her husband's permission and sets off for the well with her servant Blanaid. On the way, the two women meet Enda, a straying student who has been wandering all Ireland in search of a miracle that

---

[1] Moore, i. 155.
[2] Austin Clarke, *The Bright Temptation* (New York, 1932), pp. 226–65, 294–5.
[3] Austin Clarke, *The Sun Dances at Easter* (London, 1952).

will restore his faith. He has committed sins of the flesh but is now ready for repentance, though he has seen no miracle. Orla assures him that her 'hermit' will perform the miracle he seeks. Blanaid notices, incidentally, that Enda looks very like Flann, red hair and all. After some uncanny experiences during the night at the nunnery of Glan, Orla meets Enda again the next day.

In Part Two, to pass the time, Enda tells the two girls the story of 'The House of the Two Golden Methers' (*Altrom Tige Dá Medar*).[1] Eithne, a woman of fabulous beauty, comes to the hermit Ceasan and asks to be instructed in Christianity. Gradually Ceasan realizes that she is a woman of the *síde*. He hears her tell Angus that she is no longer his foster-daughter; she refuses to return to the Otherworld. In the *Book of Fermoy* (fifteenth-century) version of the tale, Eithne is safely baptized by St. Patrick before she dies. But in Enda's version the sorely tempted Ceasan is prevented by a flood from reaching the saint, perhaps because he is guilty of loving Eithne after the flesh rather than the spirit. When Ceasan tries to baptize Eithne himself, she disappears. This astonishing story, blending so harmoniously pagan and Christian beliefs, has a powerful effect on the romantic Orla, especially from the lips of such a handsome storyteller. Before parting from Enda, she gives him a detailed description of her 'hermit' so that he may recognize him. Enda is startled and obviously realizes whom Orla is describing.

In Part Three, Orla, now at the holy well, finds a night orgy in progress. After wild dancing, couples disappear into the woods. She soon realizes why the well is famous for curing barrenness. A big farmer chases her and she is about to yield to him when Enda appears and trips him up. Running away together, Enda and Orla find a hut, but within it proves to be a *bruidhean*—in fact, the fairy 'House of the Two Golden Methers' where Eithne was brought up.

After they have eaten a fairy meal in this magic place, Enda tells Orla a story called 'The Only Jealousy of Congal More', an imaginative adaptation of 'The Adventure of the Skin-Clad Cleric'. Enda's version gives Congal some new adventures

---

[1] For a summary of the original Gaelic story, see Dillon, *Early Irish Literature*, pp. 67–72.

after his metamorphosis into a he-goat: he finds that one of the noble ladies of his kingdom is an 'animal-lover' in a rather literal sense; flees in shame from the ignominy of being put to stud with a she-goat; develops a taste for feminine under-clothing (for eating it, that is); creates havoc as a result among some courting couples; finally, as he grows more animal, becomes enamoured of a she-goat; is felled by her mate when he approaches her; and returns to his human self as a result of this shock and the ministrations of a druid. Thereafter Congal prefers druids to his abbot-bishop, the puritanical Macuad, who will not allow even animals to have intercourse by daylight. As for his wife, whose infidelity he witnessed while a goat, Congal decides to forgive and forget.

Enda's description of Angus, who of course was responsible for Congal's change of shape in the story, leaves Orla in no doubt about the true identity of her 'hermit'. Also, they both realize at last that they are in an enchanted dwelling 'in the invisible Ireland'. They kiss, but a flight of angels drives Enda from her. Later, they awaken by moonlight in a hut. The *bruidhean* has disappeared. They decide, eventually, that they have both had the same enchanting dream. Enda challenges Orla to kiss again now that they are awake. She accepts the challenge, but it is too much for her virtue. Next morning she leaves Enda before he wakes. Arriving at the well before any of the other pilgrims, she sees the holy trout leap. Sure enough, in nine months she has a red-haired son who looks just like his father—and just like her husband too.

The Sun Dances at Easter offers several of the themes we have examined earlier in this chapter—including those of the disguised god and the *bruidhean*—all skilfully blended into a comic affirmation of Nature against Spirit. I can think of no other contemporary book, not even *At Swim-Two-Birds*, which better illustrates the continuity of the Irish comic tradition.

3

Macabre and Grotesque Humour in the Irish Tradition

'Beauty is Thought and Strength is Love and Ugliness is Generation. The home of Beauty is the head of man. The home of Strength is the heart of man, and in the loins Ugliness keeps his dreadful state.'

JAMES STEPHENS, *The Crock of Gold*
(New York, 1925), p. 281

The macabre and the grotesque—an hypothesis

ANY general consideration of the grotesque and the macabre might well begin with the following passage from Samuel Beckett's second novel in English, *Watt*:

The bitter laugh laughs at that which is not good, it is the ethical laugh. The hollow laugh laughs at that which is not true, it is the intellectual laugh. Not good! Not true! Well well. But the mirthless laugh is the dianoetic laugh, down the snout—Haw!—so. It is the laugh of laughs, the *risus purus*, the laugh laughing at the laugh, the beholding, the saluting of the highest joke, in a word the laugh that laughs—silence please—at that which is unhappy.[1]

This third, 'dianoetic' laugh is the one appropriate to macabre humour. It could almost as well be termed the sadistic laugh, save that it involves, by its very mirthlessness, some identification with whoever is unhappy; a truly sadistic laugh, I imagine, is full of glee. The concept of the macabre developed in this chapter is based on the assumption that a joke or other comic event, to be macabre, must inspire laughter which is tinged with terror. Such laughter is perhaps hardly intellectual enough to deserve the adjective 'dianoetic'.

Beckett's ethical laugh and hollow laugh are the laughs appropriate to satire and irony respectively. But why does the character in *Watt* make no mention of the beautiful as well as

[1] Samuel Beckett, *Watt* (Paris, 1953), p. 49; (New York, 1959), p. 48.

the good and the true? It seems to me that there is a laugh—call it the aesthetic laugh, if you wish—which laughs at whatever is not beautiful. Essentially, this laugh is provoked by the grotesque.

It is not quite sufficient, however, to identify the grotesque with the ugly. The word *grottesco* is derived from *grotta*, meaning 'grotto', and was first applied to designs imitating those found in excavations.[1] In view of the number of Priapic emblems and sculptures found in Italian excavations, particularly grottoes, I doubt whether the word was ever without overtones of sexual symbolism. At any rate, we all apply the word 'grotesque' to carvings and drawings of figures with exaggerated genitalia. True, we also apply it to figures in which almost any other bodily feature is distorted. But the protean quality in Nature which begets these myriad distortions may well be related in our unconscious to the grosser symbols of fertility. As we shall see in examining certain Irish artifacts, it is rare to find exaggerated genitalia in a context which does not also contain other distortions of the human or animal figure.

The primary meaning of 'grotesque' ('in or of a style of painting, sculpture, etc. in which forms of persons and animals are intermingled with foliage, flowers, fruits, etc. in a fantastic design'[2]) could scarcely find better illustration than in the multitudinous complexities of human, animal, and vegetable decoration which adorn the *Book of Kells*. On the other hand, their very multiplicity and the infinitely fertile invention which intertwined them can hardly fail to suggest, at both the conscious and unconscious levels, the infinite fertility and multiplicity of Nature. At that early period Irish art distorts Nature when it cannot ignore her. Later, especially in Irish literature, Nature is often insulted or ridiculed. Such manifestations offer proof of the life-hatred which the philosopher Arland Ussher detects everywhere in Irish folkways.[3]

In view of the facts just cited and many more to be developed in the course of this chapter, I offer the following hypothesis: *Whereas macabre humour in the last analysis is inseparable from terror*

---

[1] *Webster's New World Dictionary of the American Language*, college ed. (Cleveland and New York, 1957), p. 640. [2] Ibid.

[3] Arland Ussher, *The Face and Mind of Ireland* (New York, 1950), *passim*, esp. pp. 119–77.

and serves as a defence mechanism against the fear of death, grotesque humour is equally inseparable from awe and serves as a defence mechanism against the holy dread with which we face the mysteries of reproduction. Oversimplifying, I might say that these two types of humour help us *to accept death and to belittle life.*

The idea of associating awe with the sexual organs or representations of them may seem odd indeed, but there is a copious literature attesting to their use as magical charms, especially potent for averting the evil eye as well as promoting fertility.[1] For instance, the superstition which still regards a horseshoe as a good-luck charm stems from the object's fancied resemblance to the female genitalia.

The transition from awe to laughter by way of the pleasure associated with sex is not hard to envisage where grotesque representations are specifically sexual; but I think such a conception of the grotesque is rooted in error. It is too simple to read modern eroticism into primitive fertility worship, because contraception has made it easy, almost 'natural', for us to dissociate fertility from sexual pleasure.

Let me be dogmatic: the grotesque *never* excites desire and therefore can never be pornographic in the narrow sense of the word. The grotesque is always ugly, just as the adult human genitalia are always ugly. Any attempt to represent them as beautiful is by that very fact pornographic. However, evocations of these organs and of the sexual act in Irish literature are almost uniformly ugly. Such evocations arouse loathing rather than desire—until we laugh. What provokes our laughter? On the one hand, our aesthetic perception of an ugliness which seems excessive and absurd; on the other hand, a release of sexual repression.

The Irish wake

The Irish propensity for macabre humour may easily be traced to the world-renowned Irish wakes, at which merriment alternates with or triumphs over mourning, in the very presence of the corpse. Convivial drinking and cheerful conversation are the best-known features of modern wakes, but it is generally accepted that dancing, singing, and horse-play formed an essential part of the wakes in earlier times. Few people nowadays,

[1] See Roger Goodland, *A Bibliography of Sex Rites and Customs* (London, 1931).

even in Ireland, are aware that the old horse-play included some quite elaborate mimed dramas, reminiscent of fertility ritual. Lady Wilde went so far as to write of 'The Wake Orgies',[1] while Henry Morris believed that the wake games 'came down in unbroken descent through all the centuries from the *Cluichthe Caointe*, or "Games of Lamentation", mentioned so frequently in our pagan Irish literature'.[2] The similarity between the ancient Irish games and the funeral games so familiar in Homer has often been pointed out. In *A Handbook of Irish Folklore*, Mr. Seán Ó Súilleabháin lists 130 specific wake games, besides a number of more informal wake amusements; among the latter we find 'performing tricks on the corpse', a practice which might be the cause or effect of a macabre sense of humour but clearly has ritual status also.[3]

It is hard to obtain authentic information about the grotesque, phallic wake performances. J. G. A. Prim's account of the customs in County Kilkenny during the first half of the nineteenth century remains the frankest, though the games must already have lost some of their primitive tradition through having been translated from Gaelic into English. The most significant passage of Prim's reticent article follows:

[The games] were placed under the conduct of some peasant of the district who excelled in rustic wit and humour, who went under the title of 'Borekeen', and whose orders were carried into force by subordinate officers, all arrayed in fantastic habiliments. The 'game' usually first performed was termed 'Bout', and was joined in by men and women, who all acted a very obscene part which cannot be described. The next scene generally was termed 'Making the Ship', with its several parts of 'laying the keel', forming the 'stem and stern', and erecting 'the mast', the latter of which was done by a female using a gesture and expression, proving beyond doubt that it was a relic of Pagan rites. The 'Bull and the Cow' was another game strongly indicative of a Pagan origin, from circumstances too indelicate to be particularized. The game called 'Hold the Light', in which a man is blindfolded and flogged, has been looked upon as a profane travestie of the passion of our Lord; and religion might also be considered as brought into contempt

---

[1] Lady Wilde, *Ancient Legends, Mystic Charms, and Superstitions of Ireland*, i (London, 1887), 228–34.

[2] Henry Morris, 'Irish Wake Games', *Béaloideas*, viii (1938), 140.

[3] Seán Ó Súilleabháin, *A Handbook of Irish Folklore* (Dublin, 1942), pp. 662–4, 223–4. See also his *Caitheamh Aimsire ar Thórraimh* (Dublin, 1961).

by another of the series, in which a person caricaturing a priest, and wearing a rosary, composed of small potatoes strung together, enters into conflict with the 'Borekeen', and is put down and ex- pelled from the room by direction of the latter. . . . 'Turning the Spit' and 'Selling the Pig' are the names of two others of those games; in that called 'Drawing the Ship out of the Mud' the men engaged actually presented themselves before the rest of the assembly, females as well as males, in a state of nudity, whilst in another game the female performers attired themselves in men's clothes and con- ducted themselves in a very strange manner.[1]

Prim is careful to add that those who practised these strange rites

. . . had no idea of outraging propriety or religion in their perfor- mance, holding an unquestioning faith that such observances were right and proper at wakes, whilst under other circumstances they would shrink with horror from such indelicate exhibitions.[2]

Lady Wilde gives some further details concerning 'The Bull and the Cow' and 'Making the Ship'. W. G. Wood-Martin provides quite an elaborate account of the latter and also quotes 'a gentleman who had the opportunity of collecting accounts of many wanton orgies which disgraced wakes, particularly in the province of Munster'; according to this gentleman, 'The highly obscene manner of the dance called "Droghedy" is very objectionable . . . . Tradition also relates that females used to perform on these occasions as well as men.'[3]

In his well-known story 'Larry M'Farland's Wake', William Carleton apparently deals with a time and place when the wakes had already been expurgated by the clergy, but the emphasis on kissing games and mock marriages shows that something of the old pagan spirit still survived.[4] Elsewhere, Carleton mentions a solo dance which he had seen performed —at a wake, the context suggests—and words his account in such a way as to leave no doubt of the phallic nature of the performance:

[It] could not be danced without the emblematic aids of a stick

---

[1] John G. A. Prim, 'Olden Popular Pastimes in Kilkenny', *Journal of the Royal Society of Antiquaries in Ireland* (formerly *Transactions of the Kilkenny Archaeological Society*, &c.), ii (1853), 334 n.   [2] Ibid.
[3] W. G. Wood-Martin, *Traces of the Elder Faiths of Ireland*, i (London, 1902), 321. See the whole passage, pp. 314–22.
[4] See any edition of *Traits and Stories of the Irish Peasantry* (First Series).

and handkerchief. It was addressed to an individual passion, and was unquestionably one of those symbolic dances that were used in pagan rites. . . .[1]

Patrick Kennedy, the early folklorist, mentions with disapproval the telling of an obscene folk-tale at a wake—a common enough practice, I suspect.[2] All in all, the evidence from carefully worded English-speaking sources, mainly of the Victorian period, points unmistakably to the survival of phallic rites, carried out in a playful spirit, until very recent times. Morris, writing in 1938, deplored the absence of Gaelic accounts, but there is still hope that the Irish Folklore Commission may discover some more explicit descriptions of the wake rituals; if so, they are likely to occur in the older, less inhibited language.

I wonder if Joyce fully realized how much the grotesque obscenity of *Finnegans Wake*—a licence licensed by Freud's dream interpretation—was in keeping with the traditions of the Irish wake. At any rate, he knew that an Irish funeral was a 'funferall,' and felt that the word 'wake' implied rebirth as well as death. The wake game of 'building the fort', described by Lady Wilde, is clearly a representation of death and rebirth;[3] so is that of 'Sir Sop, or the Knight of Straw', reprinted by Morris from *Anthologia Hibernica*.[4] In so far as the grotesque is present in the phallic, it fuses with the macabre in a playful, even humorous amalgam at a traditional Irish wake.

It is true that the vestigial fertility rites confront us with an ambiguity: on the one hand they make fun of reproduction, while on the other hand they celebrate it. John O'Donovan, the great Gaelic scholar, brings out this ambiguity in describing the mock marriages at the County Kilkenny wakes of his youth. As the mock priest sprinkled each couple with water and 'put them to bed in a corner of the room', he would pronounce a mock blessing over them in Gaelic and Latin '*Crescite et multiplicamini*', adding: 'Now that ye are joined in the holy bonds of matrimony, may the full blessing of the beggars descend upon you; may ye have plenty of ragged children . . .' and so on. For all its humorous phrasing, there is a certain solemnity

[1] William Carleton, 'The Country Dancing-Master', *The Irish Penny Journal*, i (29 Aug. 1840), 70.
[2] Patrick Kennedy, *Legendary Fictions of the Irish Celts* (London, 1866), p. 23.
[3] Wilde, pp. 229–30.   [4] Morris, p. 123.

about this expansion of the Biblical injunction to increase and multiply. But O'Donovan goes on to tell us that

. . . this blessing was varied according to the genius and humour of the pseudo-priest, who sometimes gave the married couple plain advice about their future conduct as man and wife, and which was generally of so ludicrous a character as to create much laughter. His drollery was exhaustless, but generally gross, and always in bad taste. . . .[1]

Here we find the grotesque side of the observance, which belittles the mysteries of nature by treating them as the subject for crude jokes.

The 'Sheela-na-gig'

The amalgam of macabre and grotesque—in my special, sexual use of that word—which we noted in the wake games is strikingly exemplified by many of the Irish stone-carvings known as 'Sheela-na-gigs' (Gaelic *Síli-na-gig*, singular *Síle-na-gig*). All these female figures have in common either grossly exaggerated genitalia or a posture which directs attention to the genitalia—and usually a combination of both features. Between sixty and seventy existed in Ireland in 1935-6. Some are to be found on ruined churches, others on castles.[2] They range widely in date and in form, but what I assume to be the most primitive type displays the following characteristics: an ugly mask-like or skull-like face, with a huge, scowling mouth; skeletal ribs; huge genitalia held open by both hands; bent legs.[3] In some examples the mouth is smiling, the body is that of a young woman, and the genitalia are in a more natural proportion to the whole figure; however, I think M. Ó Séaghdha (O'Shea) is quite mistaken in thinking that an exaggerated

[1] John O'Donovan, ed., 'Extracts from the Journal of Thomas Dineley', *J.R.S.A.I.* v (1858–9), 32 n.

[2] Edith M. Guest, 'Irish Sheela-na-gigs in 1935', *J.R.S.A.I.* lxvi (1936), 107–29. Valuable bibliographical footnotes are included.

[3] See the plates illustrating Miss Guest's articles: plates IX, X, XI, XII, XIII, XIV. Fig. 1 in plate IX illustrates the characteristics I mention most clearly. It will be noted that the exaggerated genitalia and skeletal ribs are more common than the exaggerated mouth. See also plate XLIV in the same volume. Plates V and VI in Thomas Wright, *The Worship of the Generative Powers*, reprinted in Richard Payne Knight and Thomas Wright, *Sexual Symbolism*, 2 vols. in 1 (New York, 1957), ii. 33 and 39, being line drawings, are less reliable than Miss Guest's photographs, but they bring out the difference between the menacing and humorous types more strongly.

belly or bosom is, along with the other exaggerated features, one of the three main characteristics of the Sheela-na-gig.[1] All but four or five of the reproductions I have seen possess either shrunken breasts or none. The derivation of 'Sheela-na-gig' from 'Síle-na-gcíoch' (meaning 'Sheila of the breasts') seems to me unjustified, as indeed it does to Mr. Ó Séaghdha.[2] Miss Edith M. Guest found that the expression 'Sheela-na-gig' was current fairly recently in the neighbourhood of Macroom, County Cork, meaning 'hag'.[3] And a hag or a witch the Sheela-na-gig certainly was, but before that she must have been a goddess of creation-and-destruction, of whom there were many among the Celts. Perhaps she was incorporated into Christian churches as a representation of the deadly sin of *luxuria* or lust.[4] She does not become an unmistakably comic figure until she is represented as smiling. Neither she nor the wake games become truly humorous—sometimes even pornographic—until much of their primary significance has been forgotten, though I must agree with Johan Huizinga that the play-element is present from the beginning in all primitive ritual.[5]

R. A. S. Macalister noted similarities between the Sheela-na-gigs and representations of the Semitic goddess Anath; he even went so far as to suggest that the latter

. . . in the thin disguise of the *Mór-rígu*, 'the great queen,' otherwise suggestively named *Ana*, . . . entered Ireland in the train of the Beaker people, as one of the triplicity of war-goddesses who came in the same company.[6]

In discussing these three war-goddesses, whom she identified as the Mór-rígu or Morrígan and the Badb, accompanied by either Nemain or Macha, Marie-Louise Sjoestedt pointed to two passages in the Early Irish tale called *Togail Bruidne Da Derga* (*The Destruction of Da Derga's Hostel*) which she thought contained descriptions of one or other of these goddesses. If the passages will bear the construction she put on them, they

---

[1] M. Ó Séaghdha, 'Stair an Síle-na-gig', in *Féilscríbhinn Torna: Essays and Studies Presented to Professor Tadhg Ua Donnchadha (Torna)*, ed. Séamus Pender (Cork, 1947), p. 50. Those who do not read Gaelic will find the bibliographical footnotes to the entire article, pp. 50–55, most useful.

[2] Ó Séaghdha, p. 55.   [3] Guest, p. 127.

[4] R. A. S. Macalister, *The Archaeology of Ireland*, 2nd ed. (London, 1949), pp. 358–9.   [5] Johan Huizinga, *Homo Ludens* (Boston, 1955), p. 24.

[6] Macalister, p. 361.

are also descriptions of the Sheela-na-gig, a phenomenon apparently unknown to Mlle Sjoestedt. Both passages, according to her, describe 'a woman with a huge mouth, whose pudenda hang down to her knees'.[1] In the most recent edition of this tale, the editor's reading of the first passage is '*Tacmaicead a bél ichtarach co a glún*' ('Her lower lip was reaching her knees').[2] The second passage is less ambiguous, for it reads '*Tacmaicead a fés in t-ichtarach co rrici a glúin*' ('Her lower beard was reaching as far as her knee').[3] Both passages can clearly be read as somewhat bowdlerized descriptions of the most prominent feature observable in many of the bent-legged Sheela-na-gigs. When asked her name, the second of these women rattles off a whole list of names in one breath, while standing on one foot. Among the names are '*Nemain*' and '*Badb*'.[4] Mlle Sjoestedt points out the Badb's connexion with a rite of childbirth, which provides 'the link between the mother-goddesses and the goddesses of war'.[5]

The literary evidence thus reinforces my belief that those Sheela-na-gigs whose skeletal upper halves contrast so sharply with their sexual lower halves are indeed representations of a goddess or goddesses who can both destroy and create. Both the hideous women in *The Destruction of Da Derga's Hostel* appear before King Conaire as messengers of doom, but the descriptions of both and of the hideous man who accompanies the first verge on the ludicrous. We are told of the first woman that 'Though her snout were flung on a branch, it would stick there', while the second has lips on the side of her head. In discussing the humorous aspect of the Sheela-na-gig, Macalister makes an apposite comparison with medieval representations of the Devil:

. . . the lines of demarcation between the horrible, the grotesque, and the ludicrous are so indefinite that these crude ventures had the disastrous consequence of turning the most awful enemy of God and man into a figure of fun, a stock subject of frivolous jest.[6]

Whether or not the scowling Sheela-na-gigs represent goddesses, they are powerful symbols of a basic Irish attitude.

[1] Marie-Louise Sjoestedt, *Gods and Heroes of the Celts* (London, 1949), p. 35.
[2] *Togail Bruidne Da Derga*, ed. Eleanor Knott (Dublin, 1936), p. 11.
[3] Ibid., p. 16.   [4] Ibid., p. 17.
[5] Sjoestedt, p. 35.   [6] Macalister, p. 360.

Arland Ussher has remarked that 'it is hardly too much to say
that the Irishman treats sex as the Englishman treats death',
going on to compare the undemonstrativeness of the Irish
lover with the 'richness and splendour of feeling' displayed in
the Irish wake.[1] He is not being fair to a considerable body of
Gaelic love poetry, but anyone who knows the Irish in Ireland
can understand what Mr. Ussher means.

The Sheela-na-gig symbolically reveals to us a universal
truth of which the Irish, as perhaps the most archaic and
conservative people in Western Europe, have never lost sight.
Sex implies death, for if there were no death there would be
no need for reproduction. Besides, man has always found
woman terrifying as well as alluring. The psychoanalysts say
that this is because the female sex organ suggests castration to
him, as well as that first cruel expulsion from a nine-month
paradise.[2]

On the other hand, death, as we have seen in the wake games,
implies sex and offers an incitement to reproduction. We can
look away from the scowling face and skeletal ribs of the Badb-
like Sheela-na-gig to her distended fount of pleasure and
fruitfulness—and laugh with relief.

The phallic father-god

Where we find fertility goddesses, we may expect to find
fertility gods. Early Irish literature, as Mlle Sjoestedt has
shown, contains some very curious and grotesque ones.[3] Perhaps the most interesting of these figures is the Dagda as he
appears in *Cath Maige Tured* (*The* [*Second*] *Battle of Moytura*).
He is a sort of Hercules in regard to his huge but menial labours
and his giant (doubtless phallic) club, with which he can both
kill men and restore them to life. Like the Hercules of Euripides'
Alcestis, he is essentially a comic figure in his greed and his
primitive attire:

Hideous and pot-bellied, he wears a cowl and a short tunic like
that of the Gaulish god of the mallet; but in Irish sagas long garments are a measure of the dignity of the wearer, and this tunic is
the ordinary attire of churls.[4]

[1] Ussher, p. 149.
[2] Martin Grotjahn, *Beyond Laughter* (New York, 1957), pp. 55, 103.
[3] 'The Chieftain-Gods of Ireland', Sjoestedt, pp. 38–46.
[4] Sjoestedt, p. 39.

His mouth must have been a huge one, for his ladle was 'so big that a man and a woman could have lain together in it'.

In the camp of his enemies, the Fomorians, he is challenged to eat a huge meal of 'porridge', containing whole goats and sheep, poured into a big hole in the ground. He eats it all and scrapes the bottom with his finger.

After the feast the Dagda has intercourse with his enemy's daughter, not without difficulty, for his stomach is greatly distended, and she promises in return to serve him against her father with her magic powers. While the redactors delighted in emphasizing the grotesque obscenity of this double episode, one can recognize it as a ritual manifestation of the powers of voracity and sexual vigour which are attributes necessary to the prestige of a barbarous chieftain.[1]

In the account of the Dagda we find the three notable features that M. Ó Séaghdha has emphasized in the Sheela-na-gig: the huge mouth, the huge belly, and the exaggerated sexual organ—here represented by the club, but also implicit in the sexual encounter with the king's daughter. Elsewhere in the story, the Dagda has intercourse with a Badb-like goddess, the Mór-rígu, whom he finds washing herself, with one foot on the south bank of a river and the other on the north bank.[2]

Some of the Dagda's peculiarities persist in the heroes of a type of story usually associated with the Finn Cycle: the *Giolla Deacair* ('tiresome fellow') 'O'Donnell's Kern', and 'The Churl with the Grey Coat' all share some of his comic and churlish qualities.[3] None of the stories containing these clowns seems to be earlier than the sixteenth century.

[1] Sjoestedt, p. 41. Whitley Stokes writes in *Revue Celtique*, xii (1891), 86 n.: 'Here is omitted an account of the meeting of the Dagdae and the daughter of Indech under difficulties caused by the distention of the Dagdae's stomach. Much of it is obscure to me, and much of the rest is too indecent to be published in this *Revue*. The upshot is that Indech's daughter undertakes to practise her magic arts against her father's army.' The portion of the text which Stokes refused to print has been edited without a translation by Rudolph Thurneysen, 'Cath Maige Turedh', *Zeitschrift für celtische Philologie*, xii (1918), 401–2. I know enough Early Irish to appreciate the difficulty of the passage, but not enough to confirm or deny Stokes's and Mlle Sjoestedt's interpretation.

[2] Sjoestedt, p. 41.

[3] See the previous chapter. For translations of the stories in which these characters appear, see Standish Hayes O'Grady, *Silva Gadelica*, ii (London, 1892), 292–331.

One further phallic motif with a long history in folk-lore should be noted in connexion with the father-gods. There is a famous standing stone at Tara known as the *Lia Fáil*, about six feet in length, of which Dinneen writes thus:

. . . anciently the chief fetish of the capital, it was supposed to shriek on the inauguration of the rightful monarch of all Ireland. . . .[1]

Dinneen and others also tell us that the popular name for this stone in more recent times has been *Bod Fearghuis* ('Fergus's Penis'). The Fergus in question is undoubtedly the god-like hero Fergus Mac Roich, familiar from the Ulster Cycle of tales as the lover and general of the goddess-like Queen Medb (Maeve or Mab) of Connacht, who had a number of 'husbands'. Fergus's name means 'virility'. Mlle Sjoestedt describes him as follows:

He eats seven times as much as an ordinary man, he has the strength of seven hundred men, his nose, his mouth and his penis are seven fingers in length, his scrotum is as big as a sack of flour. He needs no less than seven women when separated from his wife Flidais.[2]

In *Finnegans Wake*, whether he hit on it independently or via some compendium of Irish lore, Joyce seems to identify the Wellington Monument, a tall stone obelisk in the Phoenix Park, Dublin, as the petrified penis of both the hero Wellington and the sleeping giant Finn McCool.

If the identification just mentioned is a little hard to pin down, there is less doubt about pages 546-54 of *Finnegans Wake*, where the founding and building of Dublin on the River Liffey are described in terms of intercourse between a chieftain-father-god and a mother-river-goddess:

. . . and there, by wavebrink, on strond of south, with mace to masthigh, taillas Cowhowling, quailless Highjakes, did I upreized my magicianer's puntpole, the tridont sired a tritan stock . . . and I abridged with domfine norsemanship till I had done abate her maidan race, my baresark bride, and knew her fleshly when with all my bawdy did I her whorship. . . .[3]

---

[1] Patrick S. Dinneen, *Foclóir Gaedhilge agus Béarla, An Irish–English Dictionary*, rev. ed. (Dublin, 1927), p. 421, under *Fál*.

[2] Sjoestedt, p. 36. Compare the description of Fergus Mac Léti above, pp. 29–30.

[3] James Joyce, *Finnegans Wake* (New York, 1939), p. 547.

This phallic scene recalls the Dagda's prowess when he coped with the river-straddling Mór-rígu, or that other occasion when he coupled with the goddess Boann, who was none other than the River Boyne.[1] Here as elsewhere, Joyce's grotesquerie is true to the spirit if not the letter of Irish mythology.

Wedding rites and the crossan

One would expect phallic rites to be more closely associated with weddings than with wakes, but this does not seem to have been true in the nineteenth century, when Irish wedding customs were first recorded by writers interested in folk-lore. One curious custom has persisted into the twentieth century, however, that of the 'Strawboys'. These are young men, disguised in straw masks—earlier they wore whole costumes made of straw—who attend wedding feasts uninvited.[2] 'They formerly demanded money, and indulged in boisterous play', says Wood-Martin,[3] while Ó Súilleabháin implies that they have been known to 'speak freely', apparently a euphemism.[4] Although they are not now known as 'crossans', it appears to me, for reasons which I will explain in a moment, that this was probably their original title.

Mr. Ó Séaghdha has suggested that the *cros(s)án* was a performer in a phallic mime.[5] The costume of an actor in Greek mime included a wide-mouthed mask, clothing padded at belly or bosom, and an artificial phallus. These three characteristics, Ó Séaghdha claims, are present in the description of a crossan found in No. 116 of *The Triads of Ireland*, edited by Kuno Meyer: *Tréde neimthigedar crossán: rige óile, rige théighe, rige bronn.* Meyer translates: 'Three things that constitute a buffoon: blowing out his cheek, blowing out his satchel, blowing out his belly.'[6] The word used for 'satchel', says Ó Séaghdha, might easily include 'leather phallus' among its meanings. Since the word *rige* means 'the act of stretching or distending',[7] *rige óile* could mean 'stretching of cheeks (in a grin)', the familiar facial expression of the Sheela-na-gig.

[1] Sjoestedt, p. 41.
[2] E. Estyn Evans, *Irish Folk Ways* (New York, 1957), pp. 286–7.
[3] Wood-Martin, ii. 35.　　[4] Ó Súilleabháin, p. 206.　　[5] Ó Séaghdha, p. 51.
[6] *The Triads of Ireland*, ed. and tr. Kuno Meyer, Royal Irish Academy Todd Lecture Series XIII (Dublin, 1906), pp. 16–17.
[7] *Contributions to a Dictionary of the Irish Language: 'R'*, arr. Maud Joynt (Dublin, 1944), col. 67.

This interpretation leads to a new etymology for the word *cros(s)án*, translated 'buffoon' by Meyer. In line with a note by Todd in his edition of the *Irish Version of Nennius*, this word has usually been derived from *cros* ('cross'). Todd's note reads:

Crossans. These were the cross-bearers in religious processions, who combined with that occupation the profession, if we may so call it, of singing satirical poems against those who had incurred church censure, or were for any other cause obnoxious.[1]

This explanation may sound plausible, though Todd supplies no references to support it, but a well-known text, *Senadh Saighri* (*The Synod of Seirkieran*), claims that devils from Hell were the first crossans, while virtually all the other references to them in Irish literature are denunciatory.[2] Ó Séaghdha proposes to derive the word not from *cros* but from *craos*, 'maw, open jaws'. He feels the more secure in doing so because the Gaelic name for the puffin and other big-beaked sea-birds is *crosán*. The human crossan would then be a licensed buffoon, associated with obscene mime and famous for his wide-mouthed mask.[3] The representative of a fertility god in such a mime would easily be identified with a demon by pious Christians. I have seen imaginative pictures of a witches' sabbath in which the Devil is portrayed with an erect phallus. Indeed, such sabbaths, in so far as they existed, were probably survivals of fertility ritual.

[1] Quoted by Ó Séaghdha, p. 51 n.

[2] See 'Senadh Saighri', ed. and tr. Kuno Meyer, *The Gaelic Journal: Irisleabhar na Gaedhilge*, iv (1892), 106–8. The nine crossans in this curious tale are described as 'shaggy' and 'jet-black'. They thus resemble the hags in *The Destruction of Da Derga's Hostel*, above, but they remind us also of the cormorant, a bird sometimes known as the 'sea-hag'. See immediately below in the text.

[3] Ó Séaghdha, pp. 51–52. Note also that the Welsh dictionary published by the Board of Celtic Studies of the University of Wales contains a most informative entry under the word *croesan*, rendered into English as 'jester; jongleur, minstrel; buffoon; lewd or abusive person'. While perpetuating Todd's derivation of the Gaelic cognate, *crosán*, the entry offers some synonyms from earlier Welsh dictionaries which seem to weigh heavily in favour of Ó Séaghdha's view of the true nature of the *crosán*, whatever the etymology of the word may be. John Davies's *Dictionarium Duplex* of 1632 gave *mimus*, *histrio*, *obscaenus*, and *scurra* as Latin equivalents for the noun (*mimus*, 'mime'; *histrio*, 'actor'). For *croesan* as an adjective we find *Fescenninus*, *lasciuus*, *obscaenus*, *petulans*, *scurrilis*, *spurcidicus* given by Sir Thomas Williems in his MS. *Dictionarium Latino-Cambricum* of 1604–7. English equivalents for the adjective in John Walters's *English-Welsh Dictionary* (1770–94) included 'bawdy, filthy in speech, obscene, ribald, smutty'. See *Geiriadur Prifysgol Cymru. A Dictionary of the Welsh Language*, fasc. x (Cardiff, 1956), p. 605.

The crossans are associated both with a particular metre and with a particular literary genre. The *snéadhbhairdne* metre in Irish bardic poetry is known also as *crosán(t)acht;* furthermore, verse in this metre interspersed with a kind of prose 'patter' is used to make up a form of entertainment also known as *crosán(t)acht.* Two long complete examples are to be found among the works of the seventeenth-century poet Dáibhidh Ó Bruadair (David O'Bruadair); it is surely significant that each should have been composed as an epithalamium. Although the allusions to fertility and the joys of marriage are decorous enough, they form a goodly proportion of each poem. The following points from the more interesting example may be significant. In stanzas xxxiv and xxxv the poet seems to identify himself with the god Manannán; as such, in stanzas xxxviii–xli he describes himself as 'a gay and jovial priest, who knows no Latin', but does know 'how to lead a docile, noble maiden,/Happy and delighted,/To her loving partner of the couch of marriage . . .'; he removes 'from guileless youth austere restrictions' and bids them 'indulge thereafter love's concealed caresses . . .'. A reference to the *Giolla Deacair* appears somewhat farther on. The penultimate section of the poem, beginning with stanza lxxx, is headed 'My own tale tonight' and shows us a crossan once more associated with a full belly: 'I myself am but an eerie, stumbling crosán,/Gentle maid I visit,/And from feats of drinking filled to waist am found then/Ear to wall reclining.'[1]

I imagine that weddings of earlier centuries were often enlivened by an invasion of masked crossans, with false bellies and perhaps false phalluses, gesturing and capering obscenely, invoking fertility and sexual licence in prose and verse, and doubtless ultimately collapsing drunkenly in the way the poet describes.

The other, earlier *crosánacht* by O'Bruadair[2] contains one very interesting passage. In an allusion to defloration typical of epithalamia in every language, O'Bruadair comforts the bride thus:

[1] *Duanaire Dháibhidh Uí Bhruadair: The Poems of David Ó Bruadair*, Part II, ed. and tr. Rev. John C. Mac Erlean, S.J., Irish Texts Society XIII (London, 1913), pp. 48–97.

[2] *Duanaire Dháibhidh Uí Bhruadair*, Part I, ed. and tr. Mac Erlean, Irish Texts Society XI (London, 1910), pp. 88–117.

Hardship unfamiliar should she then discover,
    Not yet by her encountered;
Let her not by coldness, in doing and enduring,
    Try to shun her trouble.

Many other valleys, likewise, have been plundered,
    Wounding unforbidden;
To strike across that frontier is no cause for scruple,
    Plentiful its profits.

The exploit of Cú Chulainn with his gapped spear, famous
    For its feats of frenzy,
Leaveth in this country no trace of fatal wounding,
    Since the fall of Connlaech.

It left a weighty burthen of certain magic virtues,
    After he was wounded;
Hence it is at present of the pain it causeth
    The pleasantest physician. . . .[1]

The magic spear of Cuchulain, the *gae Bulga*, able both to wound and heal, may originally have been a phallic attribute of a father-god, like the Dagda's club. In the erotic jesting of the epithalamium it has become phallic again, representing the bridegroom's weapon, which has the power of soothing where it wounds.

O'Bruadair's editor, Father MacErlean, comments as follows on the use of *crosánacht* for epithalamia:

It is worthy of notice that besides the two marriage poems of David Ó Bruadair the poem composed by Andrew MacCurtin of Clare at the beginning of the eighteenth century on the marriage of Sorley MacDonnell and Elizabeth, daughter of Christopher O'Brien of Ennistimon, is also written in this metre, which would thus seem to have been considered the appropriate metre for such compositions.[2]

If crossans were in fact ever crossbearers, they may have attained this function by a very curious route. The bearers of the phallus in Roman wedding processions sang ribald and abusive Fescennine verses, as Todd's cross-bearers sang satirical poems. Once again we have a link between the crossan and fertility rites. *Senadh Saighri* proves that the crossans were feared and hated as satirists; furthermore, the *crosánacht* metre was used

---

[1] Part I, p. 103.

[2] Part I, p. 91. For the metre and the *crosánacht* or *cluain* form, see the same page.

for satire on occasion, while the *crosánacht* as epithalamium contained a humorous and satiric element, particularly in the prose passages. The link between *crosánacht* as satire and *crosánacht* as epithalamium is explained by the fact that the abusiveness of the Fescennine verses had a magical origin, being intended to drive off demons and evil influences from the wedding rites and thus ensure the future happiness and fertility of the wedded couple.[1] Beneath their graceful decorum and their elaborate historical and mythological allusions, the bardic epithalamia of O'Bruadair are closer to their primitive source than one might at first suspect, though apparently so remote from the rustic clowning of the Strawboys.

Macabre humour in the hero-tales

No feature of the Irish hero-tales is more striking to anyone who can read them in Middle Irish than the macabre humour which permeates them. Much of this tends to be lost in translation because the translators—especially those of the nineteenth century—are usually unsympathetic to or even offended by such humour. The macabre appears even more frequently than the grotesque, though sometimes they are undistinguishable.

One faces a problem, of course, in deciding how much of this macabre humour was intended humorously at the time it was written. If we assume that all these tales of pagan heroes, at least in the form now available to us, were written down by Christian monks—and there seems no evidence to the contrary —it is natural to expect that the scribes would find the doings of Cuchulain and his like almost as foreign and quaint as we do.

One example of the macabre—and incidentally the grotesque —from the boyhood deeds of Cuchulain must stand for many such incidents in the *Book of the Dun Cow* and *Yellow Book of Lecan* version of the *Táin Bó Cualnge* (*The Cattle Raid of Cooley*), often described as the Irish *Iliad*.

Once, Cuchulain slept through a battle and only learned after it was over that King Conchobar (Conor) of Ulster was missing. Going to the battlefield to look for the King, 'He saw a man before him, with half his head on, and half of another man on his back.' This grotesque figure asks Cuchulain to help him carry his dead brother a while; Cuchulain refuses;

[1] See, for instance, Robert C. Elliott, *The Power of Satire* (Princeton, 1960), pp. 5–6.

the half-headed man promptly 'throws the burden to him'. Cuchulain throws it away. The half-headed man then attacks Cuchulain, but is finally overcome. Cuchulain 'strikes his head off with his playing-club [his hurley], and begins to drive his ball before him across the plain'.[1]

The picture of little Cuchulain nonchalantly playing hurley on the battlefield—we are not sure whether with his adversary's head or with a regular ball—is humorously macabre and at the same time very typical of the hero-tales in their older redactions.

Even at the climax of a most tragic story we may be diverted by a cruel joke, fiercer than any in Shakespeare or O'Casey. *Fingal Rónáin* (usually known in English as 'How Ronan Slew His Son') is a Middle Irish tale very like the story of Hippolytus. While the hero, Mael Fhothartaig, is dying his undeserved death from a spear thrust, his friend Congal and his fool are dying also. Even in death the fool lacks dignity:

> Meanwhile a raven was tugging at the fool's guts on the forebridge and he was contorting his mouth; the serving men were laughing. Mael Fhothartaig was ashamed and said:
>
> > MacGlass,
> > Gather in your bowels!
> > Why have you no shame?
> > —Servants are laughing at you.
>
> The three died then . . . .[2]

If one removed the macabre humour from *Scéla Mucce Meic Dathó* ('The Story of Mac Datho's Pig'), there would be almost nothing left, so important a structural element does it form in the tale. The heart of the story is a boasting contest between two groups of heroes representing Connacht and Ulster. The prize is the right to carve Mac Datho's pig at the banquet he is giving. A Connacht man says that he has carried off many a fat steer from Ulster, whereupon an Ulsterman claims to have carried off a fat steer from Connacht, namely the Connachtman's brother. After the exchange of many similar pleasantries, a Connacht man, Cet mac Mágach, sits down by

[1] L. Winifred Faraday, tr., *The Cattle-Raid of Cualnge* (London, 1904), p. 21.
[2] From a typescript translation in my possession by Professor David Greene, Fellow of Trinity College, Dublin.

the pig with his knife in his hand and invites any Ulsterman to challenge his right to be there. Man after man rises, only to be put down by Cet. First Loegaire stands up and says that it is not right for Cet to divide the pig under their noses. However, Cet reminds Loegaire of a humiliating defeat the latter suffered at Cet's hands, leaving his chariot, charioteer, and horses behind him and running away with a spear through him. 'You won't get to the pig that way,' says Cet. Loegaire sits down then.

Next comes Óengus, whose father's nickname is *Lám Gabaid*. Cet makes it clear that he gave Óengus' father his nickname by cutting off his hand. 'What would bring his son to a contest with *me*?' asks Cet. Óengus goes and sits down.

Another man gets up. 'Who's there?' asks Cet. 'Eogan mac Durthacht' is the answer. 'I've seen you before,' says Cet. He has blinded Eogan in one eye with a spear-throw at their previous encounter. Eogan subsides. 'Carry on the contest again, Ulstermen!' says Cet tauntingly. Next comes Muinremor mac Gerginn. 'Is this Muinremor?' says Cet. ''Tis I have cleaned my spears at last, Muinremor.' He may mean that the cleaning took him a long time, for only three days before, he killed three warriors of Muinremor's, including the latter's eldest son.

The next challenger is Mend mac Salchada ('Mend, son of Sword-heel', Meyer translates). Cet wonders why 'the sons of the churls with the nicknames' should come to a contest with him. 'For I was the priest who baptized that name upon him' by cutting off his heel. 'What would bring the son of the one-legged man against me?' Mend sits down.

Then a 'great, gray, very ugly warrior', Celtchair mac Uithechair, comes forward. 'Wait a little, Celtchair,' says Cet, 'unless you're in a hurry to crush me right away.' And he reminds his challenger that a spear-thrust from Cet went through Celtchair's thigh and the upper part of his testicles, so that he has had a urological disease (literally, 'a disease of urine') ever since and has not been able to beget any children. 'What would bring you against me?' Celtchair sits down then.

Then King Conchobar's son, Cúscraid, 'the Stammerer of Macha', stands up. But it soon turns out that the speech impediment which gave him his nickname was the result of a spear wound in the throat from Cet.

In this way Cet puts disgrace on the whole province of Ulster. Just as Cet is settling down to carve the pig, Conall *Cernach* ('The Victorious'), one of the greatest Ulster heroes, enters. Cet and Conall compliment each other in verse on their valour, but then Conall tells Cet to get up from the pig. Ever since he first took arms, Conall says, he has not let a day go by without killing a Connachtman and sleeping with the head of a Connachtman under his knee.

'It's true,' says Cet. 'You are a better warrior than I. But if Anluan were here, he would give you contest for contest. It is a blot on us that he is not here.'

'But he *is* here,' says Conall, drawing Anluan's head out of his belt; and he hurls it at Cet, hitting him on the chest, 'so that a gush of blood broke over his lips'. The latter gets up from the pig and Conall sits down at it. For the modern reader, at least, this is the end of the story.[1]

As far as possible, I have quoted the exact wording of the dialogue (in my own translation) to make quite clear how ironic and deliberately humorous are many of Cet's remarks. Here, at least, there is no doubt about whether the author (or redactor?) intended all the macabre touches.

The later literary tradition

The literary material that I have dealt with thus far dates from the Early Irish period. As for the material preserved in ritual or carved in stone, it seems to have been transmitted more or less intact from prehistoric times. After about 1250 we cannot speak of either macabre or grotesque humour as forming a separate literary genre. Both occur sporadically throughout later Gaelic literature—properly called Modern Irish literature —both comic and serious. My chapter on satire in Modern Irish contains many examples of both types of humour; unfortunately, the editors of Modern Irish texts, being more puritanical, more narrowly nationalistic, or simply less scholarly than the editors of Early Irish texts, usually omit the obscenely grotesque passages, leaving them to be inferred from asterisks.

[1] My partial summary of this tale, including brief passages of literal translation, is based on the text in *Scéla Mucce Meic Dathó*, ed. Rudolf Thurneysen (Dublin, 1935). For Kuno Meyer's translation see 'The Story of Mac Datho's Pig', in Tom Peete Cross and Clark Harris Slover, eds., *Ancient Irish Tales* (New York, 1936), pp. 199–207.

I do not propose to assemble here the scattered evidence for the continuity of the macabre and grotesque tradition in Irish comic literature prior to the twentieth century. What I have been trying to demonstrate is the ritual and mythical origin of an attitude that nobody familiar with contemporary Anglo-Irish literature can fail to be conscious of.

Perhaps a few remarks about Anglo-Irish literature of the eighteenth and nineteenth centuries may be in order before I pass on, however. For example, the grotesque obscenity of such poems by Swift as 'The Lady's Dressing-Room', 'A Beautiful Young Nymph Going to Bed', and 'Strephon and Chloe' takes on a rather different colouring when viewed against the background I have sketched. The scatological element in these poems does not seem to figure very prominently in the Gaelic tradition, but the acute sensitivity to ugliness shown in their treatment of sexual relations bears out what I have said about the life-hating aspect of the Irish grotesque.

After Swift, of course, all the grosser aspects of sexuality are heavily censored in Anglo-Irish literature until our own time, but macabre humour is not subject to a similar taboo. On the contrary, it flourishes in the nineteenth-century novelists, particularly Carleton and Lever. Even such reputedly gentle humorists as Mesdames Somerville and Ross exploit it frequently. An example is their story 'Lisheen Races, Second-Hand', in which the supposed death of a jockey named Driscoll inspires Slipper, a groom who appears in many of the 'Irish R. M.' stories, to the reiterated comment, 'Oh, divil so pleasant an afthernoon ever you seen.' On one occasion he adds, '. . . and indeed, Mr. Flurry, it's what we were all sayin', it was a great pity your honour was not there for the likin' you had for Driscoll'.[1]

Even Bernard Shaw exploits this Irish gallows humour in the famous trial scene of *The Devil's Disciple*, modelled after a similar scene in Dion Boucicault's *Arrah-na-Pogue*. In *John Bull's Other Island* he reveals the sadistic nature of a certain kind of Irish humour, while at the same time disapproving of it through the mouths of several of his characters. The brief but searing scene in Act IV shows all the Irishmen present, except Father

[1] E. Œ. Somerville and 'Martin Ross', *Experiences of an Irish R.M.* (London and New York, 1944), p. 68.

Keegan, laughing their heads off at the story of the pig which, when taken for a ride in Broadbent's automobile, panicked, jumped out, and was turned into bacon by the car. Many lives had been endangered by the runaway car and much damage done. Each fresh disaster, as it is described by Barney Doran, causes a fresh burst of laughter. Keegan comments, 'There is danger, destruction, torment! What more do we need to make us merry?' Later he says, 'It is hell: it is hell. Nowhere else could such a scene be a burst of happiness for the people.'

The examples I have just quoted are from the late nineteenth and early twentieth centuries, but Anglo-Irish macabre humour reached its peak a century earlier in some of the real-life exchanges related by Sir Jonah Barrington and in some of the street ballads, among which the most notorious are 'The Night Before Larry Was Stretched' and 'Johnny, I Hardly Knew Ye'.[1]

Macabre and grotesque humour in the Irish Literary Revival

The Irish Literary Revival of the twentieth century was consciously attempting to revive the Gaelic tradition. Many of the Revival writers were steeped in Early Irish literature and Gaelic folklore through the medium of translation. Others made a determined effort to learn Modern Irish—Synge and Lady Gregory most successfully, if we except true Gaelic scholars like Douglas Hyde.

This effort to revive the past, coupled with the world-wide twentieth-century affinity for the macabre and the grotesque, has given a special stamp to the recent masterpieces of Irish literature written in English. Most striking of all these, undoubtedly, is Synge's *Playboy of the Western World*, which explores the comic possibilities of parricide with a thoroughness unparalleled elsewhere in literature. Passages in Synge's *The Aran Islands* reveal some of the sources for this unique play. We know, for instance, that an old Aran man 'often' told Synge 'about a Connaught man who killed his father with the blow of a spade when he was in a passion, and then fled to this island and threw himself on the mercy of some of the natives

[1] Sir Jonah Barrington, *Personal Sketches of His Own Times*, ii (Philadelphia, 1827), 28–29; Kathleen Hoagland, ed., *1000 Years of Irish Poetry* (New York, 1947), pp. 289–92, 271–3.

with whom he was said to be related'. Eventually the parricide was gotten away safely to America. The island people's defence of their behaviour was the simple comment, 'Would any one kill his father if he was able to help it?'[1]

Another quotation from *The Aran Islands* gives Synge's testimony that the islanders were still more concerned with fertility than with eroticism:

This evening they began disputing about their wives, and it appeared that the greatest merit they see in a woman is that she should be fruitful and bring them many children. As no money can be earned by children on the island this one attitude shows the immense difference between these people and the people of Paris.

The direct sexual instincts are not weak on the island, but they are so subordinated to the instincts of the family that they rarely lead to irregularity. The life here is still at an almost patriarchal stage, and the people are nearly as far from the romantic moods of love as they are from the impulsive life of the savage.[2]

On one occasion Synge was almost mobbed by a dozen married women, 'jeering and shrieking at me because I am not married'.[3]

One further quotation from *The Aran Islands* helps to justify the cruel humour in *The Playboy* and, indeed, in Somerville and Ross and the rest:

Although these people are kindly towards each other and to their children, they have no feeling for the sufferings of animals, and little sympathy for pain when the person who feels it is not in danger. I have sometimes seen a girl writhing and howling with toothache while her mother sat at the other side of the fireplace pointing at her and laughing at her as if amused by the sight.[4]

Sean O'Casey reveals himself in his autobiography as for some years an ardent student of Modern Irish in the classes of the Gaelic League. Perhaps this has something to do with his taste for macabre humour, best shown in *The Plough and the Stars*, especially in the fourth act, which begins with the card game beside Mollser's coffin. At the end of the act and the play, when virtually every home in the tenement has been visited by death and when the sky outside is red with the flames of

[1] *The Complete Works of John M. Synge* (New York, 1935), pp. 369–70.
[2] Ibid., p. 426.
[3] Ibid., p. 418.
[4] Ibid., pp. 448–9.

burning Dublin, the curtain falls on two British soldiers singing 'Keep the Home Fires Burning'!

Gentler writers of the Revival, like Lady Gregory and Lennox Robinson, have not entirely rejected the macabre. In Lady Gregory's *Spreading the News*, a little farce performed over two years (December 1904–January 1907) before *The Playboy*, much humour is also extracted from an imaginary murder. The climactic remark is Jack Smith's 'I'll break the head of any man that will find my dead body!'

Lennox Robinson's comedy *Is Life Worth Living?* (also known as *Drama at Inish*) hinges on the drastic effect that a 'little theatre' season has at an Irish seaside resort. The plays of Ibsen, Chekhov, and others spread melancholy and soul-searching among a basically humdrum group of people. Eventually there are four attempted suicides, one more ridiculous than the other. First a man throws himself off the end of a pier:

ANNIE. Was he drowned dead?
MICHAEL. No, ma'am. Bruised. The tide was out.[1]

Then a young stage-struck couple, the husband having lost his job, try to commit suicide by gas poisoning:

. . . but sure it was a penny-in-the-slot metre and it gev out, and I suppose the young couple thought better of it, or maybe they had no change in the house; anyway, they're alive and little the worse of it.[2]

Finally the hero, Eddie, tries to drown himself, but only catches a cold.

EDDIE. But if I'm no good at living, I'm as bad at dying, for the minute I felt the cold of the water I wanted to get out of it quick and go on living, and unfortunately I'm an awfully strong swimmer so—so I just swam ashore and—and that's all.[3]

Perhaps none of the examples from Robinson, Lady Gregory, or Synge is truly macabre, since no death has actually taken place, but they are certainly *related* to the macabre.[4]

James Joyce in his youth was hostile to both the Gaelic

---

[1] Lennox Robinson, *Is Life Worth Living?* An Exaggeration in Three Acts, rev. ed. (New York, 1938), p. 43.
[2] Ibid., p. 53.　　　　　　　　　　　　　　　　　　　[3] Ibid., p. 77.
[4] Another gentle humorist, Seumas O'Kelly, exploited the Irish cult of the dead in *The Weaver's Grave*.

Revival and the Literary Revival. A growing interest in myth, legend, and folklore in general, because of the archetypal personages they present, led him to turn towards specifically Irish myths, &c., just as Yeats was beginning to turn away from them. This Irish interest of Joyce's is very evident in *Finnegans Wake*, as we have seen, but traces of it may already be found in the 'Cyclops' episode of *Ulysses*. I think it is to the earlier, more general interest in mythical and folk material that we must in part attribute the grotesque and macabre features of the 'Circe' or brothel episode of the same book. We must also remember that Joyce's model for the latter episode, Flaubert's *Temptation of Saint Anthony*, by its very nature abounded in the macabre and the grotesque. We cannot say, therefore, that the 'Circe' episode is truly in the Irish tradition, but episodes such as Bloom's pregnancy are definitely grotesque in their humour. The dog which is metamorphosed into the ghost of Paddy Dignam and then speaks like the Ghost in *Hamlet*—'Bloom, I am Paddy Dignam's spirit. List, list, O list!' —is a far-from-isolated example of macabre humour.[1]

Curiously enough, Joyce appears never to have heard of the Sheela-na-gig. At any rate, I can find no mention of it in *Finnegans Wake*. One cannot conceive, given his preoccupations with sex and with archetypes, that he would have failed to use this archetypal sex symbol if he had known of it.

Although W. B. Yeats early acquired a wide knowledge of Irish folklore and Early Irish literature in translation, he never mastered Gaelic as either a written or a spoken language. Therefore, unlike Synge, he long remained unaware of the true raciness and daring of the Gaelic countryman's speech. In his later years, however, Yeats drew on the knowledge of Irish possessed by younger men with few Victorian inhibitions. I am not sure just how much Irish F. R. Higgins ever knew, but Frank O'Connor is a real scholar in the language. By working with Mr. O'Connor on the latter's translations of Irish poetry, Yeats found several phrases like 'beaten into the clay' for his own poetry; he also may have found that better understanding of the Gaelic spirit which seems evident in the poems and plays of his very last years.[2]

[1] James Joyce, *Ulysses* (Hamburg, 1935), pp. 507, 489.
[2] Frank O'Connor, *Kings, Lords, and Commons* (New York, 1959), p. v.

I am tempted to draw an analogy between the 'Crazy Jane' of many poems and the Sheela-na-gig:

> A woman can be proud and stiff
> When on love intent;
> But love has pitched his mansion in
> The place of excrement;
> For nothing can be sole or whole
> That has not been rent.

('Crazy Jane Talks with the Bishop')[1]

'John Kinsella's Lament for Mrs. Mary Moore' unmistakably combines the macabre with the sexual:

> . . . Death who takes what man would keep,
> Leaves what man would lose.
> He might have had my sister,
> My cousins by the score,
> But nothing satisfied the fool
> But my dear Mary Moore,
> None other knows what pleasures man
> At table or in bed.
> *What shall I do for pretty girls*
> *Now my old bawd is dead?*[2]

It is in *The Herne's Egg* (1938), a play which even Yeats shrank from putting on the stage,[3] that we find the most extraordinary mixture of macabre and grotesque humour. The poet has here superimposed upon the eleventh-century saga *Fled Dúin na nGéd* (*The Feast of Dún na nGéd*)[4] a fable about a priestess, Attracta, who believes herself to have sexual intercourse with her god, the Great Herne (or Heron). It is suggested that seven men rather than one god are necessary to satisfy her—reminding us of Queen Maeve and her 'husbands' or of Fergus and his seven women. We never quite know whether the seven

---

[1] *The Variorum Edition of the Poems of W. B. Yeats*, ed. Peter Allt and Russell K. Alspach (New York, 1957), p. 513.   [2] Ibid., p. 620.

[3] *The Letters of W. B. Yeats*, ed. Allan Wade (New York, 1955), p. 871.

[4] Yeats's chief source for this tale must have been *The Banquet of Dún na nGédh and the Battle of Mag Rath*, ed. John O'Donovan (Dublin: Irish Archaeological Society, 1842). Sir Samuel Ferguson used the same source for his *Congal: A Poem in Five Books* (London, 1872), a highly serious work. See Myles Dillon, *The Cycles of the Kings* (London and New York, 1946), pp. 56–74, for a convenient summary of this and related tales.

have lain with her or not. At any rate, she loses her virginity. The sacred herons' eggs take the place of the saint's goose eggs (in the saga) as bones of contention—and as symbols of fertility.

After various episodes King Congal is killed by a fool. Attracta promptly commands an old servant of hers, Corney, to lie with her, since he is the only man available, and beget a body into which Congal's soul can enter. While Corney is still protesting because of his fear of the Great Herne, Corney's donkey is heard braying.

Attracta. Too late, too late, he broke that knot,
   And there, down there among the rocks
   He couples with another donkey.
   That donkey has conceived. I thought that I
   Could give a human form to Congal,
   But now he must be born a donkey.
Corney. King Congal must be born a donkey!
Attracta. Because we were not quick enough.
Corney. I have heard that a donkey carries its young
   Longer than any other beast,
   Thirteen months it must carry it. [*He laughs*.]
   All that trouble and nothing to show for it,
   Nothing but just another donkey.

                    THE END[1]

As I see the play, Yeats is mocking at and questioning one of his greatest themes: the intercourse between a god and a mortal ('Leda and the Swan'), and, more generally, all intercourse between the natural and the supernatural. Perhaps the natural should be enough for us; perhaps there is a rational explanation of Attracta's belief that she is to be the Great Herne's bride:

            Women thrown into despair
            By the winter of their virginity
            Take its abominable snow,
            As boys take common snow, and make
            An image of god or bird or beast
            To feed their sensuality . . . .[2]

Perhaps she should have contented herself with her seven men. And yet the ending seems to contradict this idea. What has the

[1] W. B. Yeats, *Collected Plays*, 2nd ed. (London, 1952), pp. 677–8.
[2] Ibid., p. 649.

natural world to offer, after all? 'Nothing but just another donkey.' If Yeats had ever discussed the Sheela-na-gig in his writings, he would doubtless have pointed out that while she offered a natural fear and a natural satisfaction, she was ultimately the representative of a goddess and thus of the supernatural.

Samuel Beckett: in the tradition though not of it

Those who, like myself, regard Samuel Beckett as a master humorist must base their claim almost exclusively on his treatment of the grotesque and the macabre. I imagine anybody thoroughly familiar with Beckett's work would concede that the grotesque and the sexual are almost inseparable in it. When Vladimir and Estragon are planning suicide by hanging in *Waiting for Godot*, they are particularly attracted by the idea that this method will give them an erection. Here we have a perfect marriage of the macabre and the grotesque in humour. But note the peculiar form of sexuality. Vladimir and Estragon are habitually impotent, like most of the protagonists in Beckett's later work.

It would be hard indeed to place such sterile grotesquerie under the aegis of a fertility goddess. Yet the very fact that sexuality still persists—however degraded in form—among the defeated and derelict shows what a powerful force it is. I can recall only one passage (from *Watt*) where Beckett fully acknowledges the power of human fertility, but in that passage this uncontrollable and protean force pours out an almost inexhaustible supply of grotesques—'the fortunate family of Lynch', whose ambition is to make their combined ages add up to a thousand years. In a mad race between creation and destruction, the latter consistently wins by a short head. The passage is too long to quote in full, but I must give one example of the triumph of fruitfulness in this family where each new arrival is, if possible, more diseased and deformed than the last:

And then finally to pass on to the rising generation there were Sean's two little girls Rose and Cerise, aged five and four respectively, and these innocent little girlies were bleeders like their papa and mama, and indeed it was very wrong of Sean, knowing what he was and knowing what Kate was, to do what he did to Kate, so that she conceived and brought forth Rose, and indeed it was very wrong of her to let him, and indeed it was very wrong of Sean again, knowing what he was and what Kate was and now what Rose was, to do again what he did again to Kate, so that Kate conceived again and brought forth Cerise, and indeed it was very wrong of her again to let him again . . . .[1]

What is even more startling, the ugly and diseased middle-aged spinster Ann Lynch proceeds to have twins:

Now the question that began on all hands openly to be asked was this, Who had done, or whom had Ann persuaded to do, this thing to Ann? For Ann was by no means an attractive woman, and the painful disorder under which she laboured was a matter of common knowledge, not only in the Lynch household, but for miles and miles around in every direction. Several names were freely mentioned in this connexion.[2]

In other words, no fertile woman is too repulsive and too riddled with transmissible disease not to find several males who are willing to impregnate her.

Since atomic and nuclear bombs first made it seem possible to exterminate the whole human race, there have been many works of art or entertainment dealing with a few survivors' urge to repopulate the earth. Beckett's play *Endgame* shows us two survivors whose aim is quite the opposite: Hamm and Clov want to ensure the permanent extinction of the human race. Sharing Beckett's view of fertility as a virtually inexhaustible, terrifying, and misdirected force, Hamm quite contentedly watches his parents die, while Clov eagerly kills a flea and a rat lest these creatures find mates, start the evolutionary cycle over again, and produce a human population once more. Anti-fertility is perhaps no less grotesque than its opposite, and considerably more macabre.

Beckett's relationship to the Gaelic tradition seems tangential indeed. At our only meeting he did tell me that he had attended the Abbey Theatre regularly for a year at one time. I should be surprised if he had any direct contact with Gaelic either at Portora Royal School in Northern Ireland or at Trinity College, Dublin. We have the peculiar case here of an Anglo-Irishman who, like Swift, seems to fit comfortably into the Gaelic

[1] *Watt* (both eds.), p. 103.   [2] Ibid., p. 106.

tradition yet has almost no conscious awareness of what that tradition is. Beckett might be described as *in* the Gaelic tradition but not *of* it.

I have spoken of macabre humour as a defence mechanism against the fear of death; it seems a very imperfect mechanism in the death-obsessed work of Samuel Beckett. On the other hand, I feel that his grotesque humour often fully bears out my theory that such humour 'serves as a defence mechanism against the holy dread with which we face the mysteries of reproduction'. The love affair of Moll and Macmann on the brink of the grave in *Malone Dies* is calculated to undermine the reverence for life and awe before the reproductive processes of all but the most wholesome personalities. Moll is the hag-like Sheela-na-gig in person.

The fact that these two pathetic derelicts can give vent to something like the raptures of romantic love proves nothing. Even Moll's love-letter cannot mislead us:

Sweetheart, Not one day goes by that I do not give thanks to God, on my bended knees, for having found you, before I die. For we shall soon die, you and I, that is obvious.[1]

It cannot mislead us, I say, because we have just previously read the following clinical description of the physical activities which inspired Moll's raptures:

There sprang up gradually between them a kind of intimacy which, at a given moment, led them to lie together and copulate as best they could. For given their age and scant experience of carnal love, it was only natural that they should not succeed, at the first shot, in giving each other the impression they were made for each other. The spectacle was then offered of Macmann trying to bundle his sex into his partner's like a pillow into a pillow-slip, folding it in two and stuffing it in with his fingers. But far from losing heart they warmed to their work. And though both were completely impotent they finally succeeded, summoning to their aid all the resources of the skin, the mucus and the imagination, in striking from their dry and feeble clips a kind of sombre gratification. So that Moll exclaimed, being (at that stage) the more expansive of the two, Oh would we had but met sixty years ago![2]

[1] Samuel Beckett, *Malone Dies* (New York, 1956), p. 90.
[2] Ibid., p. 89.

If the above passage be funny—and to me, at least, it is—its humour does not spring from any sense of superiority that has been conferred on the reader ('Thank goodness I'm not *that* old or *that* impotent!'). Rather, one laughs in self-defence against the uneasy suspicion that sex has betrayed everyone into at least remotely comparable absurdities. Much of Joyce's humour at the expense of sex, particularly in *Ulysses*, has exactly the same effect.

When these absurdities are found tolerable at all by Irishmen, they are found so primarily because they serve that great end, the perpetuation of the human race. But to a number of Irish Manicheans—including Beckett, Swift, and Shaw—they are *not* tolerable. Irish lovers live in constant terror of being laughed at, and, if it be true that the Irish in Ireland are a vanishing race, at least part of the blame must lie with their national sense of the grotesque.

4

Irish Wit and Word Play

WHENEVER national characteristics are discussed, we are almost bound to hear a reference to 'Irish wit'. The phrase has become a cliché, though many of those who use it really mean 'humour' rather than 'wit'. Still, any serious discussion of wit in the English language inevitably leads to the mention of several Anglo-Irish names—Shaw and Wilde being the two most likely to occur. Most recently, the late Oliver St. John Gogarty earned a reputation for wit on both sides of the Atlantic. All of this trio were renowned for their oral repartee and/or their skill as *raconteurs*, as well as for the witty lines in their plays, prose, and poetry. Shaw earned his reputation for impromptu wit on the platform, the other two at the dinner table or the cocktail bar. Curiously enough, James Joyce is almost never thought of as a wit, because he lacked the oral facility of the others. Yet I think his almost purely verbal wit, never far removed from the pun, which is so brilliantly demonstrated in *Finnegans Wake*, has closer affinities with the Gaelic tradition of wit than theirs. English-speaking wits of Gaelic stock, like Francis Mahony ('Father Prout') and, to a considerable extent, Gogarty, find their fullest expression in what might better be termed 'word play' than wit.

Actually, when we examine some of Wilde's most famous witticisms carefully, we find that, although he avoids puns, the element of verbal play in them is very important. Take his definition of foxhunting, 'The unspeakable in full pursuit of the uneatable';[1] the close resemblance in sound between the two key words adds greatly to our pleasure in the witticism. Had Wilde written, 'People unfit to be spoken of in pursuit of an animal they cannot eat', much of the wit would have evaporated. Wilde's famous critical judgement, 'Meredith is

---

[1] Oscar Wilde, *A Woman of No Importance*, Act I.

a prose Browning, and so is Browning',[1] is so worded as to give pleasure to people who are ignorant of both Meredith and Browning.

Even Shaw, whose wit relies more than Wilde's upon a skilful juxtaposition of ideas, has something of this purely verbal felicity. His most quoted witticism, 'He who can, does. He who cannot, teaches',[2] owes its success to its form rather than its content; or, at any rate, a teacher may be pardoned for thinking so.

Shaw, Wilde, Sheridan, Congreve, and other noted wits with an Irish background who belong essentially to English literature do not fall within the scope of this chapter. Their Irish upbringing or heritage undoubtedly fostered their special gift for wit, but that gift would have developed differently had they remained in Ireland or at least in constant touch, like Joyce, with the Irish cultural tradition.

I have chosen the title 'Irish Wit and Word Play' for this chapter because I am convinced that the Irish reputation for wit, in so far as it is deserved, is in the last analysis a reputation for playing with words rather than with ideas. Word play is as old as Gaelic literature, though some of the earlier manifestations of the play element are far removed from wit as we define it today.

Any of my readers who are familiar with Huizinga's *Homo Ludens* will object at this point that verbal play lies at the roots, not merely of Gaelic literature, but of *every* literature. In Huizinga's words, '. . . archaic poetry is barely distinguishable from the ancient riddle-contest'.[3] Elsewhere he says:

. . . the definition we have just given of play might serve as a definition of poetry. The rhythmical or symmetrical arrangement of language, the hitting of the mark by rhyme or assonance, the deliberate disguising of the sense, the artificial and artful construction of phrases—all might be so many utterances of the play spirit.[4]

With the omission of a word or two, this passage could serve equally well as a definition of wit. I assume *Homo Ludens* does

---

[1] Oscar Wilde, 'The Critic as Artist', *The Works of Oscar Wilde*, ed. G. F. Maine (New York, 1954), p. 952.

[2] George Bernard Shaw, 'Maxims for Revolutionists', appended to *Man and Superman*.   [3] Johan Huizinga, *Homo Ludens* (Boston, 1955), p. 133.

[4] Ibid., p. 132.

not include a chapter on 'Play and Wit' only because Huizinga felt it would be superfluous, in view of the currency of such expressions as *jeu de mots*, *jeu d'esprit*.

All I am claiming in this chapter is that the archaic, tradition-bound nature of Gaelic literature and culture preserved into modern times something of the ancient, playful attitude to language, thus creating in English-speaking Ireland a climate favourable to the growth of the great Anglo-Irish wits and ultimately of Joyce. *Finnegans Wake* is the apotheosis of the pun; now, even if the pun be the lowest form of wit, a position which I will not concede for a moment, we can be almost certain that it is the oldest form. Linguistics, psychology, our own observa-tion of growing children, all support this view. Once again, Irish archaism helps to explain the Irish comic genius.

Riddles, kennings, and other forms of word play in Early Irish

In view of the quotation from Huizinga above, riddles seem surprisingly rare in Early Irish literature: R. I. Best's biblio-graphies list only three brief texts under the heading 'Riddles'. If we adopt a slightly broader definition of the word 'riddle' than the usual one, however, it will be seen that Early Irish literature consists of very little else.

To explain what I mean, I must first quote one example of an Early Irish riddle from the text entitled *Cesta Grega* ('Greek Questions');

Caidi iat na tri duili amlabra dobeir fiss do chach? Ni ansa, .i. rosc, menma, liter.

What are the three dumb creatures that give knowledge to every one?
Easy (to say): an eye, a mind, a letter.[1]

The formula *Ni ansa* (meaning 'not hard' or 'easy'), which introduces the answer to all fourteen of the decipherable riddles in this text, probably was the time-honoured formula for answering riddles. Anybody familiar with Early Irish literature, however, knows that this ubiquitous formula can introduce almost any kind of text; any knowledge that is in the least recondite may be prefaced by a question, the answer to which always begins '*Ni ansa*' (we can disregard minor

[1] Whitley Stokes, 'Irish Riddles', *The Celtic Review*, i (1904–5), 132, 134.

differences of orthography which depend on the date of the text). Passages of *dindshenchas* (traditional place-name lore), learned treatises, even hero-tales, are introduced by the same boastful formula. We have here, I think, a reminder of the oral nature of druidic lore and traditional Irish poetry and story-telling. The *fili* had to know hundreds of tales by heart, and no doubt he was catechized orally to test his knowledge of them before he obtained his 'degree' in poetry; almost inevitably, the question became an integral part of the tale itself, or of any other traditional lore.

Another point about our riddle deserves notice, namely that the answer forms a triad. Every saying in *Trecheng Breth Féni* (*The Triads of Ireland*) implies a riddle, although the form in which we now have these pieces of gnomic wisdom suppresses the question and the '*Ni ansa*' formula; for instance:

Three fewnesses that are better than plenty: a fewness of fine words, a fewness of cows in grass, a fewness of friends around ale.[1]

Obviously, this could just as easily have been phrased as a riddle: 'What are three fewnesses that are better than plenty? Not hard: a fewness of fine words . . . .' From this example and many others that could be cited—some are included in my chapter on satire in Early Irish—it can be seen that there is an element of both wit and word play in these triads. 'A fewness of fine words' implies that too many fine words would begin to sound insincere, whereas 'a fewness of cows in grass, a fewness of friends around ale', implies that the fewer there are present, the more grass or ale there will be for each one. *Uathad*, the word for 'fewness', is really being played upon a little in this passage.

Was it Joyce who first said that the Catholic Church was founded upon a pun ('Thou art Peter, and upon this rock will I build my church')? Some of the punning riddles in Gaelic have a religious significance, e.g.:

What son eats the body of his father in the womb of his mother? —The body of the Lord which the priest eats in the Holy Church.[2]

[1] Kuno Meyer, ed. and tr., *The Triads of Ireland*, Royal Irish Academy Todd Lecture Series XIII (Dublin, 1906), p. 13.
[2] Kuno Meyer, 'Anecdota from Irish MSS., XIII', *The Gaelic Journal: Irisleabhar na Gaedhilge*, v (1894–5), 155. Also quoted above, p. 6.

Very likely such a pun is of Latin origin, but one Gaelic riddle which occurs in at least two collections cannot be translated into any other language:

What son (*mac*) has not been brought forth, and will not be brought forth, and (yet) is named a son?
Easy (to say): the *mac alla*, 'echo' (literally 'son of a cliff').[1]

One of the three groups of riddles mentioned by Best occurs in the text *Tochmarc Ailbe* ('The Wooing of Ailbe'), where the courtship of Finn and the maiden Ailbe is carried on by means of riddles.[2] Analogous to this is the curious riddling conversation between Cuchulain and Emer in *Tochmarc Emire* (*The Wooing of Emer*). Josef Baudiš points out that Cuchulain wants to marry Emer

. . . because she *understands* these riddles, while in modern folk tales the princess must marry the suitor because she fails to solve the riddles, or because the suitor solves her riddles.[3]

We should be unable to understand the veiled speech of the couple in *The Wooing of Emer* if Cuchulain's charioteer had not demanded an explanation of everything after the interview was over.

Many of the puns and kennings in this tale seem intolerably dull to a modern reader, but I feel obliged to quote at least one sample of perhaps the most famous piece of word play in Early Irish:

'Whence hast thou come?' she asked. 'From Intide Emna,' he replied. 'Where did you sleep?' said she. 'We slept,' he said, 'in the house of the man who tends the cattle of the plain of Tethra.' 'What was your food there?' she asked. 'The ruin of a chariot [perhaps rather 'the prohibition of a chariot'] was cooked for us there,' he replied. 'Which way didst thou come?' said she. 'Between the Two Mountains of the Wood,' said he. 'Which way didst thou take after that?' said she. 'Not hard to tell,' said he. 'From the Cover of the Sea, over the Great Secret of the Men of Dea, over the Foam of the two Steeds of Emain . . .'[4]

[1] Stokes, p. 135. See also Meyer, 'Anecdota', p. 155.
[2] J. F. Campbell, ed., *Leabhar na Feinne*, i (London, 1872), 150–1. The answers seem to be proverbial. For example, No. 26 in the second text: 'What is sharper than a sword?' said Fionn. 'The wit of a woman between two men,' said the girl.
[3] Josef Baudiš, 'On *Tochmarc Emere*', *Ériu*, ix (1921–3), 105.
[4] Kuno Meyer, tr., *Archaeological Review*, i (1888), 72. Irish text in A. G. van

and so on, and so on. 'Not hard to tell' is the *Ni ansa* formula
once more, introducing a passage which is actually very hard
indeed to interpret. The various unusual place-names and
phrases like 'the ruin of a chariot' (meaning 'a foal') are kennings—allusive periphrases. Elsewhere the text contains kennings
which are also puns, as when Cuchulain says he is 'the nephew
of the man that disappears in another in the wood of Badb'.
Cuchulain was the nephew of King Conchobar of Ulster;
there was also a River Conchobar which flowed into the River
Dofolt in the Wood of Badb.[1]

A knowledge of kennings seems to have been one of the
basic branches of study in the Early Irish schools of poetry.
Kuno Meyer edited a version of a well-known tale, *Scél Baili
Binnbérlaig* ('The Story of Baile the Sweet-Spoken'), which
is virtually identical with another text except that 'for many
ordinary Irish words . . . Latin, Hebrew and archaic Irish
words have been substituted'. Meyer's introduction to this
version continues as follows:

> We have here, in fact, an instructive example of that delight in
> obscure modes of diction, which Irish poetry so often shows in its
> use of kennings, extinct forms of language, antiquated native, and
> lastly even foreign words. We know that a regular training in the
> use of such expressions formed part of the curriculum of the aspiring
> *fili*; and I think that it was these various modes of expression that
> were comprehended under the name of *bérla na filed* 'the language
> or dialect of the poets,' which the young *fili*, then called *anroth*, was
> required to master in the sixth year of his apprenticeship.[2]

Those interested in following this curious tradition into regions
utterly remote from wit, though not from word play, should
consult R. A. S. Macalister's *The Secret Languages of Ireland* and
George Calder's edition and translation of *Auraicept na n-Éces*
(*The Scholars' Primer*) and related texts from the *Book of Ballymote*.[3]

Before leaving this branch of my subject, I must analyse
briefly another *locus classicus* for kennings in Early Irish,

---

Hamel, ed., *Compert Con Culainn and Other Stories*, Mediaeval and Modern Irish Series
III (Dublin, 1956), p. 26.

[1] Tom Peete Cross and Clark Harris Slover, eds., *Ancient Irish Tales* (New York,
1936), p. 161 n. [2] *Revue Celtique*, xiii (1892), 220.

[3] R. A. Stewart Macalister, *The Secret Languages of Ireland* (Cambridge, 1937);
George Calder, ed., *Auraicept na n-Éces: The Scholars' Primer* (Edinburgh, 1917).

Immacallam in Dá Thuarad ('The Colloquy of the Two Sages'), a veritable battle of wits if not of wit.[1] This text must have been highly prized, for at least thirteen manuscript copies of it are known. Whitley Stokes concluded from the language of the earliest versions that it was composed in the tenth century, though its action purports to take place during the legendary days of King Conchobar and Cuchulain.

The 'colloquy'—actually a verbal contest—occurs under circumstances which I shall describe as briefly as possible. The *anroth* Néde has been studying in Scotland; meanwhile his father Adnae, the ollave (*ollam*) of Ireland in scholarship and poetry, has died, and his post as ollave or poet laureate of King Conchobar has been awarded to Ferchertne. Néde's Scottish teacher, satisfied that the young man now has all the qualifications of an ollave, sends him back to Ireland. There Bricriu, the Ulster satirist and troublemaker, assuring Néde that Ferchertne is dead, urges the young man to make himself a beard by magically attaching grass to his chin and to assume the ollave's chair and robe. Immediately Néde has done so, Ferchertne returns from a journey. Angrily he begins to question the youthful usurper, and the battle is joined. Néde defends himself very politely against the questions of the older poet, answering each and then asking the same question of Ferchertne in reply. The entire dialogue may exemplify the oral examination in *bérla na filed* taken by an *anroth* before becoming a seventh-year student or *ollam*. An ollave's training continued to the end of the twelfth year.

One of the first questions Ferchertne asks Néde concerns his name; the young man's cryptic reply, which forms a 'rhetoric' or passage of archaic alliterative verse, is a characteristic sample of the spirit of this riddling colloquy:

Ni ansa. Robec. Romor. Rothet. Rochtot.

> *Rosre tened,*
> *Tene feth,*
> *Fogroll sése,*
> *Sopor somma,*
> *Slocreth dána,*
> *Droncherdach co teinm a tein.*[2]

---

[1] Whitley Stokes, 'The Colloquy of the Two Sages', *Revue Celtique*, xxvi (1905), 4–64.   [2] Ibid., p. 20.

I am convinced that this alliterative verse was originally evolved for the utterance of magic spells—some of which, indeed, survive in this form[1]—though it was later employed for eulogy, satire, and the preservation of all kinds of legal, genealogical, and topographical lore. The half-magical content of the passage is evident in a translation:

Not hard (to say): Very-small, Very-great, Very-bright(?), Very-hard.

> Angriness of fire,
> Fire of speech,
> Noise of knowledge,
> Well of wealth,
> Sword of song,
> Straight-artistic with bitterness (?) out of fire.[2]

Some of these cryptic statements are clarified by glosses: for instance, Néde is very small in age but very great in knowledge. When Ferchertne asks what art Néde practises, the kennings which form the latter's reply are clearly a series of metaphors for the practice of poetry: 'reddening a countenance, piercing flesh', for instance, refers to the poet's satirical powers.

When Ferchertne is asked whose son he is, he replies with a riddle, the answer to which is 'Adam'. This in itself is sufficient proof that the colloquy as we now have it must date from after the Christianization of Ireland. Here is the riddle:

Not hard (to say): I am son of the man who has been and was not born:

> He has been buried in his mother's womb [the earth]:
> he has been baptized after death:
> his first presence, death, betrothed him:
> the first utterance of every living one:
> the cry of every dead one:
> lofty A is his name.[3]

After many such exchanges, Ferchertne calls upon Néde for 'tidings'. The young man delivers an optimistic report, and asks Ferchertne for tidings in return. Ferchertne replies with a

---

[1] See Whitley Stokes and John Strachan, eds., *Thesaurus Palaeohibernicus*, ii (Cambridge, 1903), 248–50. One of these spells is quoted above, p. 6.

[2] Stokes, 'Colloquy', p. 21.   [3] Ibid. p. 33.

seven-page prophecy foretelling the tribulations which will herald the end of the world and the Day of Judgement. The Biblical origins of this passage are very evident. At the end of it Néde kneels before his elder, saying, 'Ferchertne is a great poet and a prophet', and yields up the ollave's chair and robe. Ferchertne in his turn acknowledges Néde's great gifts and wishes him a glorious future; Néde reciprocates his good wishes, and the text ends on this note of reconciliation.

The significance of this text for the history of Irish learning and wit can hardly be exaggerated. It expresses three archaic attitudes which have remained imbedded in the popular beliefs of the Irish: first, that wisdom can be demonstrated by the propounding or answering of seemingly insoluble riddles; second, that the dexterous use of verbal ambiguity is inseparable from wit and wisdom; third, that truth can be arrived at by witty dialectic. The witty and humorous cross-examination of witnesses who match their own wit and humour against the barrister's is a part of Irish legal tradition; John Philpot Curran was considered a past master at this art. To this day, obtaining information from an Irishman or Irishwoman about the simplest matters of fact often involves a battle of wits.

Irishwomen, if we can trust the evidence of the Early Irish tale *Erchoitmed Ingine Gulidi* ('The Excuse of Gulide's Daughter'),[1] have been skilled in evasion since very early times. I remember asking a young girl in the Irish tourist office in New York what was the cheapest way of getting to Ireland in the summer of 1949; 'Swim there' was her instant reply. I eventually got the information I wanted, but can you imagine receiving that sort of answer in the tourist office of any other nation in the world? Straight answers to straight questions are almost as rare among Irish people in the twentieth century as they apparently were in the tenth.

Gaelic epigram

After the archaic material just dealt with, the next step in the evolution of Gaelic wit and word play seems to have been the development of verse epigram. Robin Flower has remarked that 'a sharp and homely brevity of epigrammatic speech' is

[1] See Kuno Meyer, ed., *Hibernica Minora*, Anecdota Oxoniensia, Mediaeval and Modern Series, Part VIII (Oxford, 1894), pp. 65–69.

the universal characteristic of Irish literature 'from the first records down to the tales and popular sayings current among the peasantry to-day . . .'.[1] As I note in my chapter on satire in Early Irish, many of the early verse epigrams tend to be moralizing rather than witty; indeed, this gnomic vein persists throughout the history of the Gaelic epigram. Nevertheless, I can quote at least one famous Early Irish epigram which is witty, amoral, and most skilfully worded; note the repetition of *fetar* and *fáifea*, almost an example of word play:

> *Ní fetar*
> *cia lasa fáifea Etan,*
> *acht rofetar Etan bán*
> *nochon fáifea a hóenarán.*[2]

Kenneth Jackson's translation preserves these repetitions: 'I do not know with whom Edan will sleep, but I do know that fair Edan will not sleep alone.'[3]

Thomas F. O'Rahilly has compiled two anthologies of the verse epigrams in Modern Irish, which are known to all students of Gaelic. The first, *Dánfhocail*, consists of verses in the older syllabic metres, while the second, *Búrdúin Bheaga*, contains only verses in the stress metres which predominated after the disappearance of the 'bardic' schools in the seventeenth century.

Here is an example from *Dánfhocail* which shows the same skilful employment of repetition that we saw in the epigram on Edan; its use of antithesis is neater than that in the older poem:

> *Más bráthair bocht an bráthair méith,*
> > *is maith a ghné 's a shursaing teann;*
> *más le reimhe gheibh sé neamh,*
> > *is duine leamh an bráthair seang.*[4]

If the fat friar is a poor (i.e. mendicant) friar,
  (still) his form is fair, his girdle taut;
if 'tis with fatness he gets Heaven,
  the lean friar is a silly fellow.

---

[1] Robin Flower, *The Irish Tradition* (Oxford, 1947), p. 110.
[2] Kuno Meyer, *A Primer of Irish Metrics* (Dublin, 1909), p. 17.
[3] Kenneth Hurlstone Jackson, *A Celtic Miscellany* (Cambridge, Mass., 1951), p. 142.
[4] Thomas F. O'Rahilly, *Dánfhocail: Irish Epigrams in Verse* (Dublin, 1921), p. 29. Translation mine.

Some of the epigrams in *Dánfhocail* hinge on puns; for instance, one plays on the two meanings of *dána*: 'of a poem' and 'courageous'. Similar repetitions, antitheses, and plays on words will be found in *Búrdúin Bheaga;* for instance, one quatrain turns on the two meanings of *Onóra*: 'of honour' and 'of Nora'.[1]

The choicest example of such punning epigrams known to me occurs among the poems of Seán Ó Tuama (John O'Tuomy); it contains at least a triple pun, and runs as follows:

> *Mo mhuirinn-se Muirinn tar Muirinnibh áilne críoch,*
> *Mo mhuirinn do Mhuirinn do mhuirinn ag tál na dighe;*
> *Cé muirinn le Muirinn mo mhuirinn chun cláir ag suidhe*
> *Ní muirinn le Muirinn mo mhuirinn gach tráth gan díol.*[2]

I would not presume to offer a translation when such authorities as Richard Foley and Father Patrick Dinneen do not agree in their interpretations.[3] It is clear, however, that *muirinn* meaning 'a woman, a housekeeper', *Muirinn* as a woman's name, *muirinn* meaning 'a burden, a family', and *muirinn* meaning 'love' are all being played upon. The second line, for instance, *may* mean, 'My love to Muirinn pouring drink for a family (or 'troop of guests').' Anybody who can elucidate a quatrain like this is in excellent training for an assault upon *Finnegans Wake*.

Wit and amour courtois *in Gaelic poetry*

Because of the continuity in tradition shown by the Gaelic epigram, our brief glance at that genre has carried us forward from the ninth-century epigram on Edan to Seán Ó Tuama in the eighteenth century within a matter of minutes. We must now turn back again in time to the period between the end of the twelfth century and the beginning of the seventeenth. After their invasion of Ireland in the former century, the Anglo-Norman lords introduced into Gaelic literature

. . . the learned and fantastic love of European tradition, the *amour courtois*, which was first shaped into art for modern Europe in

---

[1] O'Rahilly, *Dánfhocail*, p. 80; Thomas F. O'Rahilly, *Búrdúin Bheaga: Pithy Irish Quatrains* (Dublin, 1925), p. 52.

[2] Risteárd Ó Foghludha (Richard Foley), ed., *Éigse na Máighe* (Dublin, 1952), p. 73.

[3] Ó Foghludha, p. 239. Patrick S. Dinneen, *Foclóir Gaedhilge agus Béarla, An Irish–English Dictionary*, rev. ed. (Dublin, 1927), pp. 771–2, under *muireann, muirn*.

Provence, and found a home in all the languages of Christendom wherever a refined society and the practice of poetry met together. In Irish, too, it is clearly the poetry of society. To prove this, we need only point to the names of some of the authors of the poems: . . . Gerald the Earl, Magnus O'Donnell (the chief of his clan), the earl of Clancarthy, and Pierce Ferriter . . . .[1]

But thanks to the Irish poets, themselves an intellectual aristo-cracy, the syllabic *dán díreach* became the vehicle of this new poetry, instead of giving way to some new style of Gaelic versification, based on French or English. To quote Robin Flower again:

In this happy union the aristocrats of position contributed the subject, the aristocrats of art the style. By their intermediation the matter of European love-poetry met the manner of Irish tradition.[2]

Thomas F. O'Rahilly's magnificent anthology of this poetry, *Dánta Grádha* (*Poems of Love*), has inspired excellent translations by Flower, Frank O'Connor, the Earl of Longford, Robert Farren, Kenneth Jackson, and Máire MacEntee. Nobody who knows anything about Gaelic literature is likely to be ignorant of the delicate wit and irony present in many of these love poems. However, as I am writing primarily for those who know nothing of Gaelic literature, it would be a sin not to discuss the subject in some detail.

Anyone familiar with this tradition as represented in Eliza-bethan, Jacobean, and Caroline love poetry knows of the 'conceits' in which the poet expresses even his despair. Naturally, the same kind of wit is present in Gaelic poetry. For instance, a poem by one Uilliam Ruadh (whose last name was perhaps Mac Coitir) congratulates a blind man on his not being able to see women and therefore not falling sick of love as the poet has done.[3] Uilliam, who once pitied the blind, now asks the same pity for himself, *i lúib na lúb ag lúib a-táim*. This pretty piece of word play reminds us of Yeats's line, 'I am looped in the loops of her hair', and may even be its source. One might lamely translate this concise Gaelic phrase as 'in the coil in

---

[1] Flower, p. 142.
[2] Ibid., p. 143.
[3] Thomas F. O'Rahilly, *Dánta Grádha; An Anthology of Irish Love Poetry* (A.D. *1350–1750*), 2nd ed., Part I (Cork, 1926), pp. 37–38.

which I am through the coils of the girl with coiling hair'. The poem ends, appropriately, in a paradox:

> *is mairg duine bhíodh 'na haice,*
> *'s is mairg nách 'na haice tá.*
> Woe to the man who is near her,
> and woe to the man who is not.

On the other hand, the Gaelic poets often use their wit to mock at love, as George Wither did when he wrote

> Shall I, wasting in despair,
> Die because a woman's fair?

Frank O'Connor has beautifully translated a poem very like Wither's, No. 99 in *Dánta Grádha*. It begins thus:

> I shall not die because of you
> O woman though you shame the swan,
> They were foolish men you killed,
> Do not think me a foolish man.[1]

Again, just as Shakespeare ridiculed the conventions of love poetry in his sonnet beginning 'My mistress' eyes are nothing like the sun', so Cúchonnacht Ó Cléirigh ridicules the hyperbole of suffering lovers. Robin Flower has rendered one quatrain of this poem with especial accuracy:

> Rope will bind me, this know I,
> Like a sponge my mouth's ne'er dry,
> Softer is my flesh than stone,
> I can't drink the sea alone.[2]

All of Flower's images are present in the original stanza, which represents very accurately the spirit of the entire poem.

Love drives men to other absurdities, not the least of which is jealousy, a foible on which the Gaelic poets gleefully ply their wit. O'Connor has translated an amusing poem about a jealous man with an ugly wife, No. 94 in *Dánta Grádha*. Here is a witty quatrain from his translation:

> Other men must watch
> Who have wives to shield,
> Why should you put up
> A fence without a field?[3]

---

[1] Frank O'Connor, *Kings, Lords, and Commons* (New York, 1959), p. 59.
[2] David H. Greene, ed., *An Anthology of Irish Literature* (New York, 1954), p. 224. O'Rahilly, *Dánta Grádha*, p. 10.   [3] O'Connor, p. 64.

The last line here reproduces exactly the image in the Irish line: *sin an fál gan ghort*.

Another clever poem, No. 74 in *Dánta Grádha*, urges a woman whose name has been linked in scandal with the poet's to earn the bad reputation she has already been given and become his lover:

> Good luck to all who blame us
> Since you have made me rue;
> They're welcome to defame us—
> Would only it came true![1]

The poet's only fear is lest people find out that he has not, after all, enjoyed her favours.

The wit in the poems we have just been examining is more often conceptual than merely verbal, but in every period of world literature libertine love poetry has fostered the *double entendre*. Again, Gaelic poetry is no exception, though many bawdy verses no doubt still languish in manuscript. However, Professor David Greene of Trinity College, Dublin, has published two Gaelic poems in which punning comparisons are made between the game of love and a board game, called *táiplis* in Gaelic, rather similar to backgammon.[2] The earlier poem, from the Scottish *Book of the Dean of Lismore*, is incomplete and difficult, but the second, ascribed to Tadhg Ó Ruairc and probably dating from the middle of the seventeenth century, is relatively easy to understand, thanks to Professor Greene's glossary of the technical terms.

Perhaps the original of the second poem was tampered with and added to by a later scribe, for the backgammon puns do not become outrageous until we reach quatrains 10-15 and the ensuing *ceangal* or *envoi*. The seventh quatrain, however, which may be an interpolation, contains two bawdy double meanings. A literal translation seems harmless enough at first:

> A pity that without me, indoors under lock and key,
> is the woman of the white-tipped, gentle hands;
> in Waterford of the white sides,
> or in Lisgoole of the quiet streams.

---

[1] Máire MacEntee, *A Heart Full of Thought* (Dublin, 1959), p. 9.
[2] David Greene, 'Un Joc Grossier in Irish and Provençal', *Ériu*, xvii (1955), 7-15.

But *Port Láirge* (Gaelic for 'Waterford') can also mean 'the harbour of a thigh', and *Lios Gabhuil* (Gaelic for 'Lisgoole') can mean 'the fort of a fork'. Insert these kennings in place of the proper names in the above translation, and at once the lines take on a very different meaning.

In the later stanzas, the backgammon terms are almost meaningless except when given a sexual reference. The poet's favourite throw of the dice, for instance, is *aon is dó* ('one and two' or 'acey-deucey'), of which Professor Greene remarks that it is 'a low throw and not a good one in any form of backgammon known to me'. Almost certainly a reference to the male sex organs is intended. The poet insists that his girl opponent should grant him entrance to 'home' or 'the finishing point', and the reference to a bed in the last line of the *envoi* makes explicit what has been implicit for several quatrains.

Although there is perhaps nothing distinctively Irish, except the language, about the wit of the poems quoted in this section, I think it is fair to say that the seed of this poetry, when imported to Ireland from the Continent, fell upon fertile soil and became completely acclimatized within a relatively short time. Nor should we forget the witty *double entendre* of the Middle-Irish poem on *Crínóc*, already referred to in Chapter 2, which antedates all the witty love poems I have been discussing. Its wit operates inversely to that of our backgammon verses, for an ostensibly erotic poem turns out to be innocuous and edifying. (See above, p. 43.) A poet capable of that degree of subtlety would have nothing to learn from the Anglo-Normans.

From Gaelic to Anglo-Irish

Can we point to any continuity between Gaelic wit and word play and their Anglo-Irish counterparts, or must we fall back upon a *post hoc ergo propter hoc* type of argument? I should like to indicate three lines of reasoning which favour continuity; none of these is conclusive in itself, but all three taken together may help convince the sceptic that Anglo-Irish wit is not a mere accident of history but the product of a cultural complex distinct from that of England, the main distinguishing feature being the close proximity in time and place of Gaelic culture —indeed, we can speak of the interpenetration of the two cultures.

First of all, there are some important personal contacts. John Philpot Curran, the only great Anglo-Irish wit who passed almost his whole life in Ireland, regarded by Byron as the wittiest man he had ever met,[1] grew up in a Gaelic-speaking district and was familiar with the Irish language from his earliest years. Also, the Rev. Thomas Sheridan, Swift's mentor in the wildest flights of word play and the author of a treatise on the pun, came of Gaelic stock. The Sheridans or O'Sheridans were a famous clan in the County Cavan. In spite of the *Dictionary of National Biography*, the Rev. Thomas Sheridan was *not* the grandson of the Rev. Denis Sheridan, head of his clan and a Gaelic speaker but also a Protestant clergyman and the father of two Protestant bishops.[2] On the other hand, whoever this Thomas Sheridan's grandfather was—we only know that Thomas's father's name was Patrick and that he was a farmer[3] —it seems virtually certain that he was a Gaelic speaker. Perhaps Farmer Patrick was a Gaelic speaker too, for the Sheridans seem to have given up their religion more easily than their language or their claim to nobility, if the Rev. Denis was at all typical of the family.

In the second place, we at last have scientific proof that the Anglo-Irish dialects spoken in country parts of Ireland are to this day saturated with Gaelic modes of thought and expression. I refer to Dr. P. L. Henry's epoch-making book *An Anglo-Irish Dialect of North Roscommon*.[4] Dr. Henry shows a scholarly reluctance to generalize, but his reviewers have been less reticent; I quote some excerpts from a review in *Hermathena* by Mr. E. G. Quin, Reader in Old Irish at Trinity College, Dublin:

It must be assumed that the vigour and vividness of certain forms of Anglo-Irish are entirely due to Irish itself . . . . No one who reads Dr. Henry's book need have any further doubt about Synge's highly-coloured language. Not all of Synge's phrases nor indeed of those in this book can be translated directly back into Irish, but this is not the point. The feeling for style is there . . . . As one reads

---

[1] William Henry Curran, *The Life of the Right Honorable John Philpot Curran*, ed. R. Shelton Mackenzie (Chicago, 1882), p. 508 n.

[2] See *A True Relation of the Life and Death of . . . William Bedell*, ed. Thomas Wharton Jones, Camden Society, New Series IV (London, 1872), p. 210.

[3] R. Crompton Rhodes, *Harlequin Sheridan* (Oxford, 1933), p. 3.

[4] P. L. Henry, *An Anglo-Irish Dialect of North Roscommon* (Dublin, n.d.).

through the examples and savours 'the vigour and vitality of the living idiom' (p. 125) it is difficult to feel that the adoption of English has in any way imposed intellectual limitations on the speakers of this dialect. On the contrary, . . . it is the English language, not the mentality and imagination of Irishmen speaking it, that has undergone a change.[1]

If this is so at a time when the vast majority of Irishmen speak English as their native language, how much more true must this have been of the seventeenth and eighteenth centuries, when Gaelic was still the native language of the majority of Irishmen? Even in Dublin, founded by the Norsemen, where a majority of the population may never have spoken Gaelic at any given moment throughout its history, Gaelic modes of speech and a Gaelic feeling for wit and word play must have been constantly present in the Anglo-Irish spoken by the common people.

In the third place, we have a vast quantity of literary references to the witty and humorous speech of the half-Anglicized Irishman, beginning at least as early as 1689, when the preface to *The Irish Hudibras* mentions '*Bogland-Witticisms*, and *sharp Repartees*, alias, *Bulls and Blunders*'.[2] From this date to the beginning of the nineteenth century, all such references show the complacent assumption that the native Irish are witty only by accident; indeed, the stereotype of the 'Irish bull' persists today, especially among Englishmen. A change in attitude begins with the Edgeworths' *Essay on Irish Bulls*, which concludes

. . . that the Irish are an ingenious generous people; that the bulls and blunders, of which they are accused, are often imputable to their neighbours, or that they are justifiable by ancient precedents, or that they are produced by their *habits of using figurative and witty language* [italics mine].[3]

In the late nineteenth century W. R. Le Fanu gives a number of examples of genuine wit spoken in the courtroom and elsewhere by uneducated Irish countrymen. For instance, a

[1] E. G. Quin, 'Irish and English', *Hermathena*, No. xciii (1959), pp. 35–37.

[2] [James Farewell], *The Irish Hudibras, or Fingallian Prince* (London, 1689), second page, unnumbered, of the preface, 'To the Reader'.

[3] Richard Lovell Edgeworth and Maria Edgeworth, *Essay on Irish Bulls* (London, 1802), p. 308.

bullying counsel said to a witness, 'You're a nice fellow, ain't you'? 'I am a nice fellow,' replied the witness; 'and if I was not on my oath, I'd say the same of you.' After two further such anecdotes, Le Fanu comments:

> It is sometimes hard to say whether such answers are given in truthful simplicity or not; but certainly the peasants, particularly in the south, do like to take in a stranger.[1]

Traces of the old patronizing attitude survive in such a comment, but the general impression given by Le Fanu's book is that very little of Irish wit occurs by accident. As one who grew up in southern Ireland when the Protestant ascendancy was gone for ever, I personally feel that, regardless of differences in education, the Irishman of Gaelic stock is generally more quick-witted than someone of my own English, Scottish, and Huguenot stock.

A favourite anecdote of mine may supply a not irrelevant conclusion to this section. Frank Feehan, a labourer from my home town of Clara, County Offaly, once told me of a lazy man who briefly 'worked' beside him in the local jute factory and was always looking for a chance to malinger. 'Frank,' he announced one day, 'me heart's stopped!' 'Well, then,' said Frank sceptically, ''twill be a great ease to your feet.' I suppose someone who had a low opinion of Irish intelligence might be able to dismiss Frank's remark as an Irish bull, especially if he was not present to observe the relish with which Frank told the story. But an unprejudiced person can see the irony and wit hidden in this seemingly casual remark, including the clear implication that ease for his feet was what the lazy workman most earnestly desired.

The word play of Swift and Dr. Thomas Sheridan

The most ingenious Irish exponents of word play between the Early Irish period and *Finnegans Wake* were Jonathan Swift and his crony the Rev. Thomas Sheridan. Dr. Sheridan was, as I have already mentioned, of Gaelic stock; he was also the father of Thomas Sheridan, the actor, elocutionist, and theatre manager, and thus the grandfather of Richard Brinsley Sheridan. If he provides a rather tenuous link with the Gaelic

[1] W. R. Le Fanu, *Seventy Years of Irish Life* (New York, 1893), pp. 199, 200.

tradition, on the other hand, Swift's influence on *Finnegans Wake* is direct and all-pervasive. J. S. Atherton's recent study *The Books at the Wake* devotes an entire chapter to Swift,[1] providing ample evidence to support L. A. G. Strong's judgement that 'The influence of Swift on Joyce goes beyond likeness and coincidence. It is assimilated into the fabric of the mind.'[2]

Swift apparently met Sheridan soon after returning to Dublin as Dean of St. Patrick's, and they were closely associated, apart from minor quarrels, until shortly before Sheridan's death in 1738.[3] Although the *Journal to Stella*, for example, shows that Swift took pleasure in puns and word play before he met Sheridan, the latter's interest in such amusements amounted almost to an obsession and unquestionably encouraged Swift's. It was Sheridan, not Swift, who wrote, under the pseudonym of 'Tom Pun-Sibi', the treatise on punning entitled *Ars Pun-ica, sive Flos Linguarum: The Art of Punning; or, the Flower of Languages; in Seventy-Nine Rules: for the Farther Improvement of Conversation and Help of Memory*.[4] Swift's name appears on the title-page of the only edition I have seen, but the *Cambridge Bibliography of English Literature* describes the pamphlet as 'mainly by Thomas Sheridan', a view supported by the reference to 'my much honour'd Patron *J—— S——*' in the book itself.[5]

The preface to *Ars Pun-ica* is a half-serious defence of the antiquity and respectability of the pun, illustrated by copious and, I think, usually authentic quotations from Greek, Latin, and French. Sheridan, we must remember, was a better Classical scholar than Swift.

As for the body of the work, it contains twenty-seven pages and but thirty-four rules; no doubt the remainder of the seventy-nine were to have appeared in the promised second part, which, unfortunately for Joyce's commentators, seems never to have appeared. The thirty-fourth is 'The Golden Rule', which 'allows you to change one Syllable for another;

---

[1] James S. Atherton, *The Books at the Wake* (New York, 1960), pp. 114–23.
[2] Quoted by Atherton, p. 114.
[3] See *The Poems of Jonathan Swift*, ed. Harold Williams, 2nd ed. (Oxford, 1958), i, 212 n.
[4] Tom Pun-Sibi, (i.e.) Jonathan Swift, *Ars Pun-ica, sive Flos Linguarum*, 2nd ed. (London, 1719).   [5] Ibid., p. 28.

by this you may either Lop off, Insert, or Add to a Word'.[1]
This rule, which proved golden indeed to Joyce and Lewis
Carroll, inspires Tom Pun-Sibi to a discourse of five pages.

Rule 30 would also have appealed to Joyce:

> *The Rule of Naturalization*, is, that PUNNING *is free of all Languages*:
> As for the *Latin Romanos*, you may say *Roman Nose—Temeraria*, Tom
> *where are you* . . . . When one says of a Thief, *I wish he was transported.*
> *A.* He is already *Fur enough* [*fur* is the Latin for 'thief'].[2]

At least these rules are presented jestingly, unlike the comparable
rules for torturing one poor word ten thousand ways which
are to be found in the tract on the Ogham alphabet in the
Book of Ballymote.[3]

At the risk of exhausting the reader's patience, I must quote
just one more rule which describes a Joycean practice: No. 21,
'*The Rule of Concatenation*', or 'making a String of PUNS . . .
'till you have exhausted the Subject'. Instead of giving Pun-
Sibi's illustration, I offer a similar passage from Swift's papers,
'The Story of the Baker':

> Is the story of the baker-man bran-new? I shall sift it to-day.
> Yeasterday I heard no such thing. Pray keep aloaf from such tittle-
> tattle . . . .[4]

From such puns it is but a short step to phonetic writing
which appears to be an unrelated series of familiar words, like
this passage in a letter of Sheridan's to Swift: 'Eye mash
aimed off knott wry tin two yew' (I'm ashamed of not writing
to you).[5] Like Joyce, Sheridan is fond of the brogue in his
punning: one such letter begins 'Deer Soar',[6] and another,
'Rave e'er end day ann'[7] (Reverend Dean). A step further
brings us to English words which prove to be phonetic Latin,
as in Swift's letter to Sheridan beginning 'Am I say vain a
Rabble is'[8] (*Amice venerabilis*). Sheridan seems to have invented

---

[1] Pun-Sibi, p. 21.
[2] Ibid., pp. 19–20.
[3] Calder, *Auraicept na n-Éces*, pp. 272–99.
[4] *The Correspondence of Jonathan Swift*, ed. F. Elrington Ball, ii (London, 1911), 407.
[5] Ibid., v (London, 1913), 82.
[6] Ibid., 119.
[7] Ibid., 139.
[8] Ibid., 434.

a favourite jargon of theirs, *Latino-Anglicus*, in which, by an inverse process, Latin is read as English:

Mi mollis ab uti, an angeli se. An has fine iis, a fine face, ab re ast as no, a belli fora que en. Andi me quis mi molli as I ples.[1]

Which, being translated, reads, 'My Molly's a beauty, an angel, I say. And has fine eyes, a fine face, a breast as snow, a belly for a queen. And I may kiss (quiz?) my Molly as I please.'

The above examples do not by any means exhaust the varieties of word play to be found in letters exchanged by the pair. The verses circulated among Swift's friends also contain word play: riddles, rhymes in *Latino-Anglicus*, and competitions in finding rhymes to the same word. Sheridan once sent Swift a harmless ballad, entitled 'Ballyspellin', in praise of the spa of the same name; the ballad, he claimed in the last stanza, had exhausted all the rhymes to 'Ballyspellin'. Swift promptly wrote 'An Answer to the Ballyspellin Ballad' containing fifteen more rhymes and a great deal of cruel comment on Sheridan, his ballad, and his male and female company at the spa. Apparently Swift meant the answer as a joke, but Sheridan's feelings were hurt, and Swift in turn was annoyed by Sheridan's attitude, as his prose character of Sheridan, 'The History of the Second Solomon', reveals.[2]

For all his skill in word play, I think Swift met his match in Sheridan. As for wit, although his major writings are full of witty irony, Swift did not excel in spontaneous repartee. Curran, to whom the next section of this chapter is devoted, far outshone him in that branch of wit.

The wit of John Philpot Curran

John Philpot Curran, whose last name suggests that his family was originally Gaelic, grew up in the small town of Newmarket, County Cork, which was then part of the Gaelic-speaking area of Ireland. Curran appears to have spent the first nineteen years of his life there, from his birth in 1750 to the year 1769, when he entered Trinity College as a sizar or charity student. His son tells us that he was 'from his infancy familiar with the native Irish language'; furthermore:

---

[1] *The Correspondence of Jonathan Swift*, v. 234.
[2] *The Poems of Jonathan Swift*, ii. 437–43.

. . . he was a frequent attendant at the weddings and wakes of his neighbourhood . . . . They appear to have had considerable influence on his mind; he used to say himself, that he derived his first notions of poetry and eloquence from the compositions of the hired mourner over the dead. It was probably amidst those scenes that he acquired the rudiments of that thorough knowledge of the Irish character, of which he afterwards made so amusing an use in enlivening a company, and so important a one in confounding a perjured witness. It may have been too in this humble intercourse that some even of his finer tastes and feelings originated or were confirmed.[1]

We may safely add, I think, that his wit was first stimulated or sharpened at these gatherings. As we have seen in an earlier chapter, it would be hard to say whether weddings or wakes provided better opportunities for merriment. During the Newmarket years he is said on one occasion to have acted as the 'voice' for Punch in a puppet show and 'mercilessly satirized the reigning vices of the neighbours'.[2]

In these surroundings he developed the spontaneity of wit and humour which dazzled Byron and made Horne Tooke compare the 'laboured and polished' Richard Brinsley Sheridan so unfavourably with Curran's 'rich and glittering ore, . . . raised from the mine without effort, and in the most exuberant profusion'.[3] Though Curran won a reputation as an orator in both the law courts and the Irish Parliament, his formal speeches were considered much inferior to his work as a debater and a cross-examiner.

So quick was Curran's wit that all the other Irishmen of his time seem, at least in his son's biography, to have been born only to act as 'straight men' for him:

'No man,' said a wealthy, but a weak-headed barrister, 'should be admitted to the bar who has not an independent landed property.' [Curran, of course, had inherited no land.] 'May I ask, sir,' said Mr. Curran, 'how many acres make a *wise-acre* ?'[4]

In another story we read of 'a gigantic and ignorant barrister' who had suffered from Curran's wit; when he

. . . half-seriously threatened to put him in his pocket—Curran being of stunted stature and size—the quick retort was, 'Do! and

---

[1] William Henry Curran, *The Life of . . . John Philpot Curran*, ed. R. Shelton Mackenzie (Chicago, 1882), p. 52.   [2] Curran, p. 6.
[3] Ibid., p. 524. See also pp. 502–3.   [4] Ibid., p. 502 n.

then you'll have more law in your pocket than you ever had in your head!'[1]

Once a barrister named Egan, a huge man, was to fight a duel with Curran and complained that his opponent offered too small a target, while he himself offered too big a one.

Curran answered, 'Very true, my good fellow. Suppose that we chalk my size upon your person, and every bullet outside the outline shall count for nothing!' They both smiled at the ludicrous idea, harmlessly exchanged shots, went and breakfasted together, and never again met in a hostile manner.[2]

Although we have seen only one example so far, Curran was undoubtedly very fond of puns. When someone said of a certain man that his iron leg was the softest part about him, 'Oh, surely,' said Curran, 'that must be *irony*.'[3] If we ignore the play on words, this remark is still appropriate—the most exacting test of a pun. Not all his puns were so spontaneous:

He called a commander of yeomanry (who dealt largely in flour) 'Marshal Sacks'—a lawyer, of a corpulent frame, 'Grotius'—another, who had a habit of swelling out his cheeks, 'Puffendorf.'[4]

When Curran first made enough money out of legal fees to own a carriage, he had painted on it the motto from Virgil *Per varios casus*, which means in the *Aeneid* 'through manifold dangers', but which Curran intended to be translated, quite acceptably, as 'through various cases'.[5]

Curran's wit, like that of most Anglo-Irishmen, often expressed itself as irony. He said of a departing Viceroy in a parliamentary speech:

Let us excuse his manners, if he could not help them; let us pass by a little peculation, since, as an honourable member says, it was for his brother; and let us rejoice that his kindred were not more numerous.[6]

Hostile judges were favourite victims of his irony; for example:

Lord Clare had a favourite dog that sometimes followed him to the bench. One day, during an argument of Mr. Curran's, the Chancellor . . . instead of attending to the argument, turned his

[1] Curran, p. 71 n.   [2] Ibid., p. 150 n.
[3] Ibid., p. 529.   [4] Ibid., p. 511.
[5] Ibid., p. 77 n.   [6] Ibid., p. 137.

head aside and began to fondle the dog. The counsel stopped suddenly in the middle of a sentence—the judge started. 'I beg pardon', said Mr. Curran, 'I thought your Lordships had been in consultation; but as you have been pleased to resume your attention, allow me to impress upon your excellent understandings, that . . . .'[1]

Even when passionately denouncing the wrongs of his country, he would make use of vivid metaphors which were not far removed from wit. During one of his courageous defences of the 1798 rebels he made this savage comment on the 'professional witnesses' who came forward for the British Government:

. . . horrid miscreants who acknowledged, upon their oaths, that they had come from the seat of government—from the very chambers of the Castle (where they had been worked upon, by the fear of death and the hopes of compensation, to give evidence against their fellows) . . . where the wretch, that is buried a *man*, lies till his heart has time to fester and dissolve, and is then dug up a *witness*.[2]

Curran's wittier cross-examinations do not seem to have survived in any readily accessible form, but here is one example of his handling of a witness, particularly interesting because of its reference to Gaelic: Once a witness under cross-examination refused to admit that he knew Irish, although he spoke very bad English. Said Curran, 'I see, sir, how it is, you are more ashamed of knowing your own language than of not knowing any other.'[3]

In the bilingual Curran the two streams of Irish wit and word play, Gaelic and Anglo-Irish, flow together to become, if not a mighty torrent, at least a pure, swift and sparkling river. Without a knowledge of Curran's Irish career, the reader might be misled into thinking that Anglo-Irish wit was an item produced exclusively for export and never offered on the home market. Indeed, he might be forgiven for thinking that Irish wit, like Scottish thrift and industry, needed the stimulus of London to make it flourish.

Joyce and Gogarty

The image of Anglo-Irish wit and word play so sharply etched by Swift, the Rev. Thomas Sheridan, and 'Fillthepot

[1] Curran, p. 159 n.   [2] Ibid., p. 214.   [3] Ibid., p. 523.

Curran' (as Joyce called him, rather unjustly) does not vary much in the centuries which follow. 'Father Prout' (Francis Mahony) and William Maginn delighted in word play, often multilingual. Richard Brinsley Sheridan, Goldsmith, Wilde, Shaw, earned a reputation in England for the wit of their speeches, writings, and conversation. In the second half of the nineteenth century a group of Trinity College dons, led by Robert Yelverton Tyrrell and Sir John Pentland Mahaffy, carried on the Dublin tradition of witty conversation and published witty parodies in Tyrrell's magazine, *Kottabos*; Wilde formed a part of their circle for a time. It was Mahaffy who supplied the perfect definition of an Irish bull, 'A male animal that is always pregnant'—itself a bull.[1]

Instead of listing names and quoting witticisms to prove a point that no one disputes—namely, that Ireland continued to produce wits all through the eighteenth, nineteenth, and twentieth centuries and to export a considerable percentage of them—I should like to deal in a little more detail with two of the principal twentieth-century figures, Joyce and Gogarty.

Oliver St. John Gogarty joined the Tyrrell–Mahaffy circle while still an undergraduate and has preserved many of their *bons mots* in his autobiographies and his rambling essay on wit and humour, *Start from Somewhere Else*. The latter book also records some witticisms by Dubliners of a slightly later generation, such as Thomas Kettle and James Montgomery; I miss the latter's best remark, however, about a river whose banks are a favourite Dublin lovers' lane: 'The trees along the Dodder are more sinned against than sinning.'

The one person whose wit Gogarty singularly fails to capture is himself. What was spontaneous in conversation becomes laboured in print; to my mind Gogarty had little gift for prose. In his poetry, however, we sometimes find the witty *amour courtois* of the Elizabethans and *Dánta Grádha*:

> Begone, sweet Ghost, O get you gone!
> Or haunt me with your body on . . . .[2]

A careful reading of his *Collected Poems* will reveal that he is one of the few successful modern explorers of this vein.

[1] Oliver St. John Gogarty, *Start from Somewhere Else* (New York, 1955), pp. 175–6. For Tyrrell and *Kottabos* see also below, Chapter 8, p. 225.

[2] *The Collected Poems of Oliver St. John Gogarty* (New York, 1954), p. 137.

To get an inkling of Gogarty's spontaneity in the flesh, one must turn to the first and ninth episodes of *Ulysses*, where Joyce presents a rather hostile portrait of his one-time friend as Malachi Mulligan but gives us a lively sense of his bubbling wit, humour, and mimicry.[1] Mulligan's sketch of a morality—or rather an 'immorality'—play in the latter episode conveys some idea of Gogarty's celebrated skill in bawdy word play.

About Joyce himself I really want to make only one point: we all know that *Finnegans Wake*, in its attempt to re-create the elusive and allusive shapes of the dream world, became the most thoroughgoing example of multilingual word play ever devised by man, but we tend to overlook the brilliant flashes of wit that are to be found on almost every page of this 'funferall', this 'pillgrimace of Childe Horrid'. Some of these contain a wisdom that deserves to become proverbial: 'Drouth is stronger than faction', for instance, or 'You cannot make a limousine lady out of a hillman minx'. The Darwinian outlook of many a co-ed might be expressed as 'the strangle for love and the sowiveall of the prettiest'. The most stolid of men comes sooner or later to rebel against 'the beast of boredom, common sense'.[2]

If one allows oneself to fall beneath the Joycean spell, certain phrases and words tend to supplant their plain English equivalents: Joyce's biographers ruefully admit the accusation in 'biografiend'; 'Irish Roman Catholics' seems a weak alternative for 'roman pathoricks'; old maids might be ready to grab the first man who passes after seeing themselves described as 'viragos intactas'; an erring husband should feel chastened by the implications of 'Promiscuous Omebound'.[3]

Not all Joyce's word play is witty, of course, though most of it is ludicrous. When we read

Your head has been touched by the god Enel-Rah and your face has been brightened by the goddess Aruc-Ituc. Return, sainted youngling, and walk once more among us![4]

we think at first of Egyptian and Aztec mythology; only when we read the magic names backwards do we realize that proprietary products, Harlene for the hair and Cuticura for the

---

[1] James Joyce, *Ulysses* (Hamburg, 1935), pp. 5–26, 189–225.

[2] James Joyce, *Finnegans Wake* (New York, 1939), pp. 13, 423, 336, 376, 145, 292.

[3] Ibid., pp. 55, 27, 432, 560.

[4] Ibid., p. 237.

complexion, reduce this lofty prose to a parody of advertising.

In his peculiar way Joyce acknowledges a debt to all his Irish predecessors who are known to him. Among the countless references to Swift is one which suggests that Joyce knew 'The Story of the Baker', quoted above: 'Old yeasterloaves may be a stale as a stub' acknowledges its Swiftian provenance by the reference to *A Tale of a Tub*.[1] Wilde's witticism about fox-hunting is borrowed in a reference to what somebody (Gladstone?) called 'the unspeakable Turk' and his massacres of the Armenians: 'the Turk, ungreekable in purscent of the armenable . . .'.[2] J. S. Atherton notes a great many other such allusions in the appropriate chapters of *The Books at the Wake*.[3]

Though Joyce and Gogarty are both dead, their spirit lives on in Dublin. Brian O'Nolan, who appeared in an earlier chapter under his pseudonyms of Flann O'Brien and Myles na gCopaleen, has for many years written a column in the *Irish Times* newspaper under the latter pseudonym. Some of his word play imitates *Finnegans Wake*, but his most outrageous puns have terminated spurious anecdotes about Keats and Chapman. The story which inaugurated this series tells how Keats and a certain Chapman were medical students together; Chapman's pet homing pigeon fell ill of a throat ailment, and Keats was asked for a medical opinion; after carefully examining the bird, he wrote that immortal sonnet, 'On First Looking into Chapman's Homer'. In another memorable column O'Nolan remarked that two famous Dublin scholars had proved that there were two Saint Patricks and no God.

---

[1] Joyce, *Finnegans Wake*, p. 598.   [2] Ibid., p. 181.
[3] See the chapter on Swift already referred to; the chapter on 'The Irish Writers', pp. 89–113; and the 'Alphabetical List of Literary Allusions', pp. 233–90. Atherton fails to note the reference to *Ars Pun-ica: 'Sharadan's *Art of Punning', Finnegans Wake*, p. 184.

5

Satire in Early Irish

Introductory

PERHAPS the most striking single fact about Irish literature in either Gaelic or English is the high proportion of satire which it contains. Even the most superficial observer can hardly fail to notice the vein of harsh ridicule running through twentieth-century Irish writing: Yeats, Joyce, Synge, George Moore all have their bitter moods, while O'Casey rarely condescends to sweeten his; Lennox Robinson, Liam O'Flaherty, Frank O'Connor, Denis Johnston, Sean O'Faolain, Austin Clarke, and many others show a similar tendency; even James Stephens and Lady Gregory bare their teeth occasionally; Padraic Colum alone remains consistently gentle; if formal satire were not out of fashion, doubtless many of these writers would have joined Eimar O'Duffy in the practice of it.

Anyone who cares to probe below the surface will soon discover the great antiquity and unbroken continuity of the Irish satiric tradition, in Gaelic at least. In order to make this vast subject less unwieldy, I have divided it among three chapters, two on Gaelic satire and the third on Swift and Anglo-Irish satire. The second of these chapters will be much the longest because its subject has never before been treated at any adequate length, to my knowledge.

The present chapter aims at no such lengthy treatment. Fred Norris Robinson's magnificent essay, 'Satirists and Enchanters in Early Irish Literature', published in 1912, has covered much of the ground already with a thoroughness that few could rival.[1] I shall summarize his argument briefly and

---

[1] Fred Norris Robinson, 'Satirists and Enchanters in Early Irish Literature', in David Gordon Lyon and George Foot Moore, eds., *Studies in the History of Religions presented to Crawford Howell Toy* (New York, 1912), pp. 95–130.

then go on to consider some aspects of Early Irish satire which
did not fall within his scope.

Professor Robinson's chief aim was to demonstrate the
magical origin of Irish satire. The word *áer* (Modern Irish
aor or *aoir*), which eventually came to mean 'satire' in the most
general sense—while retaining the earlier meanings of 'lampoon, personal attack in prose or verse, curse'[1]—must originally
have signified 'spell' or 'enchantment'. As Robinson shows by
copious reference to the literature, an *áer* was believed to have
power to cause facial blemishes, or even death, in its victim.[2]
This power could be exercised on rats and mice as well as
humans—a belief which gave rise to more-or-less humorous
references by Shakespeare, Spenser, Sidney, and other English
writers.[3]

Fear of this power, which was sometimes used as a sanction
to enforce treaties or collect taxes,[4] played a great part in
ensuring the prestige and wealth of the *fili* (Modern Irish *file*)
or poet. Many picturesque stories are told to illustrate the
layman's fear of him. One chieftain is said to have cut off his
own finger rather than deny the ring he wore on it to an im-
portunate poet.[5]

The clergy too were not exempt from fear of the poet's
satire. The great St. Columcille (Columba), for example, is
said to have accomplished two miracles in order to satisfy the
demands of poets. On one of these occasions he began to sweat
with shame at the thought of being satirized for niggardliness;
fortunately God turned the sweat to gold, which he was then
able to give the poets![6] It was a truly Christian act on his part,
therefore, to prevent the banishment of the poets from Ireland
at the Assembly of Drom Ceat, which had been convened
primarily to enact that punishment.[7] However, the power of
the poets and the size of their retinues was curbed thereafter.

---

[1] Patrick S. Dinneen, *Foclóir Gaedhilge agus Béarla, An Irish–English Dictionary*,
rev. ed. (Dublin, 1927), under *aor*.   [2] Robinson, pp. 103, 110, 114–15.

[3] Ibid., pp. 95–97. The interesting paper by James Henthorn Todd on this
subject occurs in *Proceedings of the Royal Irish Academy*, v (1850–53), 355–66, not in
the 1855 volume as Robinson says.   [4] Ibid., pp. 107–8.

[5] Ibid., p. 123. See also, for example, p. 116.

[6] Richard Henebry, ed. and tr., '*Betha Coluimb Cille*, Life of Columb Cille',
Zeitschrift für celtische Philologie, iv (1903), 297, 299, 301.

[7] Geoffrey Keating, *The History of Ireland*, ed. Patrick S. Dinneen, vol. iii,
Irish Texts Society IX (London, 1908), p. 79.

Columcille's reward was a long, though obscure, elegy by Dallán Forguill, the chief poet of Ireland.[1] According to Keating's history of Ireland, the poets had been banished three times previously.[2]

The *fili* undoubtedly inherited his magic powers from the *drui* or druid, who must have been more a wizard than a priest; Latin lives of the Irish saints often use the word *magus* to translate *drui*.[3] The fact that the words for 'druid', 'prophet', 'poet', 'judge', and 'physician' are virtually interchangeable in the Early Irish sagas and the lives of Irish saints (in both Latin and Irish) suggests that the druid originally combined the functions of all.[4]

A malevolent spell would naturally be aimed at a specific individual or, more rarely, at a clearly defined group of individuals. Very likely as a result of its origins, Irish satire in Gaelic or English usually has great difficulty in escaping from the personal lampoon towards more generalized satire. Since Ireland has adopted the English law of libel, such lampoons now rarely find their way into print, though Joyce had both 'The Holy Office' and 'Gas from a Burner' printed at his own expense.[5] Like most Irishmen to this very day, Joyce held the archaic, magical view that words are weapons—and lawful weapons. 'Sticks and stones may break my bones,/But words will never hurt me' is one English proverb that has never had much currency in Ireland.

After this very brief outline of the status and function of satire in Early Irish society (A.D. 600-1250) and of its probable origin in pre-Christian times, we can go on to consider some problems that are literary rather than sociological. In the first place, what was the nature of Early Irish satire—what techniques did it employ besides mere abuse? In the second place, how did a more generalized type of satire evolve out of—or rather, alongside—the spell-derived lampoon? The remaining two sections of this chapter will attempt to answer these questions.

[1] Myles Dillon, *Early Irish Literature* (Chicago, 1948), pp. xvi, 172–3.
[2] Keating, pp. 79, 81.
[3] Charles Plummer, *Vitae Sanctorum Hiberniae* (Oxford, 1910), i, p. clxii.
[4] Robinson, p. 98; Plummer, i, pp. clxi–clxiii.
[5] *The Critical Writings of James Joyce*, ed. Ellsworth Mason and Richard Ellmann (New York, 1959), p. 149; Richard Ellmann, *James Joyce* (New York, 1959), pp. 207–8, 348–9.

The nature of Early Irish satire

It is not easy to determine the nature of Early Irish satire, for the texts which survive are usually brief and/or fragmentary and/or obscure. The sagas often tell us that a satire was composed and had certain unpleasant consequences without quoting its actual wording. If the satire is quoted, it may consist of a single quatrain; whether long or short, it may contain language so archaic or allusions so obscure that no scholar has yet been able to elucidate it. In view of these facts, it is lucky that one theoretical discussion of satire, however brief, has survived from the period.

In the *Book of Ballymote*, compiled about 1400, there is a short treatise in Middle Irish on the various types of satire.[1] This has recently been edited, with readings from two other manuscripts, by Professor Howard Meroney, who does not minimize the difficulty of first establishing a satisfactory text and then translating and elucidating it.[2] There remains the problem of whether so late, brief, and schematic a treatise presents a reliable account of actual satiric practice in the Early Irish period. Also, though the work does give brief examples of almost all the types of satire named in it, a modern reader finds it hard to distinguish between the different types, even with the help of the examples. Still, it does give some insight into the feeling for irony and the sense of the ridiculous which were current when it was written.

The three basic types of *áer*, says the treatise, are *aisnés, ail*, and *aircetal*, which Professor Meroney translates as, respectively, 'declaration, insult, incantation'.

Declaration, now, is narration in reproach, without rhyme, as the libeller said in the house of a certain gentleman—he thought his rations meagre. 'Shall salt be sprinkled for you on your portion?' asked the attendant. 'No,' said he, 'For I have nothing to sprinkle it on. Unless it be sprinkled right (?) on my tongue, there's no need. It's bark, anyhow.'[3]

Ail is defined as 'the insult of a nickname which clings to anyone, or verbal injury, whether rhymed or not'. Since

[1] *The Book of Ballymote*, ed. Robert Atkinson (Dublin, 1887), p. 299 of the facsimile. Note that Atkinson, in the 'Contents', p. 14, gives the page wrongly as 298.

[2] Howard Meroney, 'Studies in Early Irish Satire I. "*Cis lir fodla áire?*" ', *Journal of Celtic Studies*, i (1950), 199–212.   [3] Meroney, p. 204.

aircetal means essentially 'verse', this definition is somewhat
confusing. One would expect both *aisnés* and *ail* to be distinguished from *aircetal* by the absence of rhyme.[1] The example
of *leasainm* ('nickname') cannot be misunderstood: a church
was named 'Church of the Wretched Repast' for its poor
hospitality. The other two examples of *ail*, however, are beyond
my comprehension.

Aircetal aíre, meaning 'incantation of satire' or merely
'versified satire', is subdivided into ten types, arranged roughly
in ascending order of publicity: *mac bronn, dallbach, focal i
frithshuidiu, tár n-aíre, tár molta, tamall aíre, tamall molta, lánaír,
ainmedh, gláim diceand*. Professor Meroney renders these as
follows:

'Son of womb,' innuendo, 'word in opposition,' outrage of satire,
outrage of praise, touch of satire, touch of praise, full satire, sarcasm,
and [normalizing the spelling] *glám dícind*.[2]

'Son of womb' has been studied separately by Professor
David Greene of Trinity College, Dublin, who defines it thus:

... it is a satire *in petto*, which has either not been published at all
or published to one person only. It is not surprising that the BB
[Book of Ballymote] tract, while giving examples of the other kinds
of satire, gives none of the *mac bronn*.[3]

Dallbach (literally 'blindness') or innuendo is divided into
three further sub-types: 'the firmly established, the lightly
established, and the unestablished'. The subtle distinctions
between these three elude me, but they all have in common the
fact that their victim remains anonymous: *ní feas cía diandéntar
saindruid*[4] ('It is not known about whom it is made in particular').
The example of unestablished innuendo has been translated
by Frank O'Connor, under the title 'No Names', as follows:

> There's a girl in these parts—
> A remarkable thing!
> But the force of her farts
> Is like stones from a sling.[5]

[1] Meroney, p. 207, says, 'Is not this *ail* the same as *ail*, "stone", in the sense of
a bump caused by a blow or metaphorically by a slur? Meant here is verbal hurt,
otherwise the term cannot be made to conform with the categories of prose and
verse'. [2] Ibid., p. 201 (Irish); p. 104 (English).
[3] David Greene, 'Mac Bronn', *Éigse*, v (1947), 231. For an example of *mac
bronn*, see the next chapter, p. 133. [4] Meroney, p. 201.
[5] Frank O'Connor, *Kings, Lords, and Commons* (New York, 1959), p. 53.

O'Connor's second line is introduced for the sake of rhyme, the Gaelic saying 'I don't mention her name'. Otherwise his translation is faithful.

Although the examples which illustrate it do not appear well chosen, the definition of *focal i frithshuidiu* suggests satire of great subtlety:

'Word in opposition' next, viz. a quatrain of praise, and therein is found a word on the verge of satire. . . .[1]

The next four types are not always clarified by either the definitions or the examples given in the Gaelic. Enough remains clear, however, to endorse Professor Meroney's interpretation: '*Tár* and *tamall* . . . I take to involve distinctions of plus and minus, viz. over- and understatement.'[2] The example of *tár molta* ('outrage of praise') is an unmistakable piece of outrageous and ironic flattery. Beginning with a cry of 'Halleluiah, halleluiah! *Credo, credo!*' its author pretends to believe that the victim of it has accomplished the incredible feat of reading three hundred psalters.

The example of 'outrage of satire', however, does not appear any more direct than that of 'touch of satire': both reproach inhospitality by making odious comparisons. The not-very-subtle wit of the 'touch of satire' example lies in this remark: 'The door which is not shut before me in the house of [hospitable] Brocan mac Addi, let it not be useless for a whole year —let it be taken to [inhospitable] Mac Aithcherda'.[3] Being in prose, this seems rather an example of *ail*.

As for 'touch of praise', it presumably means to 'damn with faint praise', in Pope's words, but the example hardly makes this meaning clear:

> O sons of Gartnan! O goodly pair of brothers!
> O younger! O older! O each of you two!
> Worth a hundred ounces is the yellow coif
> Which is about your mother's head![3]

I can imagine several possibilities, all of which may be wrong. The 'yellow coif' might be yellow with age and therefore perhaps originally the white veil of a nun. Or the headgear might in fact be valuable and hence the price of their mother's

---

[1] Meroney, p. 205.   [2] Ibid., p. 209.
[3] Ibid., p. 205.

shame, a gift from her lover. Or again, we might say today,
'The MacGartnan brothers are fine fellows: their mother buys
her hats from Lilly Daché', the obvious implication being that
we could not think of anything else to say in their favour.

'Full satire', the eighth type of *aircetal*, occurs

... when name and family and abode are present therein, *ut dixit*
Ua Derglega:
  My friend from Kilmallock—if it pleases you, you shall know
  him—
  A bag of wild oats [is] Cianán of the Decies.[1]

As for the example of *ainmedh* ('sarcasm'), it has so far defied
intelligible translation; no definition of the term itself is given.
Glám dícind is not defined in the treatise either, perhaps because
a definition is supplied earlier in the *Book of Ballymote*. Professor
Meroney suggests that the original meaning of this phrase was
'headless (i.e. 'endless') bite' and devotes an entire article to
it, in which he discusses the possible origin of the curious and
unreliable traditions which grew up around this type of satire.[2]

Robinson condenses the *Book of Ballymote* account of the
glám dícind, or rather the ritual prescribed for directing it
against a king 'who refuses the proper reward for a poem', as
follows:

First there was fasting on the land of the king, and a council of
thirty laymen and thirty bishops and thirty poets as to making a
satire; and it was a crime to prevent the satire after the reward of
the poem was refused. Then the poet himself with six others, on
whom the six [other] degrees of poets had been conferred, had to go
at sunrise to a hilltop on the boundary of seven lands; and the face
of each degree of them toward his own land, and the face of the
ollave [holder of the highest poetic degree] there toward the land of
the king whom he would satirize, and the backs of them all toward
a hawthorn which should be on the top of the hill, and the wind from
the north, and a slingstone and a thorn of the hawthorn in every
man's hand, and each of them to sing a stave in a prescribed metre
into the slingstone and the thorn, the ollave singing his stave before
the others and they afterwards singing their staves at once; and
each was then to put his stone and his thorn at the butt of the

---

[1] Meroney, p. 206.
[2] Howard Meroney, 'Studies in Early Irish Satire, II. "*Glám dícind*"', *Journal of Celtic Studies*, i (1950), 212–26.

hawthorn. And if it were they that were in the wrong, the earth of
the hill would swallow them up. But if it were the king that was in
the wrong, the earth would swallow up him and his wife and his
son and his horse and his arms and his dress and his hound.[1]

Obviously this 'prescription' would have been very hard to
fill. I doubt if a *glám dícind* of this kind was ever pronounced,
but if it were, its failure could easily be blamed on the non-
fulfilment of some requirement. As Robinson says, 'It may
have been largely invented, or at least embellished, by some
file with a turn for magical liturgy.'[2] Note the legalistic tone of
the whole passage, which serves as a reminder that the Early
Irish laws contain many provisions regulating the use of satire
and set penalties for its employment in unjust causes.[3]

About the contents of the treatise itself some generalizations
may be made. First of all, inhospitality and stinginess were
faults very frequently satirized; as licensed beggars, the poets
could scarcely afford to let these go unpunished. At least five
examples in the tract fall under this heading. Indeed, a well-
known tradition states that the first satire ever made in Ireland,
in the fabulous times of the Tuatha Dé Danann, was directed
against the inhospitality of Bres, son of Elatha and King of All
Ireland. The story is told in the saga entitled *Cath Maige Tured*
(*The* [*Second*] *Battle of Moytura*):

Once upon a time the poet came a-guesting to Bres' house, even
Corpre son of Etaín, poet of the Tuath Dé. He entered a cabin
narrow, black, dark, wherein there was neither fire nor furniture
nor bed. Three small cakes, and they dry, were brought to him on
a little dish. On the morrow he arose and he was not thankful. As
he went across the garth he said:

'Without food quickly on a dish:
without a cow's milk whereon a calf grows:
without a man's abode under the gloom (?) of night:
without paying a company of story-tellers, let that be Bres'
    condition.'[4]

More curse than satire, these lines had their due effect upon
Bres: 'Nought save decay was on him from that hour.'

---

[1] Robinson, pp. 108–9.   [2] Ibid., p. 109.
[3] Ibid., pp. 104–8.
[4] 'The Second Battle of Moytura', ed. and tr. Whitley Stokes, *Revue Celtique*,
xii (1891), 71.

Secondly, even if some of the examples are quatrains taken from their context in longer poems, much Early Irish satire must have been short enough to deserve the name of epigram. The longest example cited, which illustrates 'outrage of satire', appears to be a complete poem of three quatrains since it begins and ends with the same word, *lín*.[1] Any complete Gaelic poem longer than a single quatrain is likely to show this cyclic pattern; unfortunately, the single-quatrain epigram is not subject to this rule and is therefore hard to identify.

Furthermore, the examples I have quoted support the view that Early Irish satire is usually aimed at an individual or a clearly specified group of individuals. In fact, not one of the examples given in the treatise seems to ridicule vice or folly in general. Since I am going to argue later in this chapter that the development of more generalized satire was due to clerical influence, I should in fairness admit now that at least four of the examples in the *Book of Ballymote* have a clerical context; perhaps all four were composed by members of the clergy. At any rate the nickname 'Church of the Wretched Repast' is given a clerical attribution, to the 'household', or clergy, 'of Lismore Mochutu'. The example of 'outrage of praise' bears the name of Ceallach Mac Cumasgaigh, who died in 866 as Abbot of Fobhar. The 'touch of satire' is attributed to the saintly fool Mac Dá Cherda.[2] The instance of firmly established innuendo, attributed to one Paitren, attacks 'a reverend cleric' of Clonard.

Another rich and probably representative selection of Early Irish satirical epigrams and fragments is to be found in Kuno Meyer's *Bruchstücke der älteren Lyrik Irlands*. Here he edited and translated into German thirty items which he classified as '*Spott- und Schmählieder*'.[3] Almost all of these are drawn from the Middle Irish treatises on versification published by Rudolf Thurneysen under the title '*Mittelirische Verslehren*'.[4] The

---

[1] Meroney, p. 202.

[2] For Mac Dá Cherda, see J. G. O'Keeffe, 'Mac Dá Cherda and Cummaine Foda', *Ériu*, v (1911), 18–44, esp. 18–19. For Ceallach Mac Cumasgaigh, see *Annala Rioghachta Eireann, Annals of the Kingdom of Ireland by the Four Masters*, ed. and tr. John O'Donovan (Dublin, 1851), i. 505.

[3] Kuno Meyer, *Bruchstücke der älteren Lyrik Irlands*, Erster Teil, in *Abhandlungen der preussischen Akademie der Wissenschaften*, Jahrgang 1919, Philosophisch-historische Klasse, Nr. 7 (Berlin, 1919), pp. 27–37.

[4] Rudolf Thurneysen, '*Mittelirische Verslehren*', in Whitley Stokes and Ernst Windisch, eds., *Irische Texte*, Dritte Serie, 1. Heft (Leipzig, 1891), pp. 1–182.

compilers of these treatises quoted the passages, which are frequently in Old Irish, apparently without paying much heed to their content, as examples of various metres and stanza forms. Thurneysen's 'raw' texts contain a number of other satirical quotations which Meyer passed over, doubtless in part because of their difficulty.

In attempting to classify Meyer's selections, one soon concludes that many must be labelled 'mere abuse'. At least ten of the thirty fall into this category,[1] and of these ten only one (No. 60) fails to identify fairly explicitly the person attacked. It is interesting to note that none of the ten contains a main verb; indeed, only No. 83 contains a verb at all; otherwise they consist exclusively of nouns and adjectives, all of course derogatory. Six of the examples[2] are addressed directly to their victims, so that the nouns are all in the vocative case; the others employ the nominative case exclusively.

Here is an example (No. 74) in the vocative case; I give the Gaelic first so that the reader can see the alliteration, and perhaps also the pattern of assonance and rhyme, for himself. In doing so, he will probably come to share my feeling that this, like many other such satires, is a verbal firework, an exercise in virtuosity, rather than a flame of hate designed to shrivel its victim.

> *A Dalláin doburthanaig dígrádaig,*
> *   a cammáin chrínlámaig chonfathmannaig chúaránaig,*
> *A phítig phaitig phíanánaig,*
> *   a thíagánaig étig aitig úarlámaig!*

> (O Dallan, you undistinguished, unlucky man;
>   you twisted, withered-handed, shaggy-dog-haired
>   crooked one;
> you hungry, thirsty, troublesome one;
>   you odious, comic carrier of a little bag with cold
>   hands!)[3]

The humour is increased and the bitterness moderated when one discovers that the third line consists entirely of noncewords: for instance, *phaitig* ('thirsty') is presumably derived

---

[1] Nos. 60, 64, 65, 71, 73, 74, 79, 81, 83, 86.
[2] Nos. 60, 73, 74, 81, 83, 86.
[3] Meyer, pp. 32–33. I have tried to translate this and all the other quotations from *Bruchstücke* directly from the Irish, but I must admit that I lean heavily on Meyer's German.

from the noun *pait*, meaning 'a bottle made of animal skin'.[1]
This reference, like the one to the 'little bag' in the fourth line,
suggests that Dallán is a scrounger who collects scraps and
dregs in his bag and bottle.

I shall quote just one more example (No. 64) of these litanies
of abuse, in the nominative case this time:

Adastar lára i lláim, leccu phúit dar pundainn,
cenn crúaid con ar cáirig,
maite odar áilig,
lúe fri lúag, leccu chúar, úa con cúan, ni cundail.

(The halter of a mare in the hand, the cheek of a block over a sheaf,
the head of a bloody dog on a sheep,
a dun-colored stick from a dunghill,
a kick for payment, a crooked cheek, O'Concuan, not decent.)[2]

This looks like a fairly coherent description of a dirty, rude,
unkempt individual; thus it is far from typical of the random
abuse scattered in most of the examples I pass over.

In considering those of Meyer's examples which offer some
justification for their attacks, I was surprised to find only four
which denounced stinginess or inhospitality. One of these
(No. 72) has been often reprinted because of its unusual and
humorous stanza form:

> *Ro-cúala*
> *ní tabair eochu ar dúana;*
> *do-beir a n-í as dúthaig dó,*
> *bó.*[3]

(I have heard he does not give horses for poems; he gives the thing
which is native to him, a cow.)

This might be rendered as follows in the metre of the original:

> I know him;
> He'll give no horse for a poem;
> He'll give you what his kind allows,
> Cows.[4]

---

[1] See *Contributions to a Dictionary of the Irish Language*, '*N-O-P*', arr. Maud
Joynt (Dublin, n.d.), under *paitech*.

[2] Meyer, p. 29.

[3] To show the stanza form more clearly, I quote the Irish text from Gerard
Murphy, ed. and tr., *Early Irish Lyrics* (Oxford, 1956), p. 90.

[4] Prose and verse translations mine.

Another (No. 75) reproaches a certain Crunnmáel for offering bread with salt instead of butter on it, but adds that this is not surprising, since the flesh of all his household is dried up like the bark of a tree. No. 82 reproaches a certain Finn for 'evil denial'—of what, we are not told.

The fourth attack on an ungenerous person (No. 76) demands food, anticipates refusal, and threatens satire in return. The poet asks the woman in charge of the larder to give him 'bacon, a sup of milk, butter and bread'. If she does not, he will take away her honour.

A threat of satire is voiced in one other example (No. 87), which may as well be mentioned here: it simply states that two men should be satirized for what they did to a third; all three are named. Perhaps it is the opening of a poem which satirized the pair.

The 'professional' attitude expressed in some of the examples just referred to—their concern with the payment or hospitality due to a poet and their wielding of satire as a weapon to enforce demands—finds an echo in another group of examples.[1] The latter apply to their victims one or more of the following terms, for many of which one can only give approximate translations: *drúth* ('jester' or 'fool'), *crossán* ('buffoon, satirist'), *oínmit* ('fool'), *cáinte* ('satirist'), *fetánach* ('flute player'), *cornaire* ('trumpeter'), *clíaraige* ('singer'), *aés dána* ('poets'). I wonder how many of these terms are used as terms of abuse and how many in a technical sense. The examples in which they occur are just as abusive as the first ten mentioned above. In the Modern Irish period an *iomarbháigh* or 'flyting' between poets is very common, so that some at least of these examples may have been addressed by one poet to another in a satirical sham-fight. Of course a learned poet (*fili*) would feel himself superior to all of the types mentioned above except the *áes dána*. Even the *cáinte* belonged to a lower social stratum than the *fili*, though both *cáinte* and *crossán* were notorious for the practice of satire.[2] As we shall see in this chapter and the next, satire against satirists is a genre to be reckoned with in Gaelic. Perhaps one *fili* might call another a *cáinte* or even a *crossán* to belittle him.

Two of Meyer's examples ridicule unnamed women without attaching any moral stigma to them. No. 77, about the woman

[1] Nos. 66, 67, 68, 69, 78, 80, 84, 88.   [2] Robinson, p. 104.

with a remarkable talent for *crepitus ventris*, has already been quoted from the *Book of Ballymote*. The other (No. 70) comments on a woman whose face is both too red and too white, showing that her father was a blacksmith with the typical red face of his trade, while her husband is a pale-faced goldsmith.[1]

I have left until last the few examples of denunciation or ridicule that we would now regard as legitimate satire: those which reproach their victims with moral or intellectual short-comings. Actually, I am not at all certain that even the five I have so classified (out of thirty!) all belong to this category. No. 61 denounces the cowardice of a certain O'Flannáin in fairly well chosen terms: 'O'Flannáin, you slow mare, you one-legged goose, you crooked bolt in face of the war-cry of the foreigners!' Obviously the man addressed is slow-footed in approaching battle, not in running away from it. As a crooked bolt or broken lock he is unfit to bar the door against invaders.

Two examples (62, 63) seem to denounce liars or traitors. Each consists of a string of epithets which describe contemp-tuously the appearance and habits of its victim; only the last word or words accuse him of being a 'false man' or a 'lying descendant of Britán'. One man is called a 'bosom full of nits', while the other is accused of eating lice. The remaining epithets are almost equally choice: apparently any stick will do to beat a liar with.

To the modern ear, this neat quatrain (No. 85) is far more damaging, in spite—or rather, because—of its restraint. Note the repetition of the negative, *nocho*:

> *Ni fuilet a máine,*
> > *nocho mó atá a maisse,*
> *nocho mór a gére,*
> > *nocho déne acht braisse.*

> (He has no treasures;
> > no greater are his good looks;
> not great is his sharpness;
> > he does nothing but boast.)[2]

The last I shall mention of this group (No. 59) is aimed at a certain Domungort, who is described as, among other things,

[1] For a neat translation, see O'Connor, p. 53.

[2] Meyer, p. 36. I have arranged the quatrain in four lines instead of Meyer's two to bring out the structure more clearly.

a 'hump of a stolen goose' and a 'blue-black jewel of a demon'. In the tenth and last line we discover his crime: *nír lessaigis in sáithe* ('You have not advanced learning').[1] As anybody who reads learned journals can testify, scholars are a censorious lot; on the whole, however, our modern Domungorts are let off more lightly than their Early Irish counterpart.

If Kuno Meyer's selection is representative, then satire with a firm moral or intellectual basis was relatively rare in Early Irish. On the other hand, inhospitality, which the modern Englishman or American tends to regard as a mere personal idiosyncrasy, was no doubt viewed as a grievous moral blemish —it still is in modern Ireland—violating an older law than the Christian one of charity. In spite of their selfish motivation, I perhaps ought to have included the satires against those guilty of this fault among my examples of legitimate satire. As for the *methods* of satire, Meyer's little anthology suggests that these did not vary much, whether the motive for lampoon was noble or ignoble. It does seem true, however, that those examples which do not name their victim show more restraint than the others.

The longest surviving Early Irish poem, to my knowledge, which has any claim to be described as a satire is that composed by Fingen mac Flainn against the Fir Arddae, a County Clare tribe. They had refused him what he considered his due fee for a eulogy of them, whereupon he wrote this poem of seventy quatrains, beginning '*Ammo Choimdhiu néll cid dogén fri firu Arddae?*' ('O my God, what shall I do against the Fir Arddae?'). This remarkable work, dating from the ninth century and therefore in Old rather than Middle Irish, has been edited by Kuno Meyer but not translated.[2] I doubt whether it could be satis- factorily translated into any modern language, since it bristles with synonyms for 'satire' and 'satirize', but for that very reason it possesses the greatest interest for lexicographers. The whole poem may be summed up in a single line: *grómfa grómfa, glámfa glámfa, aerfa aerfa*.[3] This line, in effect, says 'I shall satirize' six times over. *Glámfa* is derived from the noun *glám*, which we have already met in *glám dícind*, and *aerfa* from the noun *áer*.

---

[1] Meyer, p. 27.

[2] Kuno Meyer, '*Fingen Mac Flainn's Gedicht auf die fir Arddae*', in Whitley Stokes and Kuno Meyer, eds., *Archiv für celtische Lexikographie*, iii (Halle, 1907), 291–301.

[3] *Archiv. für celtische Lexikographie*, iii. 297.

The whole poem, in other words, is less a satire than a threat
of satire: the poet is considering in which of the many ways
open to him he will annihilate the tribe with his mockery. He
gives an account of his grievance against the Fir Arddae, whom
he had apparently praised to the skies, but he does not, so far
as I can see, ridicule them in any way. Such a poem will hardly
fit any modern definition of the term 'satire'. Nevertheless, it
does illuminate the Early Irish poet's view of the power and
purpose of satire. It seems to end on a conciliatory note, as if
the poet still hoped to receive his just reward.

Vigorous and skilful though his poem may be, Fingen mac
Flainn tends to make himself ridiculous by such a prolonged
and tautological assertion of his largely imaginary powers. He
and his fellow poets, by giving themselves such airs, became
potential targets for satire in the more modern sense of the
word. In my chapter on parody I have analysed a Modern
Irish work, *Tromdámh Guaire* or *Imtheacht na Tromdháimhe* (*The
Proceedings of the Burdensome Bardic Company*) probably of clerical
authorship, which gives the poets their well-deserved come-
uppance.[1]

Another example of satire against satirists—the crossan is
the victim in this case—does fall within our period, namely the
Middle Irish tale entitled *Senadh Saighri* (*The Synod of Seirkieran*).[2]
In this, a pious king, Donnchadh the Stout of Ossory, dies and
is buried, whereupon 'nine shaggy jet-black crossáns' come to
sit on his grave and sing together, 'as has been the custom of
crossáns ever since'. The burden of their song is that the pious
Donnchadh is now in Hell: 'Great his reward after going into
the other world—we are his people.' Eventually an angel
comes from Heaven to reveal that these are 'nine of the band of
O'Conghedh . . . and this is the third time that they have come
into Ireland out of Hell, and as they were powerless against
the king in his life, therefore are they pursuing him after his
death'. Holy water sprinkled on the grave and the churchyard
drives off the demons, who admit that 'we were after his body
in the world, since his soul is in Heaven, and we can do no
harm to her'. They depart, but two crossans, Find O'Cinga

---

[1] See below, pp. 219–21.
[2] Kuno Meyer, ed. and tr., 'Anecdota from Irish MSS., IV: *Senadh Saighri*',
The Gaelic Journal: Irisleabhar na Gaedhilge, iv (1891–4), 106–8.

and Mac Rinntach O'Conodhran, were present and 'remembered the song and the music of the band of O'Conghedh. So this is the art that has served them ever since, and the other crossáns of Ireland from that henceforward.' It would be impossible to prove that this legend, told with great apparent sincerity, is in fact a satire, but I think the concluding words, just quoted, leave little doubt that the equation of *crossán* with demon was humorously intended. This is a more general satire than any of those previously quoted, but it does cite two crossans by name.

The development of generalized satire

In spite of the many examples to the contrary in the previous section of this chapter, some generalized satire did exist in the Early Irish period. The most brilliant and sustained example, *The Vision of Mac Conglinne*, I have discussed elsewhere in this book as an example of both parody and fantastic humour.[1] This unique work is so atypical of Irish satire that it would be quite misleading to examine it here. Because of its blithe ridicule of the clergy and its irreverent parodies of sacred literature, the *Vision* might seem to be of lay authorship, but nobody could parody devotional writings so effectively without some clerical training; if not in holy orders, its author must have been that familiar figure among Irish literary men, a 'spoiled priest'. Since the chief victims of this satire are the abbot and monks of the monastery of Cork, the reader may wonder why I call it 'generalized'. Certainly the abbot's name is given, but he has not been identified as an historical figure; furthermore, his name, *Manchín*, means 'little monk' or—to use Irish English—'monkeen'.[2]

It was under clerical influence, I am convinced, that a few rather halting steps were taken in the direction of impersonal, generalized satire and away from personal lampoon. As it moves in this direction, satire often falls into the opposite ditch and becomes mere moralizing, without humour or wit or even sarcasm. I think I have found some examples of genuine satire; at least the excerpts which follow are not lampoons.

[1] See above, pp. 17–18, and below, pp. 214–7.
[2] Kuno Meyer, ed. and tr., *Aislinge Meic Conglinne, The Vision of MacConglinne* (London, 1892), p. 136.

The chief influence on this essentially Christian type of satire is gnomic literature: not only that of the Old and New Testaments and of Classical Latin, but also that of the native pagan tradition. The oldest generalized satire in the Irish language is probably that found in two collections of proverbs and aphorisms known as *Trecheng Breth Féni* (*The Triads of Ireland*) and *Tecosca Cormaic* (*The Instructions of Cormac*). Next in chronological order come some verse epigrams which retain a strong gnomic flavour. Finally we have a few longer moralizing poems in which genuine satire masquerades as homily or prophecy.

The language of the *Triads*, according to Kuno Meyer, places them in the second half of the ninth century and 'may be described as late Old-Irish'.[1] They were therefore written down later than the *Instructions of Cormac*, whose language Meyer dates 'not later than the first half of the ninth century',[2] but the form and content of the *Triads* suggest an even more archaic tradition than that of the *Instructions*, which are attributed to the pagan King Cormac Mac Airt, who flourished in the third century A.D. The passages in the *Triads* which can be described as more satirical than proverbial are few indeed, but some examples deserve quotation:

95. Three laughing-stocks of the world: an angry man, a jealous man, a niggard.

103. Three signs of a fop: the track of a comb in his hair, the track of his teeth in his food, the track of his stick (or his cudgel) behind him.

117. Three things that constitute a comb-maker: racing a hound in contention for a bone; straightening a ram's horn by his breath, without fire; chanting upon a dunghill so that all antlers and bones and horns that are below come to the top.

234. Four on whom there is neither restraint nor rule: the servant of a priest, a miller's hound, a widow's son, and a stripper's [i.e. a young cow's] calf.

255. Three coffers whose depth is not known: the coffer of a chieftain, of the Church, of a privileged poet.[3]

---

[1] Kuno Meyer, ed. and tr., *The Triads of Ireland*, Royal Irish Academy Todd Lecture Series XIII (Dublin, 1906), p. x.

[2] Kuno Meyer, ed. and tr., *The Instructions of King Cormac Mac Airt*, Royal Irish Academy Todd Lecture Series XV (Dublin, 1909), p. xi.

[3] Meyer, *Triads*, pp. 13, 15, 17, 31, 35.

Some of the above—for example, No. 95—may have been considered mere statements of fact, but No. 103 is genuine satire in capsule form.

The form of *Tecosca Cormaic* allows scope for a long series of aphorisms on a given subject, the longest of all being that on women. In a sense, this passage could be described as satire, but I think it was primarily intended as a sober statement of fact. I shall quote a few lines to give the reader its flavour:

'O grandson of Conn, O Cormac,' said Carbre, 'how do you distinguish women?'

'Not hard to tell,' said Cormac. 'I distinguish them, but I make no difference among them.

> They are crabbed as constant companions,
> haughty when visited,
> lewd when neglected,
> silly counsellors,
> greedy of increase,
> they have tell-tale faces,
> they are quarrelsome in company. . . .'[1]

and so on for three pages more.

Another passage seems to me more genuinely satirical in that it employs ridicule, directed, so the text insists, against a personality type rather than an individual:

'O grandson of Conn, O Cormac,' said Carbre, 'who are the worst for whom you have a comparison?'

> 'Not hard to tell,' said Cormac.
> 'A man with the impudence of a satirist,
> with the pugnacity of a slave-woman,
> with the carelessness of a . . . dog,
> with the conscience of a hound,
> with a robber's hand,
> with a bull's strength,
> with the dignity of a judge,
> with keen ingenious wisdom,
> with the speech of a stately man,
> with the memory of an historian,
> with the behaviour of an abbot,
> with the swearing of a horse-thief,

and he wise, lying, grey-haired, violent, swearing, garrulous when he says 'the matter is settled, I swear, I shall swear'.[2]

---

[1] Meyer, *Instructions*, p. 29.   [2] Ibid., pp. 43, 45.

This whole passage could very well be applied today to a type of pompous fraud not uncommon in public life.

One further excerpt is of great interest in that it affords clues to the kind of personality defects which the Irish of that time thought deserving of satire. Asked what the 'code of ridicule' (*forus cuitbeda*, for which 'basis of ridicule' might be a better translation) is among the Irish, Cormac replies:

> 'A man proud of his wisdom, his gifts, his good fortune, fastidious, standing on his dignity, vainglorious,
> a lazy, violent, feeble, flighty man,
> a silly, dull, big-worded man,
> a wrathful, aggressive, masterful man,
> a man niggardly, unstable, jealous, . . . , timorous,
> violent, impulsive, incautious, loveless, . . . ,
> tedious, angry'.[1]

If we can trust this passage, the Irish sense of the ridiculous was already highly developed in the ninth century. Few of us would be exempt from ridicule on one or more of the above counts, but then, those of us who grew up in Ireland know that very few Irishmen or Irishwomen do in fact escape ridicule, especially in youth—and in later years also if it is their misfortune to achieve fame.

From such gnomic works it is but a short step to epigrammatic verses which attack vice, folly, and corruption rather than the individuals who are guilty of them. A famous Old Irish example is the quatrain which runs as follows in a literal translation: 'Going to Rome: great trouble, little profit! The King whom you seek here, unless you bring Him with you, you do not find him'.[2] Another quatrain, in Middle Irish, reminds us of Jesus' parable concerning the mote and the beam:

> Though a fault be small—the size of a fleshworm—
> Thou perceivest it on anyone from afar:
> Though a fault be as big as a mountain,
> Thou dost not perceive it on thyself.[3]

It is perhaps more gnomic than satiric. My final example from the relatively small number of such epigrams to be found in

---

[1] Meyer, *Instructions*, p. 49.

[2] Whitley Stokes and John Strachan, eds., *Thesaurus Palaeohibernicus*, ii (Cambridge, 1903), 296. Translation mine.

[3] Translated by Kuno Meyer in *Zeitschrift für celtische Philologie*, i (1897), 327.

Early Irish—in comparison with the large number in Modern Irish—truly deserves to be called a satire on gluttony:

> Bit upon bit,
> Woe to him who puts them into his belly:
> The Son of God will not be pleased with him
> For filling the privies.[1]

Though the author of this was clearly in earnest about the sinfulness of gluttony, he just as clearly wanted the reader to laugh at the incongruity of the last two lines. The imagination of a Swiftian satirist is at work there.

Late in our period we find three similar poems, undoubtedly of clerical authorship, which claim to be prophecies but are in fact rather subtle satires on the decline of moral standards among both clergy and laity. They invoke more contempt than ridicule, but their moralizing does not entirely lack wit. Each employs the technique of contrasting the past with the present, mainly by juxtaposing statements about both. The reader can make the unflattering comparisons for himself.

The best and harshest of these poems, which occurs only in the *Book of Lismore*, has been published at least twice,[2] besides being forcefully translated by Professor Kenneth Jackson. It takes the form of a prophecy in which the unknown poet describes 'the folk that will come after me'. Kuno Meyer in his edition gave it the title 'A Prophecy of the World's End', but Professor Jackson wisely included it in the 'Humour and Satire' section of his *Celtic Miscellany*. Reading between the lines, we cannot help feeling that the 'prophecy' has already been fulfilled; as the poet describes the clergy of olden times, he implicitly compares them with his own contemporaries:

> The saints who did God's will at the beginning of time were uneasy and naked, scurvy, muddy; *they* were not stout and fat.

> The men of keen learning, who served the King of the Sun, did not molest boys or women; their natures were pure.

> Scanty shirts, clumsy cloaks, hearts sad and piteous, short rough shocks of hair—and very rough monastic rules.[3]

---

[1] Translated by Kuno Meyer in *Zeitschrift für celtische Philologie*, i (1897), 457.

[2] See Whitley Stokes, ed. and tr., *Lives of Saints from the Book of Lismore* (Oxford, 1890), pp. 135–6; also Kuno Meyer, *Selections from Early Irish Poetry* (Dublin, n.d.), p. 8.

[3] Kenneth Hurlstone Jackson, *A Celtic Miscellany* (Cambridge, Mass., 1951), p. 223.

Contrasted with these are the rich, luxury-loving, silk-clad saints (or elders) of the end of the world, who are promised the torments of Hell.

Although the *Book of Lismore* poem criticizes the laity in passing, it reserves its most scathing irony for the clergy. A longer, less skilful poem, from British Museum MS. Additional 30512, broadens its attack to include the kings, warriors, and women as well as the clergy 'of the end of time', by comparison with their predecessors 'of the beginning of time'.[1] The clergy receive most space, however, and the accusations against them are on the whole more explicit.

The kings of the end of time—i.e. of today—are petty, cowardly, undignified. The warriors are boastful, foolish, treacherous, cowardly, far from wealthy; the most detailed reproach made against them is that they talk like judges by comparison with the affability of their olden-time counterparts. As for the women of the end of time, they are foolish, rude, and immodest; instead of allying themselves to young men and men they love, they will accept anybody.

Once again, the austere poverty and self-denial of the clergy of old are emphasized: 'scurvy' (*clama*)[2] is again quaintly used as a compliment. The habits or cassocks of the early clergy are described as 'yellow and old', whereas the new clergy wear satin. The former's 'soups of nettles and watercress' are mentioned, and we are told that 'they had few cakes'. Gluttony is the least of the new clergy's faults, for they also wear coloured garments, are lustful for women, and are 'faithful' (*ingili*) in their attendance at drinking-houses, whereas they neglect Mass and Nones.

The twenty-eighth and last stanza represents the whole poem as a prophecy made by Columcille (St. Columba), who flourished in the sixth century. The clergy of almost any subsequent century can thus be readily identified as those of 'the end of time'. Naturally, Columcille did not write the poem, whose language dates it at least six centuries later, but this attribution suggests that the *Book of Lismore* poem was also conceived as a pre-dated prophecy.

---

[1] The text, beginning '*Righa thosaigh aimsire*', is edited by J. G. O'Keeffe, under the title 'Past and Present', in J. Fraser, P. Grosjean, and J. G. O'Keeffe, eds., *Irish Texts*, Fasciculus IV (London, 1934), pp. 35–39. Translations mine.

[2] Ibid., p. 37; spelled *clamha* here.

On this matter of the date of our second poem, the fact that
the new 'order' or 'clergy' (*ord*) is described as 'foreign'
(*allmurach*)[1] raises the question whether this poem is a native
Irish protest against the introduction of foreign clerics during
the reforms of St. Malachy (d. 1148)[2] or even after the Anglo-
Norman invasion later in the twelfth century.

Another poem from the same MS., one which also occurs in
the *Book of Hy Many*, may express the same resentment against
foreign clergy. Unfortunately, the complete poem has never
been printed.[3] According to Robin Flower, the gist of it is that
Columcille once again 'contrasts the clerics of the latter times
with those of the earlier time'.[4] In *The Irish Tradition* Flower
translates six quatrains which denounce the later clerics'
passion for Latin: the native Irish clergy of the eleventh and
twelfth centuries were poor Latinists, on the whole; they did
most of their devotional and theological writing in Irish. Here
are two of Flower's stanzas:

> For every school will soon, I vow,
> Be following Latin learning now;
> Old wisdom now they scorn and song,
> And babble Latin all day long.
>
> The best of Latin has no might
> To stablish holy Church upright;
> We need pure hearts in these bad days,
> Piety, charity and praise.[5]

The second of these stanzas is pious rather than satirical, but
the expression 'babble Latin' in the first has the true contemptuous ring. It reproduces the tone of the original very faithfully,
for the last two lines of that stanza read as follows:

> *gan fhiss gan fhorus amhra*
> *acht Laiden do luathlabhra.*

---

[1] Fraser *et al.*, p. 37: '*Risin ord n-ard n-allmurach*'.
[2] See James F. Kenney, *The Sources for the Early History of Ireland*, vol. i: Ecclesiastical (New York, 1929), pp. 765–7.
[3] Kuno Meyer printed the first two quatrains and the last from the *Book of
Hy Many* text: '*Neue Mitteilungen aus irischen Handschriften*', *Archiv für celtische
Lexikographie*, ii (Halle, 1904), 141.
[4] Robin Flower, *Catalogue of Irish Manuscripts in the British Museum*, ii (London,
1926), 493.
[5] Robin Flower, *The Irish Tradition* (Oxford, 1947), pp. 46–47.

(Without knowledge, without the basic principles of song, / But Latin for quick speech.)[1]

Historically, on the contrary, Columcille seems to have favoured good Latinity, or what he thought was good. As a great saint and a protector of poets, he has had fathered upon him more poems and prophecies than he could have written in two or three lifetimes. In the next chapter we shall find Peadar Ó Doirnin (Peter O'Durnin), an eighteenth-century poet, casting his satire against a greedy priest in the mould of a pseudo-prophecy by Columcille, and thus linking up with the satirists of six centuries earlier.[2]

In spite of the strivings toward a more general type of satire that I have just recorded, as well as later ones—sometimes under clerical auspices too—it was the tradition of the lampoon that showed the greater staying-power. Strings of alliterative epithets are almost as common in the satires written in the seventeenth and eighteenth centuries by David O'Bruadair, Egan O'Rahilly, and Owen Roe O'Sullivan, as they are in Kuno Meyer's little anthology of Early Irish satire.

Why, then, does Early Irish lampoon survive almost entirely in the brief quotations used to illustrate learned treatises? Surely because it belongs to a part of Early Irish culture that was orally preserved by laymen. All the manuscripts which survive from the Early Irish period seem to have been the work of clerical scribes. If the lay poets knew how to write, they very likely preferred not to. The *áer*, especially, might lose its magical, archaic quality if committed to this new-fangled writing, with its Christian, anti-magical associations. In any case, many monks would doubtless balk at recording such litanies of spite, which were essentially pagan in spirit. The extravagant parodies of bardic satire in *Tromdámh Guaire* suggest something of the contempt felt by the clergy for this particular aspect of secular poetry, though there were other aspects which they admired and sedulously imitated. Only the prestige of a learned work could justify the expenditure of precious ink and parchment upon such harmful trash.

---

[1] Flower, *Catalogue*, ii. 493. Literal translation mine.
[2] See below, pp. 173–4.

6

Satire in Modern Irish

The outlines

THE first thing to be remembered is that our period divides
into two unequal parts: the classical or 'bardic' period,
which comes to an end in the first half of the seventeenth
century, and the truly modern period, which ends with the
Great Famine of 1846–7; the period since is best described as
that of the revival of Irish. The bardic era did not survive the
destruction of the Gaelic social system—begun by Elizabeth I,
partially completed by James I, repeated with devastating
thoroughness by Cromwell, and finally made permanent by
William III. It is not enough to say that the Gaelic-speaking
aristocracy who patronized the bardic poets were dispossessed
of their lands: the poets themselves were landholders, a sort of
noblesse de robe, whose dispossession accompanied or followed
that of the *noblesse d'épée*.[1]

The overthrow of the bardic institution was accompanied by
a change in poetic technique which enables one to judge with
considerable accuracy whether a given poem belongs to the
bardic period or not: syllabic metre (*dán díreach*) gives way to
stress or 'song' metre (*amhrán*). This change reflects not only
the gradual disappearance of the bardic schools but also that
of the bardic audience; most authorities believe that the stress
metres had been popular among the common people for a long
time before poems in those metres were granted the dignity of
being committed to manuscript.[2] If the dispossessed and often
starving poet wanted the favour of his new patrons—those who
were only less poor than he—he must cater to their tastes. As

---

[1] *The Bardic Poems of Tadhg Dall Ó Huiginn*, ed. Eleanor Knott, vol. i, Irish
Texts Society XXII (London, 1922), p. xli.

[2] See, for example, Osborn Bergin, 'On the Origin of Modern Irish Rhythmical
Verse', *Mélanges linguistiques offerts à M. Holger Pedersen in Acta Jutlandica: Aarsskrift
for Aarhus Universitet*, vol. ix, pt. 1 (Copenhagen, 1937), pp. 280–6.

we shall see, the change in patrons and technique was to prove a fruitful source of satire during most of the seventeenth century.

I think that anyone who surveys the satirical literature in Modern Irish with regard to content only will find, as I did, that five major categories establish themselves. They are the following:

1. Personal.
2. Social.
3. Political.
4. Religious.
5. Professional (i.e. Literary).

Of these, the first is so much the most important that it spills over into all the other categories: wherever possible, individuals are made responsible for the errors of Church and State, for deficiencies in social behaviour and literary composition.

Those who expect to find a 'literature of social protest' under the second category will not merely be disappointed— they will be scandalized. The outlook of an aristocratic caste persists long after bardic institutions have been swept away: anyone inferior in learning and (former) social status to the bardic poets and their self-appointed successors is a *bodach* or an *athach*—that is to say, a clown, a churl, a boor, a peasant, a rent-payer[1]—a member of Clan Thomas or Clan Lóbus, whose only pedigree is the fanciful one which traces him back to Beelzebub.

Political satire rarely lifts itself above the level of self-interest either, for the unhappy events of Irish history after 1600 had an all-too-direct influence upon the fortunes of Gaelic literary men; for reasons that I shall examine shortly, the bardic era produced very little political satire.

The broad category of religious satire includes the most diverse treatments of a variety of themes: denunciations of apostasy, theological dissections of heresy, outcries against clerical materialism, and humorously Voltairian criticism of clerical celibacy and other even more fundamental tenets of Roman Catholicism. The age-old rivalry between the two professions

[1] See the entries *athach* and *athech* in Kuno Meyer, *Contributions to Irish Lexicography* (Halle and London, 1906); also the entries *athach* and *bodach* in Patrick S. Dinneen, *Foclóir Gaedhilge agus Béarla, An Irish-English Dictionary* (Dublin, 1927).

of cleric and poet—though hundreds or perhaps thousands of Irishmen have succeeded in combining both—must date back to the conflict between the pagan druids and the Christian missionaries.

My fifth category, though less obvious than the others, is, even more than they, a natural growth from the specially prepared soil of the bardic institution. A professional literary caste cannot fail to be interested in a wide range of practices peculiar to their profession; their enemies—and even they themselves—will satirize the use or the abuse of these practices; some of this material falls under the heading of parody, with which I deal in Chapter 8.

As well as categories based on content, a full-length study of Irish satire should attempt what I lack space for, the establishment of categories based on form. It ought to inquire what metres are most commonly employed for satire in general; whether any metres are considered specially appropriate for certain kinds of satire; whether undiluted prose has ever been widely employed for satire; and how common a mingling of prose with verse was in the satire of this or that century.

One form widely used for satiric purposes is the epigram, usually consisting of a single quatrain in syllabic metre (*dán-fhocal*) or in stress-metre (*búrdún beag*); the manuscripts abound with examples. Some idea of the extent to which satire bulks in collections of these epigrams is given by T. F. O'Rahilly's celebrated definition of *búrdúin* (the plural of *búrdún*):

Búrdúin is the technical name for poems in stress-metre which are not intended to be sung, as distinguished on the one hand from *amhráin*, 'songs' (in stress-metre also), and on the other hand from *dánta*, 'poems in the older syllabic metres'. Short *búrdúin* . . . were often composed extempore, and not infrequently also took the form of lampoons on particular individuals and were repeated from mouth to mouth. Hence in popular use *búrdún* came to mean 'a lampoon', 'a tale-bearer's story'—the latter being the meaning of the word in West Munster speech to-day.[1]

I do not think, however, that a discussion of the satirical epigram as found in Modern Irish would be profitable in the small space that I could afford it here: the subject-matter and

[1] Thomas F. O'Rahilly, ed., *Búrdúin Bheaga* (Dublin, 1925), p. 44.

its treatment do not appear to differ greatly from those in longer satirical poems, which often consist of a string of epigrams rather than a smoothly developing argument. Irish epigram, satirical or not, is a subject in itself, which I have already discussed briefly in the chapter on wit; besides, we have seen several Early Irish examples in Chapter 5.

The bardic period

The most striking fact about bardic satire is that we have so little of it. Professor Eleanor Knott does not find this surprising:

> Naturally, not many complete satires have been preserved. A few scurrilous quatrains or passages occur here and there, usually in illustration of some metrical or linguistic usage, and consist, when the words are at all interpretable, mainly of rows of disparaging epithets. But there are also more subtly expressed examples.[1]

That first word, 'Naturally', requires some interpretation; what Miss Knott chiefly has in mind, I think, is that our main source of bardic poetry has proved to be the *duanairí* or poembooks kept by aristocratic Irish families, into which poems in their praise, composed by the various poets who visited them, were copied. Naturally, no satires found their way into such books, though we do come across poems full of humorous effrontery, in which the poets cadge shamelessly for horses and other gifts worthy of the laudatory verse they offer.[2]

'But', the reader may ask, 'why shouldn't a poem-book contain satires on the enemies of the particular family that owned it?' In order to answer this very pertinent question I must supply a little more detail about bardic practice. Contrary to the popular view, each noble family did not normally support just one hereditary poet, whose allegiance was pledged to it alone. Rather, a successful and generous chieftain would be visited by a number of poets, either singly or in a bardic company (*dámh*). These poets would also visit other chieftains, any of whom might, then or later, be the enemy of any other.

---

[1] Eleanor Knott, *Irish Classical Poetry, Commonly Called Bardic Poetry* (Dublin, 1957), p. 62. This book is the best brief summary of what is known about the bardic poets as well as their work; I have relied heavily on it throughout the first three sections of this chapter.

[2] See especially *The Book of Magauran*, ed. Lambert McKenna (Dublin, 1947), p. 311.

Hence comes the peculiarity of bardic poetry which Miss Knott describes as follows:

In Tadhg Dall's verses, and those of most bardic poets, the only living individual referred to is, with rare exceptions, the chief addressed. We might expect O'Donnell to be congratulated on his triumphs over O'Neill, or *vice versa*, but no. . . . This assumed ignorance . . . of feuds, or of rival claims to leadership . . . seems to have been based on a convention agreed on by the poets and acquiesced in by the chiefs themselves. As to the chiefs' real opinion of it, we have some evidence, perhaps, in [a poem addressed to Turlogh Luinech O'Neill by Tadhg Dall Ó Huiginn] . . . . To the poets it was probably more acceptable . . . mainly, no doubt, in order to preserve amicable relations between themselves and any chief upon whom, in the vicissitudes of things, they might one day come to depend.[1]

A profession with such a keen sense of the importance of public relations would undoubtedly be very sparing in its employment of satire. Just as a skilful union leader makes far more use of strike threats than he does of actual strikes, so the bards were often content to brandish the weapon of satire without actually hurling it. I have come across two very similar poems, one written by Gofraidh Fionn Ó Dálaigh (Geoffrey Finn O'Daly) in the fourteenth century, the other by Ádhamh Ó Fialán (Adam O'Phelan) some two centuries later, in which the aggrieved poets begin by threatening satire, then plead for redress, and end with something not too far from their usual vein of compliment. O'Daly, one of the greatest poets of the whole era, begins very fiercely indeed:

> Ere the flood of my anger swells
> to scorch thy cheek,
> I will give thee a warning. . . .

> (From the 2nd quatrain.)

The poem is addressed to Gerald Fitzgerald, fourth Earl of Desmond, whom Geoffrey accuses of condoning an underling's burning of the poet's corn. Toward its end we find this oblique compliment:

> I know of no battling, however fierce,
> O Earl of the fair Greeks' Isle,

[1] *The Bardic Poems of Tadhg Dall Ó Huiginn*, i, p. xlvi. Compare pp. xli–xliv.

which thou checkest not—thou showest it—
though thou chastisest not my robber.

(Quatrain 56.)[1]

O'Phelan retains much less dignity; by his forty-eighth quatrain he is practically grovelling:

Were I to send anyone a single verse of satire on thee, O hair like to gold-cloth, I should find no place left for me in Eire. . . .[2]

No doubt the class of satire called *mac bronn* ('son of womb', 'embryo') was much practised in bardic days; this type was either not communicated by the poet at all, or communicated only to one person. Professor David Greene of Trinity College, Dublin, has published a bardic poem in which the poet threatens to bring his embryo to monstrous birth:

I am nine months pregnant, my time for childbearing has come; (my) side is heavy from the concealed spite, the satire of the *ollamh* is a pregnancy. (Quatrain 4.)

I will not conceal it, it is enough; a certain noble lord is the father of the pregnancy—it is I who conceal its harm. (Quatrain 16.)

I will unloose on him its oppression of me. . . . (From Quatrain 17.)[3]

An exception—the only one known to me—which triumphantly proves the rule is a bardic poem which compares Tomaltach Mac Dermot and Tomás Maguire, two fifteenth-century chiefs, very much to the detriment of the latter. The opening quatrains run as follows in Kenneth Jackson's translation:

There are two chiefs in the land of Ireland, the one mere dregs, the other a choice man of slender fingers; an old churlish starveling cripple and a bountiful man of noble lineage.

It is not wrong to compare them, a rod of alder and a rod of yew, a stick of twisted alder wood and my manly very generous timber.

The beggarly tainted chief of Ulster and the brave king of Connaught, the bright cheerful merry lad and the surly grudging man.

Mac Dermot of Moylurg and Maguire the refractory; it is justice gone askew to compare them, meagre rye beside wheat.

[1] Lambert McKenna, ed., 'Historical Poems of Gofraidh Fionn Ó Dálaigh. X', *Irish Monthly*, xlvii (1919), 563, 568.   [2] *The Book of Magauran*, p. 352.
[3] David Greene, 'Mac Bronn', *Éigse*, v (1947), 232, 235.

Tomaltach deals in pure feats of valour, Tomás in vice and arrogance; his paws are always in the scales, so that half my poems have rotted away.[1]

This fifth quatrain—there are at least eighteen more in similar vein—makes it pretty evident why the poet diverged so sharply from an unwritten rule of his order: he was so badly paid for his poems—if paid at all—by Maguire, that he saw no point in continuing to be polite to such a skinflint. His poems had 'rotted away' in the sense that they were wasted on Maguire.[2]

Of the satires which do survive from bardic times, by far the most interesting fall into my fifth category—professional. However, for the sake of orderliness, I shall deal briefly with the other four categories first. One of the most redoubtable satires of the period does not survive; John O'Donovan's account of it runs as follows:

In 1414, as we are informed by the Four Masters, Niall O'Higgin, a famous poet of Westmeath, composed a satire for Sir John Stanley, Lord Lieutenant of Ireland, which caused his death; and it was remarked that this was the second *poetical miracle* performed by the same Niall.[3]

Two of the most famous personal satires which do survive are reputed to have caused the deaths, not of their victims, but of the satirists. Aonghus na n-aor Ó Dálaigh (Angus 'of the Satires' O'Daly) composed a series of bitter quatrains on virtually all the leading Irish and Norman-Irish families in the opening years of the seventeenth century, charging them with poverty and inhospitality:

Little fly on the edge of the gable, if thou didst know how to steal thou wouldst carry off with thee easily my share of bread and butter beside the Finn.[4]

Angus was supposedly bribed by Lord Mountjoy and Sir George Carew to write this spiteful poem, with a view to stirring up rivalry and ill will among the enemies of England. It is said that a servant of one of his victims murdered Angus,

[1] Kenneth Hurlstone Jackson, *A Celtic Miscellany* (Cambridge, Mass., 1951), pp. 255–6.   [2] Jackson, p. 346.
[3] John O'Donovan, 'Introduction to the Poem', in Aenghus O'Daly, *The Tribes of Ireland: A Satire*, tr. James Clarence Mangan (Dublin, 1852), p. 17.
[4] Knott, *Irish Classical Poetry*, p. 65.

but retribution must have been slow, for the satirist did not die until 1617.[1]

Tadhg Dall Ó Huiginn (Blind Teigue O'Higgin) may have met a similar fate at the hands of six men of the O'Haras whom he had satirized for raiding his house; if so, these men must have been better literary critics or more conscious of their dignity than the description of them in the poem would lead us to believe; one would have thought that such men would react more quickly to crude scurrility than to the relatively restrained mockery of Tadhg. I think it is worth quoting in full in Miss Knott's prose translation:

A troop of six that came to my house, I shall give a description of them; scarce of milk was I the next morning, from the thirst of the six vagabonds.

It was a long time, seemingly, since a bit of cow's produce had entered their bodies, the twice three whom I have mentioned.

I was able—'tis a pity—to bring them from death to life; needs must they drink my milk, so great was the thirst from the dry bread.

I in want, and they in necessity—I am in a strait between the two; it is hard for me to repress these verses, yet it is sinful for me to make them.

It is best not to conceal the satire if any deserve censure; as I satirized the troop of six it is unfitting not to tell it.

The first that I saw, he was the best equipped of the band, a youth whose vest was not worth more than a groat; one whom feasting or gaming never impoverished.

The second man, as I found, coming in front of the company, was a miserable fellow whose marrow had gone from him, I shall not leave him out of the reckoning.

The munition of the third wretch was an old javelin and an untempered, gapped ax; he and his makings of an ax in an encounter, I pity such a battle-equipment.

The equipment of the fourth fellow who flux-smitten marched with them, four shafts, that never knocked a splinter out of a target, slung across his rump.

At the heels of the four others comes the fifth rogue, in a short smock not worth a groat, I do not think his mantle was any better.

The likeness of a fellow not worth a fleshworm was along with

[1] O'Donovan, pp. 22, 23, 27.

the five; a gaunt (?), transparent sort of fellow, he was a poor commodity on inspection.

I beseech God who shed His blood, since it is but decay for them to be alive—it is scarcely to be called living—that none may slay the troop of six.[1]

This poem is much more effective than the litanies of epithets which were common enough in the period and which grow even more frequent later. My own favourite line is *nachar lom ól ná imbeirt* ('one whom feasting or gaming never impoverished'). Note the brevity of the Irish by comparison with the English.

Of social satire there is virtually none; the poets are too secure in their status to fear the competition of any other class. The perennial moralizing about the wickedness of the age that we find in all medieval European literatures occurs in Ireland too, but its tone is too earnest to deserve the name of satire. On the other hand, discussions of the foibles of womankind—equally familiar from other literatures—are light enough in tone to be classed as wit.

One would suppose from the tone of the English poet Edmund Spenser's denunciation of the Irish 'Bardes and Rhythmers'[2] that they were constantly stirring up the Irish against the English. No doubt they were, but they also stirred up the Irish against the Irish. The bardic system throve on a constant diet of tribal warfare and cattle raids—the legality of the latter is constantly defended in bardic poetry. Although the Elizabethan adventurers seem to us at least as predatory as the Irish chieftains, Spenser came from a country in the early stages of capitalist development; to him the Irish system was as anarchic and out of date as that portrayed in the poems of Homer. The poets did not become nationalists until it was already too late to unify defeated Ireland against the invader. Miss Knott writes of Tadhg Dall Ó Huiginn (1550–91) that

He shows in most of his poems a calm acceptation of the contemporary strife, as though it were the natural order. Poetry flourished on it, and for him, like most bardic poets, the profession

---

[1] *The Bardic Poems of Tadhg Dall Ó Huiginn*, vol. ii, Irish Texts Society XXIII (London, 1926), pp. 185–6.

[2] O'Donovan quotes a long passage from Spenser's *View of the State of Ireland* in his 'Introduction', pp. 19–21.

was the thing. . . . We may take him as a typical figure, thoroughly adapted in mind and customs to the existing order; utterly unaware of the imminent dawn of a new world.[1]

In view of these facts, the almost complete absence of satire against the English before about 1650 becomes more understandable. After all, during the bardic period Ireland had survived the Anglo-Norman invasion, whose chief result had been—I exaggerate, of course—to supply the bardic poets with more and wealthier patrons. How were the poets to know that the Elizabethan invasion was of a totally different kind?

A notable exception to the above general statement is the sixteenth-century poem by Laoiseach Mac an Bhaird which ridicules an unnamed 'man who follow[s] English ways', comparing him unfavourably with a certain Eóghan (Owen) Bán Mac Donnchadha.[2] While the butt of the poem cuts short his hair, Owen wears his long. Owen also refuses to wear doublet and hose, an English boot with a 'jewelled spur', or any other elaborate features of Elizabethan dress:

A blunt rapier which could not kill a fly, the son of Donnchadh does not think it handsome; nor the weight of an awl sticking out behind his rear as he goes to the hill of the assembly.

In general, Owen prefers 'the wild life', sleeping on rushes instead of a feather bed:

. . . to the good son of Donnchadh a house of rough wattles is more comfortable than the battlements of a castle.

All those things that Owen does not like are presumably favoured by the unnamed lover of English ways, and they make him ridiculous:

You are unlike Eóghan *Bán*; men laugh at *you* as you put your foot on the mounting-block; it is a pity that you yourself don't see your errors, O man who follow English ways.

Lest we mistake this for mere social satire, the political moral is expressly stated in the second-last quatrain:

[1] *The Bardic Poems of Tadhg Dall Ó Huiginn*, i, p. xlv.
[2] Jackson, pp. 236–7.

A troop of horse at the mouth of a pass, a wild fight, a ding-dong fray of footsoldiers, these are some of the delights of Donnchadh's son—and seeking contest with the foreigners.

By the time this poem was written, the dangers of the Elizabethan invasion must have been clear enough—to one poet at least.

Those members of the Irish clergy who practised bardic poetry had a keener sense of urgency about the new invasion, for it brought with it a new religion and a new system of church organization. Apostasy suddenly became a frightening and deeply shocking problem. Right at the end of the bardic period we find a long and dignified satire on this subject—aimed at individuals, yet managing on the whole to avoid mere scurrility. This is the poem by Eoghan Ó Dubhthaigh (Owen O'Duffy), a Franciscan, which begins '*Léig dod chomortus dúinn*' ('No more of your comparisons for us') and is entitled in John O'Daly's translation *The Apostasy of Myler Magrath, Archbishop of Cashel*. Actually the poem attacks four Protestant bishops in all: Magrath; Matthew Sheyn, Bishop of Cork, who does not appear to have been an apostate; William Casey, Bishop of Limerick; and another bishop not clearly identifiable. Quatrains 1–24 ridicule Sheyn for claiming that the Blessed Virgin was just like any other woman; the poet professes to have searched everywhere for 'a mother's son better than Christ' without finding one. He proceeds to compare Sheyn's mother and his poor boyhood home with the Virgin and her heavenly mansion. Quatrains 25–79 begin by comparing the wives of Magrath, Sheyn, and Casey with the Virgin; Magrath comes in for special notice because Myler is but the anglicized form of Maolmhuire (the *maol*—'servant'—of Mary). Myler is no longer the servant of Mary but a servant without Mary ('*maol gan Mhuire*'), he is the servant of Annie his wife, and so on. Various Protestant practices, such as the eating of meat on Friday, are denounced, and the inevitable end of all this heretical conduct—Hell—is frequently mentioned. Quatrains 80–87 significantly denounce several bardic poets by name for their unwillingness to write poems in praise of the Virgin and their sycophancy toward a certain unnamed earl, who has come that year (*c.* 1577) to Ireland and is clearly an English sympathizer and possibly a Protestant:

They compose, for a pittance of pence,
A poem most difficult to honour the Countess;
The sycophant falsetongued bards
Shall be howling some day *in profundis*!

(Quatrain 86.)[1]

Quatrains 88–92 form a hymn in praise of the Virgin, while
93–97 seem to me to provide a dignified and powerful ending
to the satire. Quatrains 98–101 contain a random repetition of
miscellaneous themes already worked out earlier, while 102–6
absurdly request the Virgin to box the ears or punch the jaws
of the errant bishops. I note that a manuscript in the British
Museum contains only 97 quatrains of this poem, though I do
not know whether they correspond to O'Daly's Nos. 1–97.[2]
I will end this analysis of the poem by quoting Quatrains 93–
97 from O'Daly (with my punctuation):

England and Ireland all over
I perceive have become unwise:
They are fonder of food and women
Than of the Virgin, God, or Heaven.

The bishops and their wives in woe shall be,
Wailing their matins in bitter tears;
Foot to foot in the depths of hell,
In flames of fire face to face.

You clergy with the wives, who reject vespers,
Christ will expel you from his right hand;
His wife on the arm of each bishop leaning
In hell at vespers at his side.

Bitter vespers, ah woe! they shall be,
By which you shall then suffer torments;
Sad music this at the vespers,
The howling of the bishops and their wives.

Oh! that your mind was fixed on God,
As it is on feasting and on women;
You would not be wretched and blabbering and foolish,
And heaven would be your portion at the end.[3]

---

[1] Eoghan O'Duffy, *The Apostasy of Myler Magrath, Archbishop of Cashel*, tr.
John O'Daly (Cashel, Co. Tipperary, 1864), p. 9.
[2] Standish Hayes O'Grady, *Catalogue of Irish Manuscripts in the British Museum*, i
(London, 1926), 55–56. This volume will be called 'O'Grady, *Catalogue*' for the
remainder of this chapter. [3] O'Duffy, p. 9.

Professional satire

Since professional satire is so peculiarly a product of the bardic age and survives almost entirely in syllabic metre, this seems the appropriate place to deal with the topic once for all. Subject matter, technique, and the relationship of the poet to his public all undergo satirical criticism. The most comprehensive satire on the whole bardic institution is *Imtheacht na Tromdháimhe* (*The Proceedings of the Burdensome Bardic Company*), also known as *Tromdámh Guaire*. This riotous attack on bardic techniques, pedantry, subject matter, and social behaviour is analysed below in my chapter on parody, so I shall do no more than mention it here. Since a cleric outwits the poets in this work, I assume it was of clerical authorship. In its earliest form, it is found in the fifteenth-century *Book of Lismore*, though the language suggests that it may date from the thirteenth or fourteenth century. One of the most interesting features of this tale for us at the moment is the stress it puts on the bardic poets' wanton use of satire or the threat of satire to enforce their will; one poet goes so far as to say, 'I would rather that Guaire would be satirized than that I should live and he not satirized.'[1]

A poem by Geoffrey Finn O'Daly (d. 1387) contains some very cynical comments on bardic subject matter; at this late date it is hard to tell whether they were intended satirically or as the literal truth. The poet is trying to mollify Maurice Fitzgerald, first Earl of Desmond, one of whose enemies he had apparently praised:

> O Muiris, abate thy anger!
> Do as Gearoid asks of thee!
> Thy peace, spite of thy offence,
> If thou deniest me thou art not just.
>
> In our poems we promise the Gaoidhil [Gaels]
> a kingdom they never get.
> You should not pay attention to it,
> 'tis our custom!

---

[1] *Imtheacht na Tromdhaimhe; or The Proceedings of the Great Bardic Institution,* ed. Owen Connellan, Transactions of the Ossianic Society V (Dublin, 1860), p. 87. See also Maud Joynt, ed., *Tromdámh Guaire,* Mediaeval and Modern Irish Series, II (Dublin, 1941), pp. vii–xi.

Two races to whom poems are sung
are in cool-streamed Eire,
The Gaoidhil known to fame,
And the Goill [Gauls, foreigners] of Britain, isle
of varied beauty.

In poems to the Goill we promise
the driving of the Gaoidhil from Eire;
in those to the Gaoidhil we promise
the driving of the Goill east overseas!

(Quatrains 43–46.)[1]

Satire or not, this sheds a blaze of light on what we have already seen of the lack of patriotism among the bardic poets. Remember that O'Daly is flattering a 'Gaul' or Anglo-Norman lord in the language of the Gael.

One of the bardic poets—we cannot be sure which, but he probably lived in the fourteenth or fifteenth century—wrote a scathing little poem of eleven quatrains on the fulsome flattery so common in bardic poems. It begins, '*A lucht chumas bréag san dán*' ('O folk who shape a lie into poetry'). Some of it sounds in deadly earnest, as the poet promises Hell to all lying poets and to their unfortunate patrons, too—probably because they will become guilty of pride and vanity. But the examples he gives of the poets' offences against truth are highly amusing: 'You put a comely, handsome lock of hair upon a bald forehead'; 'To a man who is parchment-yellow and tanned' the bards will attribute 'a complexion like a swan or like lime . . .', and so on, each example more untruthful and more absurd than the last.[2]

Several poems, including one by Séamus Mac Cuarta (James Courtney), who died as late as 1732, satirize or parody bad poets by stringing platitudes together: 'The Pope is in Rome to the east; the Fianna used to have hounds; fires are made of turf (peat).'[3] Dáibhidh Ó Bruadair (David O'Bruadair), indignant at having to write in the popular stress-metre for an uneducated audience, writes a poem of this kind which contains

[1] Lambert McKenna, ed., 'Historical Poems of Gofraidh Fionn Ó Dálaigh. IX', *Irish Monthly*, xlvii (1919), 513.
[2] Thomas F. O'Rahilly, ed., *Measgra Dánta: Miscellaneous Irish Poems*, Part I (Cork, 1927), pp. 21–22 and note on p. 71. Translations mine.
[3] Ibid., p. 5. See also the preceding poem, pp. 3–4, and the notes to it, p. 63.

a great deal of humour, but the final quatrain turns it into a satire on his audience:

An uair nach cluinim cion ar chéill i nduain
's an uair nach sultmhar rith do réir na suadh,
an uair nach fuilid fir na féinne suas
is guagán gliog dom thuigse an dréacht is dual.

(When I see how people set no value on poetic wit,
And when to run in steps of sages brings to no one any joy,
When the heroes of the Fenians stand no longer up erect,
An empty jingle is the only poetry which suits my mind.)[1]

Whereas the author of *The Proceedings of the Burdensome Bardic Company* reproaches the poets for not making themselves understood, David O'Bruadair attacks his public for not understanding him, and his fellow poets for not being able to write in strict syllabic metre:

Nothing but the merest mumbling can the best of those attain
Who are striving now to fashion poems in the speech of Scot. . . .

If anyone could write a piece of poetry correct in form,
Prudently embroidered in the style and metres of the school,
When the tale was told, a clever Scottic yeoman would assert
That its sense to him was such that Dutch could not be more
    obscure.[2]

There is not much laughter in this second poem of O'Bruadair's and there is even less in two similar poems written much earlier in the seventeenth century: '*Mór do-ghníd daoine dhíobh féin*' ('It is a great deal that some people make of themselves') by Fearfeasa Ó'n Cháinte (O'Canty)[3] and '*A mhic, ná meabhraigh éigse*' ('Son, do not study poetry') by Mathghamhain Ó Hifearnáin (Mahon O'Heffernan). The first attacks ignorant critics of poetry, while the second deplores the debased popular taste in poetry and warns against taking any risks: 'Praise no man, nor any satirize . . . but and if thou praise, laud not a Gael . . . to chant a panegyric of the Gael means odium earned . . .'.[4]

---

[1] *Duanaire Dháibhidh Uí Bhruadair: The Poems of David Ó Bruadair*, ed. and tr. John C. Mac Erlean, Part I, Irish Texts Society XI (London, 1910), pp. 78–79.
[2] *Duanaire Dháibhidh Uí Bhruadair*, Part III, Irish Texts Society XVIII (London, 1917), p. 195.   [3] O'Grady, *Catalogue*, pp. 555–7.
[4] O'Grady, *Catalogue*, p. 393. For an attractive verse translation see the rendering by Máire MacEntee in *The Oxford Book of Irish Verse* (Oxford, 1958), pp. 326–7.

One poet seems to have taken the seventeenth-century change in poetic fashion philosophically, if we can trust '*Ionmholta malairt bhisigh*' ('A change for the better is to be commended') by Eochu Ó Heodhusa (O'Hosey or O'Hussey). Actually, he is only pretending to like the new-fangled verse, the better to make fun of it. This reads like such a witty and civilized work of art even in prose translation that I should like to quote it entire as a fitting farewell to much of what was best in bardic poetry:

A change for the better is to be commended: I have found at this time an exchange poor but fortunate, which has turned out profitable for me.

I have abandoned the delicate series of keen and earnest admonitions for a common sort of easy art which brings me more praise.

By the obscurity of carven ornament I used to earn disgust: many protested that my verse was unworthy of favour.

Henceforth, though great is the luck, I renounce a single groat of the profit thereof, if one stanza of my poetry passes the understanding of anyone in the world.

Free and easy verse on the open road!—since that is what is asked of me, I will discharge the debts, by the leave of the Earl of Tyrconnell.

The dunces of the world would not beat me in softness and artlessness: I have gone out in the rain like the rest—a wise course.

I have abandoned—what greater luck?—my hard mysterious ways: if he hear some of my verse it will make the Earl laugh.

Lest I be put out of the protection of those from whom splendour was won (?), I refuse to let Tyrconnell's prince go upon a jury to try me.

Through bad verse many a one is full of love for me this year: I would earn more affection but for fear of the Earl.

Aodh's son, the sober-minded, a man who found my hard (verse) very soft, it is easy for me to be brave now that he is away in England.

Every poem I composed hitherto used almost to break my heart: This new fashion that has come to us is a great cause of health.

If the chief of Bearnas find fault with any quatrain that is made by me, there will be many opposed to him: a change for the better is to be recommended.[1]

[1] Translation by Osborn Bergin, *Studies*, vii (1918), 618–19.

Notice how this poem, while simultaneously doing so many
other difficult things, manages to achieve the main purpose of
a bardic poem—the paying of compliments to a chieftain. The
Earl of Tyrconnell's taste in poetry is praised obliquely, but
with the greatest skill.

1650–1850

As we move out of the bardic era into the more modern
period we find both continuity and change in Gaelic literature.
From one point of view, making a comparison with Scots
literature, we see a sharp and sudden break in technique and
diction, as if the fifteenth- and sixteenth-century Scottish
Chaucerians were immediately followed by the age of Fergusson
and Burns, which in fact occurred two and a half centuries
later. A courtly tradition, it would seem, had suddenly been
replaced in Ireland by a rustic one. But because a two-hundred-
and-fifty-year gap did not intervene, the continuity in the
Irish tradition is much easier to see than it is in the Scots.
Burns has much more in common with Dunbar and Henryson
than his lowly social status as ploughman or revenue officer
would suggest. As far as literature went, he was a sophisticated
and self-conscious artist, schooled in a technical virtuosity
foreign to the poets of London or Paris in his day. His education
was no better and no worse than that of the Irish poets in the
days when Catholic schools were proscribed in Ireland: he
learned to read and write young, as they did in the 'hedge
schools'; from then on, the poetic education of Irish and Scots
came from reading and—far more important—from voluntary
apprenticeship. If the bardic schools died out, the concept of
apprenticeship did not; one wonders whether it did not survive
from Celtic times in the Lowlands of Scotland, in spite of the
change in language there.[1] Whenever and wherever possible,
the Irish poets of the eighteenth century gathered in courts of
poetry for mutual criticism, instruction, and encouragement,
as Daniel Corkery has so well described in *The Hidden Ireland*.[2]
Burns, of course, was a man of genius, far superior to David

---

[1] See Kurt Wittig, *The Scottish Tradition in Literature* (Edinburgh, 1958), pp. 60–
61, 70–72, 185–98 and *passim* for Gaelic influence on Scots poetry. As clues to
Burns's apprenticeship see his two verse epistles to 'Davie, a Brother Poet' (David
Sillar), and three to John Lapraik.

[2] Daniel Corkery, *The Hidden Ireland*, 3rd imp. (Dublin, 1941), pp. 90–125.

Sillar or John Lapraik, but the mere fact that these men of his own class had public standing as poets made him ready to think of himself as a poet and to learn from them by correspondence and talk. Let us never forget that it was far easier and far more natural for a man to be a poet in the tiniest Irish or Scottish hamlet in the eighteenth century than it is in the best-educated groups in New York or London today.

Personal satire

That Irish satire should so frequently take the form of personal lampoon or even invective seems to me implicit in its origin as magic and in the persistent belief, still alive in the nineteenth century, that satire had the power to inflict actual physical harm on its victim. John O'Daly remembered his mother's fear of a beggarman named O'Farrell in the first decade of the last century; she gave him 'about 7 lbs. of wool, which he indignantly threw in her face, vehemently swearing that he would satirize her to death' if she did not give him twice that much, 'which', writes O'Daly, 'she was obliged to do.'[1]

In the early Irish period the devout were addicted to a form of prayer known as a *lorica* (Latin for 'breast-plate'). In it God was asked to protect every part of the worshipper's body individually, joint by joint and organ by organ. This type of prayer probably derived from a pagan spell; at any rate the careful enumeration of each part of the body has magical precedent. In the same way, a full-dress Irish lampoon seeks to ridicule every part of its victim's body—though editors seem always to insert asterisks for the portions dealing with the genitals. No doubt such satires were composed throughout the bardic period, though I do not know of any complete ones.[2] Two exhaustive examples are to be found in Dinneen's edition of the poems of Aodhagán Ó Rathaille (Egan O'Rahilly): the first is an attack on O'Rahilly by Domhnall na Tuile, the other Egan's reply.[3]

---

[1] 'Erionnach' (pseud. of George Sigerson), tr., *The Poets and Poetry of Munster*, 2nd series (Dublin, 1860), p. 218 n. John O'Daly was the anonymous editor of the Gaelic and presumably the author of this note, since Sigerson was not yet born in 1808, the latest possible date for this incident.

[2] See the passage already quoted above (p. 131) from Knott, *Irish Classical Poetry*, p. 62.

[3] *Dánta Aodhagáin Uí Rathaille: The Poems of Egan O'Rahilly*, ed. Patrick S.

Such poems are as tiresome to the modern reader as the Scots 'flytings', for the victim of such satire is not allowed to retain any individuality; it would be impossible for any human being to display all the blemishes assigned to him, so that the ridicule of known foibles cannot be the purpose of such lampoons. If the satirists are in earnest, they must desire to wound rather than to arouse laughter or punish wickedness. Otherwise, the practice of satire, especially in such flytings between poets, becomes a mere exercise in vocabulary, phrasing, and versification. The technical term for a flyting in Irish is *immarbág* (later *iomarbháigh*); when we examine the earlier uses of this word (which is also the technical term for the comparative degree of adjectives), we find that it has two main areas of meaning: 'strife, contention, a contest; act of contending', and on the other hand 'wordy dispute, boastfulness; act of boasting'; one striking example of the latter use occurs in the tale *Bricriu's Feast*, where the wives of the Ulster heroes are boasting about their husbands' prowess. The primary meaning of the word can be used in, for example, a phrase meaning 'a competition in running and archery'.[1] If we bear both these meanings in mind and think of an *iomarbháigh* as something between a contest in verbal athleticism and a boastful display of poetic muscle, we shall avoid taking a sham fight too seriously. 'Counter-boasting' is Miss Eleanor Knott's ingenious translation. When the disputants try to overcome each other by force of argument rather than mere virtuosity in invective, the more usual descriptive term seems to be *conspóid*, 'disputation'. The most famous of all poetic contests, however, *Iomarbháigh na bhFileadh* (usually translated as *The Contention of the Poets*) has no satiric intent at all. An elaborate sham fight, which several poets entered in order to show off their traditional learning, it represents the swan song of the bardic order.[2]

Even after the bardic period was over, a number of poets might join in an *iomarbháigh* like the celebrated one between Seán Ó Tuama (John O'Tuomy) and Aindrias Mac Craith (Andrew Magrath). *An Mangaire Súgach*, 'The Jolly Peddler',

Dinneen and Tadhg O'Donoghue, Irish Texts Society III, 2nd ed. (London, 1911), pp. 238–51 (text and trans.).

[1] Entry *immarbág* in *Contributions to a Dictionary of the Irish Language*, 'I', fasc. 1 Dublin, 1952).

[2] Knott, *Irish Classical Poetry*, p. 74.

was the latter's nickname, better known than his real name. O'Tuomy, having set up as a tavernkeeper in Croom, County Limerick, composed a rather smug advertisement for his house in four of the stanzas that have since come to be known as 'limericks'. Magrath, who was actually one of O'Tuomy's closest friends, composed a longer poem in the same metre, using some of O'Tuomy's very rhymes and phrases but twisting them to make O'Tuomy sound like the worst kind of *faux bonhomme*. Mangan's translation of both poems in *The Poets and Poetry of Munster* captures much of their spirit if not the letter.[1]

To illustrate *An Mangaire's* method, let me quote two lines from O'Tuomy's first stanza:

Muna mbeidh duine ar mo chuideachta dhíolfas
Mise bheas thíos leis in antráth.[2]

(If there is no one of my company who will pay,
It is I will suffer loss by it untimely.)

The next stanza makes it clear that O'Tuomy is asserting his readiness to give free drinks to those who cannot pay. Magrath, in his seventh stanza, twists the words as follows:

Gloine má thugair do dhuine gan díol
Is i mbille bheidh thíos air in antráth![3]

(If you give a glass to anyone without payment,
It is on a bill it will be [put] down to him untimely!)

'Two young children of poetry' then took up the cudgels against Magrath, still employing the same metre and some of the same phrases, but when a certain Seán Ó Tuathail (John O'Toole) dared to attack O'Tuomy, *An Mangaire* used the limerick metre to lay him low. The opening lines of the four poems run as follows:

1. *Is duine me dhíolas leann, lá . . . .*
   (I am a man who sells ale at times. . . .)

2. *Is duine thu dhíolas steanncán . . . .*
   (You are a man who sells ditchwater. . . .)

---

[1] These translations have been reprinted in Kathleen Hoagland, ed., *1000 Years of Irish Poetry* (New York, 1947), pp. 186–9.

[2] *Éigse na Máighe, .i. Seán Ó Tuama an Ghrinn, Aindrias Mac Craith—An Mangaire Súgach*, ed. Risteárd Ó Foghludha (Dublin, 1952), p. 128.

[3] Ibid., p. 129.

3. *Ní duine thu acht straoille fann-bháird.* . . .
    (You are not a man but a *streel* of a feeble bard. . . .)

4. *Ba mhinic tu ag díol na steanncán.* . . .
    (It was often you sold ditchwater. . . .)[1]

What was perhaps the most famous *iomarbháigh* among the rustic poets of the eighteenth century grew out of a series of hurling matches near the village of Faha in County Kerry between the married men and the bachelors of the district. The married men won, but the bachelors bribed an elderly poet, Teigue O'Scannell, with whisky to compose a satire against the 'old men'; a poet named O'Hegarty countered for the married; then the youthful Eoghan Ruadh Ó Súilleabháin (Owen Roe O'Sullivan) weighed in with the verbal earthquake known as *An tArrachtach Sean* ('The Old Monster'), which by itself would have earned him immortality.[2] This fairly long poem was preserved until recently by oral tradition alone, but it must be easier to remember than to translate, for it pullulates with synonyms, like most Irish satire, and many of its epithets are difficult to render precisely in English. I offer the following very tentative translation of the often-admired fifth stanza in Dinneen's edition. Perhaps Frank O'Connor might be persuaded to give us a translation of the whole poem some day.

When a girl united to an old man sees
    A handsome gallant in his prime on horseback,
Spiritedly, powerfully, maturely, cleanly, nimbly,
    Bravely, strongly, with full power, swiftly,
Her heart starts up and fills her with love for him;
    There comes a shedding of genuine tears and weeping in her
        heart;
She says, 'That a sickness without end may lay hold of my kin,
    Who tied me for ever to an old monster!'

Here the *iomarbháigh* has moved beyond the merely personal to the level of social satire.

The weapons sharpened in sham fight were often used to express a real grievance: for instance, Feardorcha Ó Dálaigh

---

[1] *Éigse na Máighe*, pp. 128–32.
[2] *Amhráin Eoghain Ruaidh Uí Shúilleabháin* [i.e. *The Poems of Owen Roe O'Sullivan*], ed. Patrick S. Dinneen, 2nd ed. (Dublin, 1902), pp. 67–72 (text only). See also pp. xv, 125.

(O'Daly), believing that a certain Dr. Whaley, a Dublin astrologer and almanac maker, had been instrumental in having his (O'Daly's) brother hanged, wrote a ferocious satire on him in the last years of the seventeenth century. With almost superstitious awe, John O'Donovan describes this as 'the bitterest, most wicked and diabolical satire ever written in the Irish language'. He goes on to summarize it as follows:

The poet first describes the hellish practices of the Astrologer, whom he describes as in league with the Devil, who since he began to view the moon and the planets, had, with his Balor-eye, destroyed their benign influence; so that the corn-fields, the fruit-trees, and the grass had ceased to grow; the birds had forgotten their songs (except the ominous birds of night), and the young of animals were destroyed *in utero*. He then begins to wither this Antichrist of Ireland with imprecations, awful in the highest degree; implores that the various diseases which waste the world may attack him, and calls down upon his guilty head the curses of God, the angels, and of all good men.[1]

I quote just one quatrain, which has the ring of an incantation:

Mallacht Dé ort 'sa naomh-Mháthar,
Mallacht na n-Apstal ort 'san Phápa:
Mallacht na Sagart ort 's na m-Bráthar,
Mallacht na m-baintreabhach 's na n-gárlach.

(The curse of God on thee and of His holy Mother,
The curse of the Apostles on thee and of the Pope:
The curse of the priests on thee and of the brothers,
The curse of the widows on thee and of the orphans.)[2]

David O'Bruadair, a poet much given to satire and invective, lashed 'a churlish boor who attacked a lady of the Barrys, a relative of the Earl of Barrymore', in an extraordinarily elaborate combination of stress and syllabic metres. I give an attempted translation of the first three quatrains, which reproduces the alliteration to some extent but ignores the assonances and rhymes; the poem begins, '*Is olc an ceart fulang an fhámuire*':

> Dirty the deed to coddle this corner-boy,
>   Sluggish the soul and meagre in mercy
> That fears to face this tattered tear-away,
>   This louser with a loy, this gouty gloater.

[1] O'Donovan, p. 28.   [2] Ibid., p. 31. Translation mine.

Gouty he goes with his weapon of war
To lash at ladies gentle and graceful;
Yet no mayor has more of imbecile English
Than this ghost of a goose when back from battering 'em.

Battering of beauties with anxious ardour
    Is the martial might of this cocky cur,
Fierce with the furious strength of a scaldcrow
    Grabbing a gosling from a gaggling goose.[1]

The poet finally passes sentence upon the churl; Father Mac Erlean translates as follows:

I order his cloak to be kneaded in bovine excretion,
And also his ears to be clipped of a neat little circuit,
A shovel well filled with the cowdung he cast at the maiden,
And boots to be plied on his bottom like polishing brushes.[2]

Three poems of invective, which we might classify as political if they were not so intensely personal, represent an attitude supposedly foreign to the Anglo-Saxon tradition—indeed, I cannot think of anything else in Irish tradition, even in pre-Christian times, which parallels it. These three poems, all by Munster poets, are three wild yells of triumph over the deaths of three public enemies. The earliest is Egan O'Rahilly's poem on the death of Murtagh O'Griffin, a renegade Irishman and apostate Catholic who acted as steward of a barony near Killarney. It begins:

Thou hast taken [Murtagh] from us, O death,
    Too late is the time for everyone;
Snatch Tadhg quickly from us to the churchyard,
    It is not fitting to separate him from him for ever.[3]

The poem goes on to adjure the gravestone to hold Murtagh down, so that he cannot return from the dead. Murtagh's torments in Hell and the sins by which he earned them are then bitterly described. Fortunately the poem is short, consisting of only 32 lines.

Even more ferocious, but probably modelled on the preceding, is the poem by Seán Clárach Mac Domhnaill (Mac

---

[1] *Duanaire Dháibhidh Uí Bhruadair*, Part I, p. 80.
[2] Ibid., p. 87.
[3] *Dánta Aodhagáin Uí Rathaille*, p. 97.

Donnell) on Colonel Dawson of Aherlow, a notorious oppressor
of the Irish. Douglas Hyde has translated the first verse thus,
preserving much of the alliteration and assonance:

Squeeze down his bones, O ye stones, in your hall of clay,
Yon reeking, gore-sprinkled boar, old Dawson the grey.
Sheathed was his sword when the foeman called to the fray,
But he cheated and sold, and slowly slaughtered his prey.[1]

Last and least effective in this unpleasant series are the verses
by Seán Ó Murchadha na Ráithíneach (John Murphy of
Raheen) on a bailiff named David Gleeson who was murdered
in Cork in 1737. They begin:

Now may the poets laugh and freely rejoice,
For the flat-footed, hard, accursed bailiff is dead;
I pardon Death all the ravage he ever made
Since he has tripped up the lout David, the old devilish *bum*.[2]

In the four poems just quoted, the satirists had at least the
excuse that they were expressing public opinion. There are
other satires, directed against people too unskilled to reply,
which lack that excuse. Perhaps we are not meant to take Owen
Roe O'Sullivan's 'Curse on Kate O'Leary' very seriously,
since the occasion for it was her keeping his stockings as a
pledge for fourpence which he owed her.[3] In fact, the humour
of the poem may lie in the very solemnity of the curse bestowed
for so trivial a cause. Father Patrick Dinneen says of it:

This psalm of imprecations is as solemn and sombre as anything
we know in literature. It proves that Eoghan's genius was adaptable
to many moods. The tone is that of a Pontiff pronouncing solemn
excommunication against an heresiarch.[4]

Less humorously meant, one feels, was David O'Bruadair's
short satire on a servant girl or barmaid who refused him a
drink, though her employers were friends of his. James Stephens
made a free translation of this, beginning:

The lanky hank of a she in the inn over there
Nearly killed me for asking the loan of a glass of beer. . . .

---

[1] Douglas Hyde, 'Unpublished Irish Poem by John Claragh Mac Donnell',
Journal of the Cork Historical and Archaeological Society, iii (Mar. 1894), 58.
[2] Corkery, pp. 113–14.
[3] *Amhráin Eoghain Ruaidh Uí Shúilleabháin*, pp. 73–75.
[4] Ibid., pp. 125–6.

and ending:

May she marry a ghost and bear him a kitten, and may
The High King of Glory permit her to get the mange.[1]

These last two lines reproduce substantially the eighth and
twelfth lines of the sixteen-line original. The sixteenth line was
too obscene not only for O'Bruadair's editor but for at least one
scribe, who wrote instead '*Finis go salach ciodh suairc*', which
means roughly, 'It ends dirtily though wittily'. One can say
this much for O'Bruadair, however: he deliberately does not
give the girl's name:

Although according to the law I hide her pedigree from you,
Little would it matter if she were to bear a ghost a cat.[2]

It is a relief to turn from the ruthless, if highly accomplished,
lampoons of the Munster tradition to gentler forms of satire,
where humour predominates. Of the three poems I am about
to discuss, only one is by a Munsterman—and he was a Franciscan when he wrote it. I mean *Leastar an Bhráthar* ('The Friar's
Bad Butter') by Father William English. Apparently another
friar had collected a keg full of butter from various farmers'
wives while seeking alms for his community. This he en-
deavoured to sell at the Cork Butter Market, but when the keg
was opened the butter proved to be all the colours of the rainbow, if we can believe Father English. All the nations of
Europe came to claim their own colours: green for Ireland,
red for England, white for France, yellow for Spain, 'and the
King of Scandinavia found an enormous quantity of blue in it'.
Unfortunately, there was no butter left for Frederick the
Great of Prussia, who promptly started the Seven Years War
out of pique:

I think the Pope died of jealousy for not receiving Peter's portion
of the bad butter as was wont. . . . All Europe is at sixes and sevens
on account of this butter that the Friar collected.

The only solution for the disturbed international situation is
to churn some more butter and send it to the King of Prussia:

[1] James Stephens, *Collected Poems*, 2nd ed. (London, 1954), p. 185.
[2] *Duanaire Dháibhidh Uí Bhruadair*, Part II, Irish Texts Society XIII (London,
1913), pp. 220–1.

Since you [the butter] began the war, secure peace for us, and like Achilles' spear, wound and heal.[1]

Peadar Ó Doirnin (Peter O'Durnin), the County Louth poet, is the first northern figure we have come upon in the later period; humour seems more congenial than satire to northern Irishmen, as O'Durnin's poem on a drunken farmer named Turloch O'Hamill exemplifies. Turloch, his pockets full of money after a fair, rented an old coach and had the driver bring him on a triumphal progress to all the inns on a very circuitous route home. Turloch bought drinks for the house wherever he went, and was soon being followed by a crowd of hangers-on. When the old coach stuck in a rut, his retainers pushed so hard that it fell to pieces and Turloch rolled out on the road. The poet begins by marvelling at the mysterious ways of Providence. Who would be less likely to become rich than the improvident Turloch?

He never amassed store nor a chest of gold, but would scatter freely in the tavern; he would sit under a table from Sunday morning until Saturday would dawn on him; he would not take advice from his wife or my lord; he would not harrow, plough or hedge; do you not see that at last Fortune has put in a coach worthy Turloch O'Hamill?

After describing Turloch's progress, the poet begins to recommend the golden mean, reminding us of the fall of Icarus ('*Icarus óg Mac Daedaluis*'), who flew too high, and the burning of Phaethon by the sun. Finally he tells us of the anticlimax in Turloch's story when 'he drops from his coach out on his rump'. It is said that Turloch reformed as a result of the publicity given to this song, which was known as *Toirdhealbhach Cóir* ('Worthy' or 'Honest Turloch').[2]

Riocard Bairéad (Richard Barret), a County Mayo poet (1748–1819), composed a satire with a similar title, *Eoghan Cóir* ('Owen the Honest and Humane', is James Hardiman's rendering). This was a mock elegy on 'one of the most rapacious "land-agents" of his time'. Barret was a great admirer of Swift

[1] Richard Henebry, 'An Unpublished Poem by W. English', *Zeitschrift für celtische Philologie*, i (1897), 141–5.

[2] David Comyn, 'Gaelic Literary Studies: Unpublished Poems of Peadar Ua Doirnin', *The Gaelic Journal: Irisleabhar na Gaedhilge*, vi (1 Oct. 1895), 101–4. Translations mine.

and adopted his irony here. Everybody is mourning for Eoghan:
'The like of the bawling and keening was never heard in the
land before'. The poet does not wonder at this, however, in
view of Eoghan's lovable character and his generosity. Two
men (doubtless bitter enemies of Eoghan) are singled out as
being particularly distressed:

I suppose that, under gravestone or sod, any person would be
preferable to the two than the poor, simple man, Eoghan Cóir.

The only edition of this poem I have seen has a rather pointless
final stanza; the true ending, to my mind, is that of the second-
last stanza with its ironical sting:

According as he was to others, may Christ be the same to him.[1]

Unlike the bards, the later poets do not make much use of
irony or understatement in their satires. Perhaps the appalling
times they were living through made detachment hard for
them, though Swift found inspiration in those very times for
his supreme piece of irony, *A Modest Proposal*; but then, Swift
was looking at eighteenth-century Ireland from above, not
from underneath. The only other completely ironical poem
that I have come across in the period is a very trivial example,
John O'Tuomy's pseudo-love poem to Seón Anna Prior which
begins, '*Mo theastas-sa díbh innsim do chléir na gceacht.*'[2] It describes a woman of supreme beauty whom he met, and the last
line reveals her name—Seón Anna Prior. The joke is that Seón
was no beauty but 'a messenger of the poets and a constant
butt of their wit'.[3]

In concluding this section I want to stress that it aims only
at illustrating *types* of personal satire. I could have used twice
the space without exhausting the material that I have studied.
Let me point out once again, to those who would make too
hasty generalizations about the Irish character, that the
literary—or rather the magical—tradition favoured the lampoon over more general types of satire.

---

[1] Roderic O'Flaherty, *A Chorographical Description of West or H-Iar Connaught*,
ed. James Hardiman (Dublin, 1846), pp. 292–3. Translations mine.
[2] *Éigse na Máighe*, pp. 143–4.
[3] Robin Flower, *Catalogue of Irish Manuscripts in the British Museum*, ii (London,
1926), 195. This volume will be called 'Flower, *Catalogue*' for the remainder of this
chapter.

Social satire

I mentioned briefly at the beginning of this chapter that social satire during the period 1650–1850 was predominantly of one kind: ridicule and denunciation of the lower classes from the standpoint of the educated minority. The two lowest classes in Early Irish society were those of the *athach* or tenant farmer and the *mogh(a)*, the slave or serf—also known as a *biatach* (Anglo-Irish 'betagh') or food-producer. We cannot be sure which class was identified with 'Clan Thomas'—perhaps both were. In any case, though the Gaelic nobility and the bardic class tended to lose both their land and their status during the invasions of the sixteenth and seventeenth centuries, the lower classes of Gaelic society tended to rise in the world —if not absolutely, then relatively as their old rulers fell. One of the harshest accusations in that great seventeenth-century satire *Pairlement Chloinne Tomáis* (*The Parliament of Clan Thomas*) alleges that the 'Clan' made their peace with the invaders, and indeed profited greatly by doing so.

In three of the four provinces of Ireland the invaders always formed a small minority, so that although the landlords might change, the tillers of the soil necessarily remained the same. Perhaps the new money economy benefited the latter more than the old partly feudal economy had. Also, the land must have produced more under a fairly rapid transition from pasturage to tillage. The end of cattle-raiding—and indeed the end of warfare after 1691—must have made life somewhat easier for the tenant farmer, at least until the subsequent enormous increase in population correspondingly increased the competition for farms and drove rents sky-high.

In the 'plantation' or colonization of Ulster (begun in 1608) a serious attempt was made to replace the Gaelic lower classes as well as the Gaelic landlord. But even here, at first, 'the new landlords found that the spare-living and industrious Celt would generally outbid the Scot or the Englishman when it came to paying rent'.[1] Naturally, he could also outbid the equally Celtic nobleman or bard who had lost his land. It is remarked in *The Parliament of Clan Thomas*

that it would be easier for themselves [the Clan] to raise and pay

[1] Edmund Curtis, *A History of Ireland*, 5th ed. (London, 1945), p. 232.

rent than for the gentry, because they would reap and thresh and get wages for lea-burning and harrowing . . .

besides practising a multitude of petty economies;

. . . it wouldn't be like that with the poor gentleman who'd be ashamed to do those deeds, so that, consequently, he falls into heavy debt and loss of his holding: and thus it's ourselves will get his holding, says they.[1]

The name 'Clan Thomas' does not seem to be older than the satire, which must be dated, on internal evidence, somewhere between 1645 and 1660. This extravaganza in prose and verse is divided into two books, the first of which is sometimes known as *Eachtra Chloinne Tomáis* (*The Adventures of Clan Thomas*), a name also sometimes given to a burlesque romance otherwise known as *Táin Bó Geanainn* (*The Cattle Raid of Gannon*).[2] Robin Flower thinks that the second book 'is perhaps a later addition'. Nevertheless, to the modern reader the second book is the more attractive of the two, since it possesses greater unity and perhaps a little more sophistication than the first, though both are clearly aimed at the widest possible audience—including the 'Clan' itself. Book Two deals solely with a single meeting of the alleged parliament, held under Cromwell's Protectorate.

The first book is indispensable to the understanding of the second, however, since it introduces us to the origins of Clan Thomas. A civil war is supposed to have taken place in Hell, resulting in the expulsion of Beelzebub and his legions. Beelzebub begot Dracapéist, who begot Lóbus Laghrach, who begot Liobur Lobhtha, who begot Tomás Mór (Big Thomas) upon a human mother.[3] All these lived in Ireland. When St. Patrick banished the demons from Ireland, he allowed Big Thomas to remain, as being half human. Thomas accepted Christianity, though reluctantly, and he and his descendants were enjoined to spend their time 'in toiling, ploughing and husbandry for the support of their noble elders in all kingdoms of the country . . . .'[4]

[1] Francis MacManus, 'The Satire of Clan Thomas', *The Bell*, vii (Dec. 1943), 234.

[2] Richard Irvine Best, ed., *Bibliography of Irish Philology and Manuscript Literature*, ii (Dublin, 1942), 187.   [3] Flower, *Catalogue*, p. 424.

[4] Francis MacManus, 'Clan Thomas', *The Bell*, vi (Sept. 1943), 523–5.

Book One continues by giving a history of the misdeeds of Clan Thomas (also known as Clan Lóbus) from the time of St. Patrick down to the seventeenth century and a mock record of the proceedings of their parliaments, supposedly held in 1632 and 1645. The use of the word 'parliament' in itself suggests an attempt to discredit the lower classes by associating them with an English institution which had wrought dire destruction in Ireland under Cromwell.

The vocabulary of *The Parliament of Clan Thomas* in the original Gaelic is so copious—especially in terms of abuse—that I have had to rely on Francis MacManus's spirited rendering, part of which was published in *The Bell*, a Dublin monthly, in 1943 and all of which Mr. MacManus very kindly permitted me to read in typescript. A delightful feature of his translation is his attempt to render into English all the contemptuous surnames and nicknames lavished upon Clan Thomas in genealogies, roll-calls of the Parliament, &c. For instance, the Clan are addressed as 'kinsmen of Big Thomas, son of Putridpelt, son of Filthyfork, son of Dragonmaggot, son of Beelzebub . . .'.[1] This of course translates the Gaelic names in the genealogy which I have already given. A group of messengers sent out by the Clan are named 'Mightybum Mahon, Barney Bigbelly, Niall O'Nettles and Crookedcrown Con O'Hollowgut'.[2] The roll-call of the Parliament in Book Two contains thirty such appellations.

These names may strike the reader as representative of a very elementary kind of humour. To tell the truth, nothing about the satire except its contempt for the lower classes suggests that it was addressed to a very cultivated audience. The clownish behaviour of the Clan, especially, is described in rather tedious detail.

The most successful satirical device used by the author or authors is to make the Clan convict themselves by their own remarks, as in the verse prayer which wishes 'more power' to Cromwell and the verse 'Acts' or decrees passed by the Parliament.[3] Both of these occur in Book Two, as does the speech by the head of the Clan, Sir Donal O'Puffprattle, in which he

---

[1] *The Bell*, vi. 528.
[2] Ibid., 527.
[3] For translations of these, see *Dánta Aodhagáin Uí Rathaille*, pp. 177–87.

blames all their misfortunes and faults on their excommunication by the Pope:

'. . . as a result of that excommunication, we are so execrated that we are bronchial, wheezy, filthy, gusty, stinky, belchy, clumsy, snotty, barbarous, loose-gobbed, slop-mouthed, lazy, lousing, lag-legged, ugly, doggish, big-booted, bag-bellied, whining, foul-fed, slow, withered, awkward, lying, rowdy, grumbling, detestable, spiteful, untrustworthy, without custom, teaching, manners, faith or conscience, without love for God or man, and yet again, without love for wives or each other. The person who would beat and scorn us the most, him we mostly love; and to him who should do us good, it is evil we would do in return. And we prefer the Saxon from London to the lord under whom we were born and reared and our ancestors before us, who used give us provisions and full nourishment.'[1]

He goes on to describe their tavern drinking and fighting and their tedious talk of farm work. 'The hour we're drunk, bawling and swearing great oaths, we brag that I'll go with your wife or daughter as soon as ever I reach home.'[2] Their wives kick them; they use their fists on the women they court. In short, their whole code is the precise opposite of chivalry.

When Sir Donal proposes to send money to Rome to have the excommunication lifted, one man opposes the expenditure from sheer parsimony, while another denies the value of the clergy's favour: 'In spite of everything I give the friars, it's not any the less my sheep die . . .'.[3]

Book Two also contains at least one effective indictment of the gentry, though it does not appear to have been intended as such. A gentleman, James of the Falcons, happens upon the Parliament and denounces it:

'O ye rabble of churls, it's ye that we, ourselves, have been nurturing! Don't ye know that it was from hell your ancestors came and that we are of the beloved children of God? And that we had ownership of Ireland for a thousand years before your ancestors came out of hell? And that we gave ye old boots and old hose and the old clothes we had put on our own bodies? Moreover, that we gave ye the intestines of our animals and whichever of them that the hounds or the wolves killed? And that we gave ye reaping, threshing and lea-burning rights, and the desert fields just for the labour of fencing them? And that we gave ye the keeping of cow, sheep and horse and put ye ploughing and driving for us? And that when we saw ye improving, we put seven or eight of ye into a single townland, sowing and ploughing at a rent, and we let your children go to school with our children, so that they picked up a little learning? Then, every single man of ye wished to make a lawyer or a cleric out of his son. When we let ye have your own way, ye went wild beyond our control, because it's usual for ye to be ungrateful towards us.'[1]

This nobleman's account of the generosity of his class will scarcely overwhelm the modern reader with admiration and wonder. We cannot be sure, however, that the author was himself aware of his character's warped perspective.

The last parliament of the Clan finally breaks up in disgust when their emissary to the Pope betrays his trust in typical Clan Thomas fashion.

With that, they began bashing and battering one another stoutly, tearing out hair and whiskers, swearing great oaths that never again nor at the last day of the world would they come to court or Parliament, and affirming that all which had overtaken them was God's justice because of their distrust and disrespect for the gentry who would free and fetch them from prison, whomsoever of them would be there on account of his own evil deeds.

And in that fit of wrath, they scattered east and west, having taken the oath of the anvil that never would they foregather in the same place to see justice or right done—but let the strongest man be uppermost.[2]

So ends *The Parliament of Clan Thomas*, but not its influence on Gaelic literature, which, says Robin Flower, 'was immediate and wide'. He lists the following works as having been written under its influence in different parts of Ireland: *Cath Lisín Uí Dhúnagain* (*The Battle of the Little Fort of O'Dunnigan*), apparently yet another name for *Táin Bó Geanainn*, which has already been mentioned; Seán Ó Neachtain's *Sgéal Éamuinn Uí Chléirigh* (*The Story of Edmund O'Clery*), a burlesque romance rather than a satire; Robert Nugent's *Crosánacht ar Chlainn Tomáis* ('Crosánacht on Clan Thomas'), not yet edited so far as I know; *Cómhairle Mhic Lámha* ('Mac Lavy's Advice'), which I discuss later as a religious satire; and Egan O'Rahilly's *Eachtra Thaidhg*

Dhuibh ('The Adventures of Black Tadhg'), which I discuss under the heading of political satire. Flower also mentions 'poems by Aodh buidhe Mac Cruitin [Hugh MacCurtin] . . ., Art Mac Cubhthaigh [Art MacCooey] . . . and others'.[1]

David O'Bruadair has been regarded as a possible author of *The Parliament of Clan Thomas*. If he was not in fact the author, then his name should be included among those influenced by the work, for several of his poems express hostility toward upstarts and one contains two clear allusions to the genealogy of Clan Thomas. This last poem, a short one, strikes me as peculiarly discreditable to O'Bruadair, in that it describes how he cheated a weaver of the price of a piece of linen by flattery. An introductory quatrain begins as follows: 'A surly packman of Clann Órluith got well beaten once by me . . .'. (Órluith was the wife of Big Thomas.) The remaining four stanzas consist mainly of flattery addressed to the weaver but include a denunciation of Fate, 'Who hath left me with nought, and stingy Lóbus with everything.'[2] The four final quatrains taken alone would form a touching lament over lost dignity. Let us hope that the introductory quatrain, which makes the whole poem a satire, is but a later interpolation.

However, in a rather similar short poem, O'Bruadair repaid a Cromwellian settler's hospitality by questioning his breeding. James Stephens gives a free rendering of this in his poem 'Blue Blood', the point being that all his guests thought this man 'a king for sure' until he finally opened his mouth to chat after dinner and revealed himself as a lout, the descendant of a line of louts.[3]

An entire chapter, or possibly even a book, might be written about the ramifications of the Clan Thomas literature, all apparently springing from a single root, but I must hasten on to one other field of social satire before concluding this section of my chapter. Ireland has had her fair share of poems and songs denouncing the evils of fashion, the flightiness of women, and similar commonplaces of social satire the world over. But there is one aspect of Irish society which the satirists of our later period denounce with peculiar vigour and personal feeling.

---

[1] Flower, *Catalogue*, p. 424.
[2] *Duanaire Dháibhidh Uí Bhruadair*, Part III, pp. 11, 13.
[3] Ibid., Part II, pp. 14–15. Stephens, p. 186.

I mean the custom of 'made matches', especially where this leads to the marriage of an old man with a young girl, or a young man with an old or ugly woman. As on other subjects, Brian Merriman's *Cúirt an Mheadhón Oidhche* (*The Midnight Court*) says the last word on this custom. The unmarried girl in the poem, who cannot find a suitable husband because she is poor—though young and beautiful—denounces the male sex as follows:

> 'Their appetite wakes with age and blindness
> When you'd let them cover you only from kindness,
> And offer it up for the wrongs you'd done
> In hopes of reward in the life to come:
> And if one of them weds in the heat of youth
> When the first down is on his mouth
> It isn't some woman of his own sort,
> Well-shaped, well-mannered or well-taught; . . .
> But some pious old prude or dour defamer
> Who sweated the couple of pounds that shame her.'[1]

When an old man denounces a friend of hers who made a cuckold of him and produced a child the day after the bridal night, she defends the wife briskly:

> 'How else would he come by such a wife
> But that ease was the alms she asked of life?
> What possible use could she have at night
> For dourness, dropsy, bother and blight . . . ?
> Is there living a girl who could grow fat
> Tied to a travelling corpse like that
> Who twice a year wouldn't find a wish
> To see what was she, flesh or fish . . . ?'[2]

The poet himself is seized by frustrated women at the end of the poem. They cry, 'You're thirty at least and still unmarried!' just as the Aran Islands women were to taunt John Synge a century later. Only Merriman's awakening from his dream of the 'midnight court' at which the male sex were on trial saves him from the beating to which he has been sentenced.[3]

In a review of Richard Foley's first edition of *The Midnight Court*, the late T. F. O'Rahilly cited a number of earlier poems

---

[1] Frank O'Connor, *Kings, Lords, and Commons* (New York, 1959), pp. 141–2.
[2] Ibid., p. 156. [3] Ibid., pp. 165–6.

on the subject of unequal marriages. There are, for instance, *An Seanduine* ('The Old Man') and *An tSeanbhean*('The Old Woman'), two songs attributed to *An Mangaire Súgach,* and also, of course, the appropriate passages of Owen Roe O'Sullivan's *An tArrachtach Sean (The Old Monster)*, mentioned earlier under the heading of personal satire. O'Rahilly quotes an unpublished poem by O'Sullivan in which 'two young women complain bitterly that they are tied to two *sgraistí* ['sluggards']'; the four lines of Gaelic that he gives *verbatim* may be translated thus:

'My curse on the gang that tied me tightly to the shambling fellow without strength in his limbs; he hasn't thought of courting me for a month, but a long cough is constantly troubling him.'[1]

O'Sullivan's poems were written before Merriman's, as *An Mangaire Súgach*'s were written before O'Sullivan's. Also before O'Sullivan, O'Rahilly notes,

we find a song written by a Clare poet, Seón Ó Huaithnín, in the name of one 'Peggy Turruidhe,' who had been persuaded into a similarly ill-assorted marriage. . . . Her husband, however, is not wholly worthless, for she thus refers to him:

A chnagaire bhig dhóite, gan maith ar bith ar m'eólas—
acht gur maith an clóca ar mo chloinn an fear tighe.

['O dried-up little half-pint, without any good in you at all, to my knowledge—
except that the husband is a good cloak over my children.']

The sentiment here is precisely that which Merriman puts into the mouth of Aoibheall; and indeed Merriman's use of the same word, *clóca*, in this connection (l.896 of the Cúirt), would suggest a conscious reminiscence of Ó Huaithnín's poem. Still another effusion of this type is the *Leabhar Eóin* composed by Uilliam Mac Gearailt (? date) for the wife of one Henrigh Ó Briain (Nat. Lib. xxv., 130).[2]

O'Rahilly makes the point in his review that 'Merriman's "revolt", as such, had nothing unique about it', nor was there anything particularly foreign and 'un-Irish' in his ideas. O'Rahilly clinches his argument by quoting a Connacht folk-song, of which he remarks

. . . in its own way it is as revolutionary as anything in the Cúirt,

[1] *Gadelica*, i (1912–13), 191 n.   [2] Ibid., 191 n.

but surely it would be unreasonable to argue that its peasant author was inspired by the theories of Continental philosophers.

The Gaelic lines which he goes on to quote may be translated as follows:

Woe be on marriage! It's a pity it ever existed. A person tied up in its shelter has difficulty in getting free of it. It's a shame that whoever isn't pleased with his wife doesn't just come out to drive her to the fair as he would sell a cow or a sheep.[1]

Before leaving this subject altogether, I want to cite just one more example of the masculine viewpoint to counterbalance the preponderance of feminine protests against marriage. I have not been able to find a text of *An tSeanbhean*, but the poem known as *An Fear Brónach d'éis a Phósda* ('The Sorrowful Man After His Marriage') may supply its place. The opening line of the latter song is arresting indeed: '*Da mbiadh ba ag an gcat is maith do pósfaidhe é*', meaning, 'If the cat had cows, he'd marry himself well!' The supposed speaker of the poem is a man who owned no cows and therefore had to marry 'the blear'd hag-daughter' instead of his own fair colleen. In his otherwise clumsy translation George Sigerson summed up the man's estimate of his plight crisply:

Without a rag on earth 'twere better to be,
Than have sheep, three cows, and a goblin wife with me![2]

The social problem of late and unequal marriages besets rural Ireland even today, as her modern novelists and sociologists of many lands have amply documented. It is little wonder that *The Midnight Court* has been translated into English at least four separate times in the past thirty-five years: by Arland Ussher, Frank O'Connor, the Earl of Longford, and David Marcus; I have quoted O'Connor's brilliant and faithful translation here. The Gaelic has been twice edited in this century—by Richard Foley both times—in 1912 and 1949.[3]

Political satire

Gifted as the Gaelic Irish are for politics and satire, they have never achieved that happy combination of the two

[1] *Gadelica*, i. 191.   [2] 'Erionnach', pp. 160–1.
[3] Brian Merriman, *Cúirt an Mheadhón Oidhche*, ed. Risteárd Ó Foghludha (Dublin, 1949). See p, 194 below for the first edition.

exemplified in the best work of Swift. Generally speaking, the satire directed against each other by the Irish and British in Ireland hardly rises above imbecility. The British ridicule the Irish for speaking English badly; the Irish ridicule the British for not having Gaelic names. No wonder Swift despaired of human reason—not to mention human goodwill.

We must admit that political satire is often hard to recognize or define. Standish Hayes O'Grady regards a certain Gaelic panegyric of Queen Elizabeth I as ironical because it calls that lady 'pre-eminently quiet, docile to reproof . . .'. The warring factions of York and Lancaster are described as 'two Saxon houses, with their steadfast forces, that lived in kindly neighbourliness . . .'.[1] But David O'Bruadair took the poem seriously enough to answer it, and his modern editor agrees that it was intended as praise.[2] One hardly knows which view to support; irony often defeats itself, and the better sustained the irony is, the more difficult it is to identify.

Then again, many a poem will begin with ridicule and end in passionate lamentation. Such is Pierce Fitzgerald's well-known song, *Seaghán Ó Dighe* ('John O'Swill', a name for John Bull). The union of John with a beauteous maiden, obviously Ireland, is ridiculed by comparing it to the marriage of Vulcan with Venus, but the mood of the poem soon changes to a tearful one.[3]

And again, what might at first appear to be satirical exaggeration often proves to be no more than the literal truth. Many political poems by David O'Bruadair describe bitterly the successive disasters which befell Ireland during his lifetime (1630? – 1698). We can hardly call them satires, though they contain occasional passages of ridicule. Usually their denunciations of the Cromwellian and later expropriations seem to fit the historical facts.

Very occasionally he takes heart and laughs at the new settlers, somewhat in the mood of the *Parliament of Clan Thomas*. After lamenting the expulsion of the Gaelic chiefs from their property (in a poem written in 1652), he goes on thus:

To take their places, then, will come the fat-rumped jeerers,
After crushing them, their culture, and their cities,—

---

[1] O'Grady, *Catalogue*, pp. 544–5.
[2] *Duanaire Dháibhidh Uí Bhruadair*, Part III, p. 65.   [3] 'Erionnach', pp. 40–43.

Laden all with packs and plates and brass and pewter,
With shaven jaws and English talk and braggart accent.

(A bunch of 'carpet-baggers', in other words.)

Every dowdy, then, will wear a cape of beaver,
And don a gown of silk from poll of head to ankle:
All our castles will be held by clownish upstarts,
Crowded full with veterans of cheese and pottage.

This will be the horde, though fretful 'tis to tell it,
Who in moated mansions fair will then be dwelling:—
        Judy Hook and mother Hammer,
        Robin Saul and father Psalm,

        The man in breeches salt a-selling,
        Gammer Ruth and goodman Cabbage,
        Mistress Capon, Kate and Anna,
        Russel Rake and master Gaffer![1]

(The last six lines are written in a mixture of Irish and English
in the original.)

O'Bruadair thus opened a vein of satirical humour that was
to be worked for more than a century. Gaelic speakers found
English names irresistibly comic. Several poems exploiting
this fact are described in the British Museum *Catalogue of Irish
Manuscripts*. An English rhyming poem of Irish origin is also
known. It begins:

The Fairs, the Blacks, the Blonds, the Brights,
The Greens, the Browns, the Greys, the Whites,
The Parrotts, Eagles, Cocks and Hens,
The Snipes, Swallows, Pies, Robins, Wrens, . . .[2]

Best known of all such poems, perhaps, is one by Owen Roe
O'Sullivan, written in Gaelic except for the planters' names,
which rhymes those names according to Gaelic rules. It makes
an effective introduction to Gaelic stress metre for the English-
speaking reader. Here is the penultimate stanza:

        Lysight, Leader, Clayton, Compton *is* Coote,
        Ivers, Deamer, Bateman, Bagwell *is* Brooks,
        Ryder, Taylor, Manor, Marrock *is* Moore,
        Is go bhfaiceam-na traochta ag tréin-shliocht Chaisil na búir.[3]

---

[1] *Duanaire Dháibhidh Uí Bhruadair*, Part I, p. 37.
[2] Ibid., p. 38 n.
[3] Corkery, pp. 217–18.

Is means 'and'. Each stressed syllable rhymes with the corre-
sponding syllable in the lines above and/or below it: of course,
the reader must always bear in mind the Irish countryman's
pronunciation of English. The Gaelic words in the last line,
which mean 'And may we see the boors routed by the mighty
descendants of Cashel', rhyme with the English ones in the
lines above.

To return to O'Bruadair for a moment—he sometimes
denounces fellow Irishmen in his political writings for betraying
their cause by disunity and insubordination. The poem by him
known as *Longar Langar Éireann* ('Ireland's Hurly-Burly') or
An Longbhriseadh ('The Shipwreck') treats the Irish irregular
troops in the Williamite war as a peculiarly unpleasant branch
of Clan Thomas. There is little laughter in this poem, however,
except when he gives this rapacious *canaille* humorous Gaelic
names, which his editor translates as 'Frank Friendly and
Charlie Chum'.[1]

Far different in mood is the poem *Caithréim Thaidhg* ('The
Triumph of Tadhg'), written in 1690, a year or two earlier
than *Longar Langar Éireann*. Tadhg (Anglo-Irish 'Teigue' or
'Teague'), often used as a generic name for an Irishman, here
characterizes the temporarily victorious Irish forces of James
II. O'Bruadair describes fairly humorously the dismay of the
temporarily defeated English planters ('John') at seeing Tadhg
in power in his own land:

The thing that has wounded John sorely and others too
Is that Tadhg from the mountain should rise to so high a rank,
That '*Cia súd*' should be thinking of nothing but revelry,
And 'Who's there' should now be a plundered old driveller. . . .
Look at Simon, with sweat running down off him ceaselessly,
Unable to breathe, and in danger of being choked,
With pains in his tongue and his side and posterior,
Lest he lose the small farm that he hath not yet parted with.[2]

This short-lived triumph must have been very sweet to a
vindictive man like O'Bruadair. It was the last that Irish arms
were to win for over a century.

My next example of political satire, *Eachtra Thaidhg Dhuibh*

---

[1] *Duanaire Dháibhidh Uí Bhruadair*, Part III, p. 171 n.
[2] Ibid., pp. 129, 135.

Uí Chróinín ('The Adventures of Black Tadhg O'Cronin'), might well have been dealt with as personal satire, along with the poem in which its author, Egan O'Rahilly, celebrated the death of Tadhg's friend and fellow extortionist, Murtagh O'Griffin. Tadhg Dubh receives honourable mention in that poem, in the line 'Snatch Tadhg quickly from us to the church-yard . . .'. 'The Adventures of Black Tadhg', a prose lampoon which fills twelve pages in Dinneen's edition of O'Rahilly, might also claim consideration as social satire. Modelled on *The Parliament of Clan Thomas*, it reads like a burlesque of the hero-tales, or even, at times, of the Bible. The opening lines, for instance, trace Tadhg's genealogy back via Lóbus to the Devil. But Tadhg is 'worse than his ancestor, for holy water doesn't drive him away'.[1]

However, in spite of O'Rahilly's personal and class hostility to Tadhg, I feel that the major animus of the satire is political. Tadhg, a Catholic Gaelic Irishman, was making himself a willing tool for the Protestant English plunderers of the estate of the second Viscount Kenmare. Lord Kenmare, a Catholic though not an Irishman, had forfeited the estate for his life-time as a punishment for supporting James II against William III. Tadhg O' Cronin also plundered the English John Asgill, purchaser of the forfeited lands, but the chief sufferers were the Irish tenants on the estate. They were in danger of being replaced by Protestant tenants, besides being cheated of the hated 'hearth-money', a tax imposed by the English Crown and zealously collected by Tadhg and his like, but rarely passed on in full to the Treasury.[2]

Tadhg, like the characters in *The Parliament of Clan Thomas*, convicts himself out of his own mouth, as follows:

'Ye black, bold, vehement, ill-mannered *bodachs*,' said Tadhg, 'was it not enough for you that I banished Lord Kenmare from his country by my cunning and my tricks, and that I gave his daughter and his lordship to his inveterate enemy? And it was not through a desire to serve either of them, as I knew that I could twist that old gentleman, John Asgill, on my finger, and that I would have the profits of the estate myself, as I have; for I never had a master whom I did not deprive of his inheritance which I kept myself in

[1] *Dánta Aodhagáin Uí Rathaille*, p. 288. Translation mine.
[2] Ibid., pp. xvi–xix.

his stead. At first I collected hearth-money. I was not a slow villain at that trade. I did not leave a cabin without plundering, and I gave no return for that money but wrangling and dispute.'[1]

The plot of the satire may be briefly summarized as follows. After Tadhg's genealogy has been given and his person described, we are told how he and Murtagh O'Griffin seized power and created a wilderness wherever they went. Then, in 1713, they summoned a parliament of Clan Thomas from all over the province of Munster. When Tadhg takes his seat in the chair of state at the parliament, men tremble and horses take fright at his hideous ugliness, which is further described. The Clan are full of grievances, in reply to which Tadhg makes the speech from which I have already quoted at length. He tells of his new plans, which involve the plundering of a Gaelic lord, Mac Carthy Reagh. He says that only four of the neighbouring English planters are 'traitors'—that is, hostile to Tadhg.

Warriors of the Clan are sent off to kill these four traitors, with what success we never learn. Also an emissary is sent to the Pope, as in *The Parliament of Clan Thomas*, to have an excommunication removed from the Clan. Then twelve leaders of the Clan are elected and also twelve 'people of perjury' to swear whatever the twelve leaders need to have sworn. An enemy of Tadhg's is disgraced, and Black Owen O'Sullivan, who collects hearth-money for Mac Carthy Reagh and cheats him as Tadhg cheats Asgill, is promoted instead.

In a passage which shows the double edge often present in Irish satire, Clan Thomas ask how to get rid of the few last remnants of the old Gaelic nobility; Tadhg advises them not to worry but to leave the nobility to God, who has done away with most of them already because of their constant warfare with one another. Then the whole parliament cries out, in English, 'The Great God of Heaven and Earth preserve our most Gracious Protector', Black Tadhg.

However, immediately thereafter the Clan split up into two factions, led by Mahon O'Cronin, a relative of Tadhg, and Young Richard Stack. Richard's faction is defeated and five hundred of them are slain. Mahon dies soon afterwards of the pox. We are given his epitaph, and the tale concludes formally with the traditional summary:

[1] *Dánta Aodhagáin Uí Rathaille*, pp. xviii–xix.

That is the life and description of Black Tadhg O'Cronin and of Murtagh O'Griffin, and the Rout of the Hill of the Three Men. . . .[1]

As the eighteenth century advances, the plaintive note in Gaelic political writing becomes louder, and the aggressive, satirical note correspondingly diminishes. I shall conclude this section by citing two late-eighteenth-century poems which mingle English and Gaelic for satiric ends.

The first of these, *Tagra an Dá Theampall* ('The Argument of the Two Churches'), by the Ulster Poet Art Mac Cubhthaigh (MacCooey or MacCoy), can also be regarded as religious satire. Two neighbouring churches, one Protestant, one Catholic, are heard arguing together by the dreaming poet. After an introductory stanza in Gaelic, the Protestant church opens the argument in English, the Catholic one replies in Gaelic, and they continue alternately, each church speaking five stanzas but the Catholic one getting the last word. The question at issue is which of them will finally hold the allegiance of the Gaelic race.

Theology plays only a small part in the arguments of the Protestant church, whose outlook is mainly political:

> In Hibernia fair, in Scotland we reign,
> In England great, and Hanover;
> So what need we care for France or for Spain
> Or for Charley, your rakish rover.

Only in the sixth stanza does the Catholic poet allow the Protestant church to offer purely doctrinal arguments. However, he does play fair in that stanza, permitting the opposition to deliver some sharp blows:

> Your clergy maintains the Scripture contains
> But mystical dreams and stories—
> False doctrine that leads your senses away
> From heavenly grace and glory;
> Inventing such schemes for money to gain,
> Of Limbo they treat laborious,
> Until Luther the Great, and Calvin of late,
> Renounced their shameful chorus.

(As usual, the rhymes are acceptable in Irish rather than English prosody. The reader will find a great deal of internal

---

[1] My synopsis of this tale, which apparently has never been translated, is based upon the text in *Dánta Aodhagáin Uí Rathaille*, pp. 287–98.

rhyme or assonance if he gives an Irish-English pronunciation to 'dreams', 'leads', 'schemes', 'treat'.)

The Catholic side of the argument mostly lays stress on the political and military consequences of having God on one's side. The Protestants are reminded that pride goes before a fall; for instance, the fifth stanza recalls the fate of the Egyptian armies in the Red Sea. At the same time there is regret for the past Irish defeats which permit Luther to torment Ireland, along with the 'New Lights, or Seceders, Old Presbyterians, Swaddlers, or Quakers . . .'.

Luther and the Huguenots are denounced for their folly in destroying the old unity of the Catholic Church 'from Nicaea and Ephesus . . . to Constanti-Grecian-Nople', and for 'injuring the most pure Virgin'. But in the concluding two lines (in Gaelic, as I have already indicated) we find a judicious mixture of the religious and the political; the Catholic church says: 'Thanks to the powers of the Son of God, you will not remain in full sway or King Charles will put sorrow on you.'[1]

Perhaps the most famous of bilingual political songs is that made up by Donnchadh Ruadh Mac Conmara (Denis Roe Macnamara, 1715–1810), to please both the English and the Irish of St. John's, Newfoundland. The complimentary English lines alternate with denunciatory Gaelic ones, somewhat in this manner (I give the lines translated from Gaelic in italics):

> As I was walking one evening fair,
> *And I of late in St. John's town,*
> I met a gang of English blades
> *Whom their foemen's strength had beaten down.*
> I boozed and drank both late and early
> With these courageous men of war;
> *'Twould be sweet to watch the hurly-burly*
> *As those Saxons ran from the Gaels afar.*

He goes on to praise Newfoundland and its women:

> Here you may find a virtuous lady,
> A smiling fair one to please your eye.
> *What a pack of whores, all sleazy and shady!*
> *Let me out of their sight before I die!*

[1] Énrí Ó Muirgheasa [i.e. Henry Morris], ed., *Dánta Diadha Uladh* (Dublin, 1936), pp. 375–9. Translations mine.

After some further ambiguous stanzas, he concludes with the
following Jacobite sentiments:

> We'll fear no cannon, nor war's alarms,
>   While noble George will be our guide.
> *O Christ, may I see the Pretender's arms*
>   *Safe home from exile—and that brute destroyed!*[1]

When the Irish had lost their country and were in the process
of losing their language, they could still occasionally take
heart and laugh at their conquerors. Their language, like the
culture it represented, was still a protecting hedge from behind
which they could snipe at the English; but there must have
been small satisfaction in launching an attack whose essential
condition was that the enemy should never become aware of it.

Religious satire

Since Ireland is a country powerfully moulded for good and
ill by religious influences, we need hardly wonder at the bulk
and vigour of the satirical literature which handles religious
themes. In his collection entitled *Dánta Diadha Uladh* (*Religious
Poems of Ulster*), Henry Morris placed thirteen poems, or about
one-sixth of his material, under the heading *Cáinte agus Dánta
Conspóideacha* ('Satires and Controversial Poems'). The similar
material scattered through Douglas Hyde's *The Religious Songs
of Connacht* would bulk even larger if gathered into one section
of that ill-ordered book. The religious satire of our period, in
verse or prose, can be divided up under three main heads with
regard to subject matter:

1. Attacks on Protestants or apostates from Roman Catholicism.
2. Attacks on the Roman Catholic clergy.
3. Attacks on specific Roman Catholic or Christian beliefs
   and on religion in general.

I don't think I am merely expressing a Protestant's pre-
judice when I say that the first of these divisions is the least
satisfying—or, at any rate, the least amusing—of the three.
There are very good *a priori* reasons why this should be so.

---

[1] John O'Daly, *The Poets and Poetry of Munster*, tr. James Clarence Mangan
(Dublin, 1849), pp. 5–6. Translations mine.

Most Irish Roman Catholics were and are imbued with the belief that theirs is the only true Church: apostasy therefore fills them with a horror compounded almost equally of awe and of disgust. How could a man dare to provoke God's wrath in this way? How could he lower himself so far as to capitulate to the Devil? These are attitudes to apostasy that we find over and over again in Modern Irish literature; they do not make for effective satire. Denunciation there is in plenty, but very little laughter and no comprehension at all. The satirist must get inside his victim, understand him through and through, in order to rend him with his laughter. That is what Burns does in 'Holy Willie's Prayer', but Modern Irish offers no parallel to that masterpiece.

Sometimes, as in the bardic poem which begins '*Truagh liom, a chompáin, do chor*' ('Pitiful to me, O companion, thy plight'), we find a controversial writer more in sorrow than in anger, but this attitude fosters satire no better than does horrified indignation.[1] Even such a congenitally irreverent jester as *An Mangaire Súgach* turns solemn about the apostasy of Donough O'Hedderman, a Dominican friar who became a Protestant clergyman in 1736.[2] More amusing is the burlesque *barántas* or warrant composed by the same poet over thirty years later; this authorizes the apprehension of one Murtagh O'Hurley so that he can be served with a *mittimus* to Hell, on the grounds that he has left the Roman Catholic priesthood to become a Protestant clergyman.[3] However, in spite of the string of humorously disrespectful adjectives which *An Mangaire* applies to O'Hurley, his main accusation, as we come to realize, is that these apostates have given themselves up to drink and women—the two temptations which the poet himself, at least in his younger days, was notoriously unable to resist. Furthermore, as we shall see, *An Mangaire* had once incurred the charge of apostasy himself.

The satirists are convinced that the apostates have changed their religion purely for worldly advantage: they have deserted their faith, their nationality, and often their class because of the superior material and social status of Protestants in

---

[1] Ó Muirgheasa, pp. 320–37 (text only).
[2] *Éigse na Máighe*, pp. 80, 83 (text only).
[3] Ibid., pp. 234–7 (text only).

eighteenth-century Ireland, where Catholicism was virtually proscribed. No doubt this triple betrayal made laughter difficult, but one would expect some wittier complaint than the perpetual cry that priests have turned Protestant in order to have wives and eat meat on Fridays. To our authors, the only really funny (or ironic) thing about Protestants and apostates is that they are going to Hell and don't know it. An Ulster song addressed to one Dominic O'Donnell, who 'was a priest on Sunday and a minister on Monday', assures him that when he is in Hell with troops of devils hanging from him, *then* he'll know which is better, priest or minister.[1]

In attacking their own clergy our poets have to be more circumspect, for they cannot be sure of having public opinion on their side, except in notorious cases of abuse; hence, probably, the large number of anonymous quatrains attacking individual priests or the whole order. Yet Douglas Hyde, on the basis of his very wide knowledge of the literature, sums up the matter thus:

> When we see that the bards were so ready to speak their minds openly about the priests in cases where they had occasion for censure, our respect for that priesthood which gained and preserved the reverence and love of the people must be all the greater.[2]

One striking example that bears out Hyde's contention is Peter O'Durnin's satire on the parish priest of Crinchoill or Crinkle in County Armagh. This is said to have been recited at a bishop's visitation between 1758 and 1769 and to have won relief for the offending priest's flock, who had a real grievance against his exactions. The satire, in verse and prose, somewhat on the lines of *crosánacht*, bears the title *Tairngire* ('A Prophecy') and claims to be an utterance of St. Columcille, to whom many prophecies are traditionally ascribed. The opening poem foretells that one of themselves will rob the Gaels worse than any of their enemies; it then lists the five severe wounds to be inflicted by the following: the Viking Turgesius; 'Murrough of the Leinstermen', who brought in the English; 'Harri and his daughter', Henry VIII and Elizabeth I; Cromwell's army; and 'unlucky James' II of England, whose defeat proved so disastrous for Ireland. A

---

[1] Ó Muirgheasa, pp. 281–2 (text only).
[2] Douglas Hyde, *The Religious Songs of Connacht*, i (London, Dublin, 1906), 191.

prose passage then describes, with apt quotations from the Apocalypse and the Gospels, the sixth severe wound, an unrighteous clergy, reproaching them for their worldliness in giving honour to the rich and dishonour to the poor. A second poem describes the parish priest himself in broadly humorous terms as he goes about the parish collecting his 'cess' in a basket which grows larger by the year. No matter how poor a man is, he must fill the basket, or the priest will wait beside him to the death. The priest is quoted refusing to absolve a man until he pays up, and the words *ciseán líonta* ('a full basket') echo through the poem. A final prose passage describes how not only the priest but his lubberly cess-collector and his lively horse have to be supported; the priest has threatened all offenders with a horse-whipping, so that the satire ends with a prayer: 'May God protect you and me from the fury and the rage of that same man.'[1]

Douglas Hyde translated a song of similar import, 'The Priest and the Poor Man', in which the priest is affable to the rich farmer and savage to the poor man whose wife is dying; he says to the latter:

> 'Go and be hanged, you mean churl,
> Hell is your portion, if any,
> I never got for this three quarters
> Out of your pocket one penny.'[2]

Owen Roe O'Sullivan made a relatively gentle attack on the clergy of his day, contrasting their hostility to the poets with the attitude of the Church in happier times, when it was charitable and humane and on good terms with men of letters. The whole poem is addressed to a priest who is presented as an exception to the current rule. O'Sullivan's characteristic and personal grudge is that a poor man can hardly look at a girl without being excommunicated, whereas the rich can have all the women they like if they bribe the clergy. He appeals to the Church to share a third of its wealth with the 'old stock' among the people, who have become impoverished. The poem concludes with a compliment to his priest friend, who delights in poetry, and a final lash at 'the mercenaries on the altar'.[3]

---

[1] D. Comyn, *Gaelic Journal*, vi (Jan.–Feb. 1896), 155–7. Translations mine.
[2] Hyde, i. 157.
[3] *Amhráin Eoghain Ruaidh Uí Súilleabháin*, pp. 65–66 (text only).

A satire against the clergy which ought to be edited in full is *Cómhairle Mhic Lámhaigh* ('Mac Lavy's Advice'), an Ulster production 'probably composed in the first half of the eighteenth century in Cavan or Monaghan'.[1] This occurs in a number of manuscripts, but even Douglas Hyde has edited only a part of it; he says of the portion which he has not edited that it is 'salt and bitter and heavy-smiting'. I regret the unavailability of this work all the more because what I have seen of it suggests that it is that great rarity in Modern Irish, a piece of *sustained* irony. Mac Lavy's advice to his friend 'Archy' is that he ought to study Latin, enter the Church, and turn his back on the 'poor world'—materially, not spiritually, poor. It paints a dismal picture of the average peasant's lot: hard work, dirt, poverty, hunger, a nagging wife, and squalling brats. This is contrasted with the priest's lot: '. . . the true rule/Which binds upon thee prosperity and glory'.[2]

After the poem follows a prose tale, which Hyde edited and translated, 'The Farmer's Son and the Bishop'. This is offered to Archy as an example of the price he ought to be prepared to pay to attain the priesthood. A certain farmer had been very generous to a hermit, whom he persuaded to recommend his (the farmer's) son to a bishop as a candidate for the priesthood. The bishop examined the young man in Latin on an island, so that the farmer and his friends could see the interview but not overhear it. The son made such a hash of his Latin that the bishop beat him as well as rejecting him. However, the friends thought the beating part of the ceremony of ordination. When the son returned to them, they

. . . asked him where was his bull or charter of priesthood.

He said that he had no charter but the bull of the race of stoop-headed Conor Mac Lopus of Cavan to the Vicarage of Lurgan—the will of the people.

They swore by the God of the elements that he never could have a better charter than that. . . .

The reference to Mac Lopus (i.e. Lóbus) and the whole tone of the passage link it to *The Parliament of Clan Thomas*, whose influence is clear throughout the satire. Archy is told, in some of its closing words:

. . . it is the good advice to you to take the same grade of priesthood,

---

[1] Flower, *Catalogue*, p. 380.   [2] Hyde, i. 171–9.

and if blows of a stick be struck on you, it is small damage compared
with every comfort and ease that you will get on the head of it. . . .[1]

Only one satire that I know of accuses the clergy of sexual
irregularities, namely *The Midnight Court*, in a typically daring
passage, where it also suggests that the clergy ought to marry:

> 'A pardon and a job for life
> To every priest that takes a wife!
> For many a good man's chance miscarries
> If you scuttle the ship for the crooks it carries;
> And though some as we know were always savage,
> Gnashing their teeth at the thought of marriage,
> And, modest beyond the needs of merit,
> Invoked hell-fire on girls of spirit,
> Yet some who took to their pastoral labours
> Made very good priests and the best of neighbours.
> Many a girl filled byre and stall
> And furnished her house through a clerical call.
> Everyone's heard some priest extolled
> For the lonesome women that he consoled;
> People I've known throughout the county
> Have nothing but praise for the curate's bounty,
> Or uphold the canon to lasting fame
> For the children he reared in another man's name;
> But I hate to think of their lonely lives,
> The passions they waste on middle-aged wives,
> While the girls they'd choose if the choice was theirs
> Go by the wall and comb grey hairs.'[2]

Other portions of the same poem, which attack the sacrament of matrimony, would lend themselves to discussion under
our third heading—attacks on specific beliefs and on religion
in general—but they have already been discussed as social
satire. It is hard to know how to classify *An Mangaire Súgach*'s
poem on 'his breaking off with the priest and with Minister
Cromie', translated by Edward Walsh as 'Lament of the
Mangaire Súgach'. No doubt his regret that the clergy of both
sides 'do not tolerate me as either a Protestant or a Papist' is
ironically exaggerated, but is he attacking the two clergymen
involved or the want of charity in the Christian churches as a
whole? Apparently the priest had excommunicated him for

---

[1] Hyde, i. 181–91.   [2] O'Connor, pp. 159–60.

not repenting of his sexual sins, whereupon he went to the minister in a fit of pique, but the latter wisely doubted the sincerity of his conversion:

> Their parson says that I am an inveterate gambler and that I confess myself a Protestant in (his) presence, but when I leave him, I would sooner go to Mass and am neither Protestant nor Papist.[1]

The edge of the satire, to my mind, lies in the following stanza, very well rendered by Walsh:

> Lo! David, Israel's poet-king, and Magdalene,
> And Paul, who of the Christian creed the foe had been—
> Did Heaven, when sorrow filled their heart, reject their vow
> Though they were neither Protestant nor Papist now?[2]

The *ceangal* or *envoi* of this poem makes it clear that *An Mangaire* was no more anti-Christian than Villon, for it pleads that, like St. Peter, who denied Christ three times, *An Mangaire* should be pardoned and admitted into Heaven. Unlike the other ten stanzas, it does not end with some variant of the mocking phrase '*protestan ná pápaire*' ('Protestant nor Papist').[3]

Criticism and ridicule of the Christian faith find a natural outlet in the popular ballads narrating the quarrels of Oisín and St. Patrick about the merits of Finn and his warriors. In Robin Flower's words:

> The hero and the saint rail upon one another in good set terms. The extreme expression of this conflict is in the quatrain which the Irish-speaking peasantry of today still declaim with a peculiar pleasure:
>
> If I saw God and Oscar hand to hand on a hill, were I to see Oscar down, I would say that God is a strong man.

Both Douglas Hyde and Frank O'Connor have translated this quatrain, together with others equally blasphemous that accompany it. Flower goes on:

> This is not, as some have thought, evidence of a pagan reaction or of medieval anticlericalism; it is with the poets who composed and the peasants who repeat the poems merely the delight in developing the implications of a situation to their last extreme.[4]

---

[1] *Éigse na Máighe*, p. 196. Translations mine.

[2] Kathleen Hoagland, ed., *1000 Years of Irish Poetry* (New York, 1947), p. 192.

[3] *Éigse na Máighe*, p. 198. The first line of the Gaelic poem is '*A dhalta dhil an dainid libh mo chás anois . . .*?'

[4] Robin Flower, *The Irish Tradition* (Oxford, 1947), p. 102.

We shall see that the most radical of all the satires here quoted has a pious ending which bears out Flower's contention. The Irish rebel in word rather than deed—if not, they would be the least conservative people in Europe rather than the most. Swift, Shaw, and Joyce are never more Irish than when they violate the bounds of good sense, good taste, and even sanity for the sake of a jest. The Irish obey what I may call 'The Law of Total Ridicule' in satire proper, just as in invective they obey 'The Law of Total Hate'.

Many of these ballads, as well as many similar prose tales, were preserved chiefly by oral tradition. Hyde translates an amusing folk-tale, 'Oscar of the Flail', which contains several passages like the following:

> 'Patrick,' says Ossian, 'for what did God damn all that of people?'
> 'For eating the apple of commandment', says St. Patrick.
> 'If I had known that your God was so narrow-sighted that he damned all that of people for one apple, we should have sent three horses and a mule carrying apples to God's heaven to Him.'[1]

After reading the above, preserved in the mouths of illiterate people, we need hardly postulate the influence of Voltaire upon *The Midnight Court*. In the words of T. F. O'Rahilly, 'There is no need to conjecture foreign influence when elemental human nature working in home surroundings is sufficient to account for all.'[2]

There *is*, however, reason to conjecture that our last example, *An Siota* [or *Sotach*] *agus a Mháthair* ('The Chit [or 'Lout'] and His Mother') was composed under the influence of *The Midnight Court*. To quote O'Rahilly once more,

> In ideas, as in metre, its kinship with the Cúirt is undeniable; and if it is not Merriman's composition, it certainly is that of a disciple of his, and almost certainly the work of a fellow-Clareman.[3]

That 'The Chit and his Mother' *is* later than Merriman's poem seems guaranteed by the fact that the oldest manuscript of the latter is dated 1789, whereas two copies of the former are dated 1815 in verse. If this date be correct, 'The Chit' cannot be the work of Merriman, who died in 1805, though no scholar has yet put forward any convincing supposition about its author's identity.

[1] Hyde, i. 211.   [2] *Gadelica*, i. 191.   [3] Ibid. 193.

This poem consists almost entirely of an argument between a beggarwoman and her illegitimate son, which he begins by asking for his patrimony; naturally she tells him that he has none, for his father gave her nothing. He reproaches her for her folly rather than her sin, and she replies that there are many women worse than she is. The son says he will die in despair if he does not get help soon; the mother, shocked, counsels prayer and patience. 'I've exhausted my patience and I'm none the better for it,' he says. Besides, though his mother says her prayers every morning, all she gets is potatoes, while other beggars get meat. She abuses him for not knowing 'that it was for the poor that Heaven was appointed as an inheritance'. He suggests that she hurry to Heaven if it is a place where there is plenty to eat and drink, so she has to explain that nobody goes to Heaven until after death, as well as to clear up various other misconceptions of his. 'If there is nothing in Heaven but glory and songs,' he asks, 'how would the poor empty belly get any sport there? Sweeter to me would be the bubbling of a pot with meat in it . . . than all the saints in Heaven thumping out their share of tunes.' He tells his mother that when she goes to Heaven she'll never get out of it alive. She ripostes that Hell, not Heaven, is *his* destination, but he consoles himself with this reflection:

'If no sinner ever goes to Heaven, whoever is blessed will have plenty of room there; and if everyone who follows my way is evil and damned, then Hell was full a year and a score ago, and they won't snatch me for want of room for me.'

When his mother quotes St. Peter as saying that anyone who abandons Christ on earth will not obtain Heaven, the lad comments that St. Peter has no right to be hard on anyone after his own betrayal of Christ—'Short is the struggle that he himself withstood.' In reply to her further denunciation of him he promises to make public her evil courses. Her answer to his rather veiled accusations is startling, in view of her piety:

'As for lust, it's not a very serious matter; it's a thing that is the love and desire of everyone. . . .'

In her opinion it is far worse 'to abandon Christ and the law of the clergy', as her son does. He promptly turns on the priests, saying that 'their deeds and their teaching are seven acres apart'. She leaps to their defence; Christ and the Apostles appointed them 'to marry and baptize and say Mass for us, and to be charitable . . .'. He questions their charity, saying that they are very free with their blessing, 'but if it was worth a halfpenny they would not part with it until Doomsday. As for marriage, it's a very dear business—three golden guineas, and a crown to the clerk. . . . *Till the Bishop is paid* [in English in the original], *nobis* will not be said . . .'. The old woman defends marriage, but her son returns to his attack on the priests: 'If you were dead tomorrow,' he says, 'and I were to bring you to the priest tied up in a sack, he would not say Mass until he got money in his hand. . . .' She claims that it is only right for the clergy to obtain a livelihood, which no doubt was divinely appointed for them. Her son then twits her with the fact that in Ireland this livelihood seems to be going mostly to the 'prime stock' of Luther. This arouses her to a longer speech than usual, in which she compares the Protestants to a scourge with which the Lord chastises his erring child, but 'short is the time after his anger is appeased till he values the child a thousand times more than the scourge'. Her son jeers at her parable, whereupon she tells him the story of the Prodigal Son, which he does not find any more convincing, since

'. . . it is sure and certain among the learned Protestants that there is not a tribe on earth worse than *Papists*, and wasn't he who sold Christ one of themselves?'

His mother replies with a denunciation of the 888 errors of the Protestant Bible and inquires who ever heard of a prophet or a saint from the prime stock of Luther? Protestants, she says, 'do not follow Christ but the wealth of the temple [a usual word for a Protestant Church, as in France] and there is the damnation of thousands upon the Protestant Bible'. Nothing has prepared us for the son's next and final speech, which in effect is a retraction of all he has said. We see that the whole poem may be no more than a dramatic exercise, a cathartic release of tension, or an elaborate joke. He wishes that 'at the end of life no one may be damned' and recalls Christ's promise: 'If a man were as black as the beetles, 'tis what He said, "Turn unto me and I myself will make you white".' The lad then tells his mother to buy him a shirt next day, for he is going to get married and not continue wrangling with her. The poet concludes with eight lines in which he asks us to decide which of the couple was better, gives the date 1815, and ends with a conventional prayer:

If there is folly in it, may Christ set it right; God's mercy upon us, and let us beseech it diligently. Amen.[1]

After such a detailed analysis, any further comment of mine on this satire will probably seem superfluous. Let me just point out that we find crammed into this poem, which contains only 232 lines in the edition that I have relied on, virtually all the themes of religious satire: ridicule of Protestantism; of the Catholic clergy; of fundamental concepts like prayer and penitence, heaven and hell, the sacrament of marriage and the authority of the Bible. Yet all this ridicule is medieval in spirit, just as the final retraction is medieval too. The author of this nineteenth-century poem looks back, far beyond Voltaire's eighteenth century or Descartes' seventeenth, far beyond Montaigne or Machiavelli, to the twelfth and thirteenth centuries of the goliards and the *Vision of Mac Conglinne*. Just a generation after 1815, it looked as though Gaelic literature might die out altogether, yet so vigorous a poem can hardly be claimed to embody the decadence of a tradition.

[1] The best text is that edited by 'An Seabhac' in *Béaloideas*, vi (1936), 315–22. I have summarized it as best I could with the help of Douglas Hyde's translation of an inferior text in *The Religious Songs of Connacht*, ii. 297–315.

7

Swift and Irish Satire in the English Language

The disappointing quality (and quantity) of Anglo-Irish satire

IN an earlier chapter I remarked very briefly on the satirical *temper* so noticeable in twentieth-century Irish writing and suggested that formal satire was scarce in recent Anglo-Irish literature only because of the present unfashionableness of satire as a distinct genre. The more I have thought about the matter, however, the more incomplete this answer seems. Frank O'Connor has blamed the deficiency in part on faulty technique. Recalling how anxious 'A.E.' was to develop a satirist among the young Irish writers whom he fostered, O'Connor continues as follows:

> None of us could ever fashion a story or a play into a stiletto to run into the vitals of some pompous ass. Oliver Gogarty, like Brian O'Nolan of our own time, could make phrases that delighted everybody, but the phrases never concentrated themselves into the shape of a dagger; they were more like fireworks that spluttered and jumped all over the place, as much a danger to his friends as to his enemies. Irish anger is unfocused; malice for its own sweet sake, as in the days of the bards.

Later in the same brief article he makes a more significant point:

> Just pick up a copy of George Moore's *Hail and Farewell*; read again the satirical descriptions of Martyn, Gill and Plunkett, and, without bothering to ask yourself if any publisher today would publish it, ask yourself what the damages would be if he did. Damages for so-called libels have become so preposterous in England and Ireland that the English have had to legislate against them, and no insurance company will even quote a rate for insuring publisher and author against 'libels' concerning Irish people.[1]

[1] Frank O'Connor, 'Is This a Dagger?' *Nation*, clxxxvi (1958), 370–1.

Here, I think, stands a great stumbling-block in the way of Anglo-Irish satire, or at any rate of lampoon, which appears to be what O'Connor chiefly means by 'satire'. We have seen in the two preceding chapters what a long and vigorous career personal satire had in Gaelic; the Early Irish laws did try very hard to regulate it, but they became a dead letter, while it was almost impossible for English law to take cognizance of libel in a language which had no status under that law. When English became the language of the majority of Irishmen, however, laws against sedition and the developing law of personal libel eventually drove the Anglo-Irish lampoon underground. Anonymous ballads circulated orally,[1] manuscripts, and occasional privately printed works like Joyce's 'The Holy Office' and 'Gas from a Burner' serve to keep the lampoon alive, but barely so. Publication on the Continent or in the United States protected Joyce and Oliver St. John Gogarty from some libel actions, but this could be no solution for writers who lacked the necessary international reputation. Besides, there is little satisfaction in lampooning a fellow Irishman if one can never be sure that the victim will see the satire in print.

O'Connor's mention of George Moore's *Hail and Farewell*, in which so many Irishmen are satirized under their own names —though with some pretence of objective reporting—reminds us that Moore 'got away with it' and makes me wonder why. Did the application of the law of libel suddenly become much more severe after the First World War, or were there special factors operating in Moore's favour? A great deal of legal knowledge would be required to answer that question. One thing is certain: Moore's blend of fiction and autobiography inspired several Irish imitators, the most notable being Oliver Gogarty, in *As I Was Going Down Sackville Street* and its inferior successors,[2] and Sean O'Casey, in his six volumes of autobiography reissued as *Mirror in My House*.[3] We do find, however,

---

[1] By definition, such material is hard to locate in print until long after the events it records. For a fine example from the 1880's, see 'The Hackler from Grouse Hall' in Colm Ó Lochlainn, ed., *Irish Street Ballads* (Dublin, 1946), pp. 78–79, 207–9. See Michael McLaverty, *The Choice* (New York, 1958), pp. 208–9, 227, for a fictional treatment of such balladry in a present-day setting.

[2] Oliver St. John Gogarty, *As I Was Going Down Sackville Street* (New York, 1937); *Tumbling in the Hay* (New York, 1939); *Rolling Down the Lea* (London, 1950); *It Isn't This Time of Year at All!* (New York, 1954).

[3] Sean O'Casey, *Mirror in My House*, 2 vols. (New York, 1956).

that those most severely lampooned by these two writers were either already dead—Moore in Gogarty, 'A.E.' and Countess Markievicz in O'Casey, for example—or, like De Valera, politicians who ignored libel as an occupational hazard. In spite of such precautions, Gogarty's first autobiography gave rise to a libel action by a relatively obscure person, who won substantial damages. It is significant, too, that Yeats did not publish *Dramatis Personae*, his acid reply to *Hail and Farewell*, until after Moore's death.[1]

Joyce in a sense lampooned Gogarty under a fictitious name in *Ulysses*, though I am one of those who feel that the portrait of Malachi Mulligan is essentially realism rather than satire. Other old scores were paid off in the same way: for example, the unflattering portrait of Vincent Cosgrave as Lynch. By an inverse process, unpleasant minor characters in Ulysses, such as Privates Carr and Compton, were given the names of people who had incurred Joyce's wrath.[2] Years after Joyce was dead, Reuben J. Dodd, Jr., who was mentioned unfavourably under his own name, sued the British Broadcasting Corporation on the basis of a radio programme in which references to him were read from *Ulysses*.[3] Otherwise the book escaped libel actions, I believe—partly, of course, because it was outlawed for so long in Great Britain and Ireland.

I am not going to discuss malicious autobiographies and autobiographical *romans à clef* any further in this chapter. They seem to me a spurious form of satire in that their ultimate aim is to inflate their authors rather than to deflate the foolish and the evil. The lampoons and general satires mentioned in the following sections all spring out of motives which, though mixed, include selfless indignation and a desire for abstract justice.

In the eighteenth and nineteenth centuries, when the law of personal libel was still in its infancy, though the law of seditious libel was very stringent, Anglo-Irish satire suffered under a different sort of handicap. The creation of great satire demands a spice of danger: it cannot be achieved by denouncing or ridiculing the weak and impoverished. *The Parliament of Clan*

---

[1] See Joseph Hone, *W. B. Yeats* (New York, 1943), pp. 416, 471–2.
[2] See Richard Ellmann, *James Joyce* (New York, 1959), p. 472.
[3] Ellmann, p. 38 n.

Thomas and its progeny would have lacked all zest if they had been directed at the underdog; what justifies them and makes them exciting is the fact that from the Gaelic writer's viewpoint the underdog seemed rapidly to be achieving the position of 'top dog'. Similarly, satires against the clergy in Voltaire's day were vigorous and exciting because the clergy were powerful; satirizing the clergy of modern France would be pushing an open door.

What handicapped Anglo-Irish satire after 1700 was the lack of a worthy opponent: the native Irish had been so hamstrung by the penal laws which were passed against Catholics after the victory of William III that there was nothing to fear from them. Earlier, the Gaelic Irish had been feared and hated, but conditions were never stable long enough to permit the creation of a distinctive Anglo-Irish culture, except perhaps briefly in the period 1250–1350. During the eighteenth century, Anglo-Irish literature was entirely the work of Protestants of English stock, who virtually formed a British garrison in their adopted country; if they were to write effective satire, it must be directed against the British government in Ireland or powerful individuals associated with that government. In effect, this would be cutting their own throats or, at the very least, 'rocking the boat'. Only a very courageous, self-assured, and unconventional personality—a Jonathan Swift, in fact—would dare to risk isolation from his own kind by doing this. And he would need the power and prestige Swift had in order to continue doing it with relative impunity.

After 1800 many Catholic Irishmen employed English, their native language, with considerable literary skill, but, except for Thomas Moore, they showed little aptitude for satire. Freedom of speech and of the press was frequently curtailed in Ireland throughout the nineteenth century, but I think it is fair to say that the native Irish writers in English did not make use of the opportunities for political satire that were available to them. Satire, especially when it employs irony, perhaps demands greater sophistication than they or, especially, their audience possessed in the new language. A greater obstacle, however, to political satire was their deep emotional involvement in the miseries of their country. Even an Irish nationalist of English stock, John Mitchel, found irony impossible to sustain in face of the enormity of the Great Famine. Lacking the necessary detachment for satire, Irish nationalists vented their indignation in factual indictments of the British misgovernment of Ireland; the facts were never in short supply. The political and legal oratory of Daniel O'Connell and Father John Kenyon, the pamphlets of James Fintan Lalor, often strike a vein of broad irony, but a brief squib by Timothy Daniel Sullivan is almost the only example of true political satire by a Catholic Irishman (other than the *déraciné* Thomas Moore) that I can cite throughout the nineteenth century.[1] If they wished to attempt social satire of the 'Protestant ascendancy', Catholic novelists found themselves handicapped by their ignorance of the *mores* of their opponents. William Carleton ridiculed his own Catholic background in a few early stories, but gave up the practice;[2] Irish loyalties were too strong for either side to have much respect for a renegade from the other. The best satire on the Protestant Irish after Swift was written by Maria Edgeworth in *Castle Rackrent* while she was still English enough not to feel that she was betraying her own kind. Even today, the sense that England and Northern Ireland are 'watching' inhibits self-criticism within the mainly homogeneous culture of the Irish Republic.

As I have already hinted in the previous chapter, Swift added a new element, sustained irony, to the Gaelic comic tradition. Much of the rest of this chapter will be devoted to Swift's relationship with that tradition and to his influence on both Gaelic and Anglo-Irish satire. Most of the writers of the Anglo-Irish Literary Revival who seemed gifted for satire (Joyce, O'Casey, and Synge, for example) had too much compassion in their hearts to become pure satirists. The few major twentieth-century satires I shall analyse all seek nourishment back beyond Swift in the well-springs of Gaelic fantasy which fed *The Vision of Mac Conglinne*.

Anglo-Irish satire before Swift

Anglo-Irish satire virtually begins with Swift. Centuries before him there was a brief flowering of satire in the Middle

---

[1] T. D. Sullivan, 'Rackrenters on the Stump', in David J. O'Donoghue, ed., *The Humour of Ireland* (London and New York, 1908), pp. 298–305.

[2] See David J. O'Donoghue, *The Life of William Carleton* (London, 1896), ii. 4–13.

English 'Kildare Poems', whose sources are English and French rather than Irish: 'The Land of Cokaygne' and the poem known as 'A Satire on the People of Kildare' (though more probably about the people of Dublin) are the most valuable products of this first crop. They are Anglo-Irish in dialect and in the use of a few Gaelic words, but, as I have said, their sources are not native.[1] By 1366, as the passing of the Statutes of Kilkenny proves, the magnetic attraction of Gaelic culture was growing too strong for many of the 'old English', who had adopted Irish ways and speech. For centuries after that date English culture in Ireland was moribund, its greatest figure being Richard Stanihurst, whose translation of the *Aeneid* is notorious for its clumsy versification and uncouth vocabulary.[2]

The only Anglo-Irish satire between the Kildare poems and Swift ambitious enough to deserve notice is James Farewell's *The Irish Hudibras* (1689),[3] a burlesque of the Sixth Book of the *Aeneid*, in which Nees (Aeneas), a comic Paddy complete with brogue and bulls, visits St. Patrick's Purgatory in Lough Derg instead of Hades. The nub of the satire is that Irishmen are criminal barbarians who speak bad English. Some realistic passages describing Irish customs and living conditions are all that a modern reader would find tolerable. Farewell, whoever he was, knew some colloquial Gaelic and was familiar with the names of some of the legendary Irish heroes like 'Finn Mac-Heuyle' and 'Osker, great Mac Osin', whom he places in St. Patrick's Purgatory. But if he shows some imagination, he has no wit. His verse is the feeblest doggerel, providing a striking contrast with the polished versification of his Gaelic contemporary David O'Bruadair.

Swift and the Gaelic comic tradition generally

At the opposite pole from Farewell, Swift had a complete mastery of the English language and of English verse technique. He apparently knew no Gaelic whatever, and even went so far as to assert that 'It would be a noble achievement to abolish

---

[1] For texts, see W. Heuser, *Die Kildare-Gedichte*, in *Bonner Beiträge zur Anglistik*, xiv (Bonn, 1904), 141-58. See also St. John D. Seymour, *Anglo-Irish Literature 1200-1582* (Cambridge, 1929), pp. 103-14.

[2] Seymour, p. 9 and pp. 145-65.

[3] [James Farewell], *The Irish Hudibras, or Fingallian Prince* (London, 1689).

the Irish language in this kingdom . . .'.[1] Yet he fits perfectly
into the Gaelic tradition, so perfectly that he had a perceptible
influence on it.

In one or another of his writings Swift displays all the most
strongly marked features of the Gaelic comic tradition. In
Gulliver's Travels he shows himself a master of fantasy: as a
medievalist recently pointed out to me, no other work in
English exemplifies so well the Early Irish *immram* (voyage)
tradition and its marvels.[2] In my chapter on fantasy in Irish
humour I have already indicated the striking analogies between
Parts One and Two of *Gulliver* and the leprechaun material
in *Aidheadh Fhearghusa*; I suggested that some Gaelic student of
Swift's acquaintance might have supplied him with a literal
translation, such as his 'Description of an Irish Feast' is based
on. According to Charles Wilson's *Swiftiana*, the Gaelic poet
who wrote the original, Hugh MacGauran, gave Swift the
translation of his *Pléaráca na Ruarcach*.[3] If Wilson's story is true,
MacGauran might well have known *Aidheadh Fhearghusa* also
and translated or summarized it for Swift. 'The Description
of an Irish Feast' dates from 1720, so that Swift's possible
encounter with MacGauran would have antedated the publication of *Gulliver* by several years.

In macabre and grotesque humour Swift has no equal until
we come to Joyce and Samuel Beckett. The author of 'Verses
on the Death of Doctor Swift' could make a jest even of his own
death, while 'A Beautiful Young Nymph Going to Bed' and
'Strephon and Chloe' are as grotesque and life-belittling poems
as ever came out of Ireland. Long before the publication of
these poems, while Swift was still at Trinity College, Dublin,
he may have helped to compose the scandalous 'Tripos, or
Speech, Delivered at a Commencement in the University of
Dublin (Held There, July 11, 1688) by Mr. John Jones, Then
A.B., Afterwards D.D.'[4] Jones, a classmate and friend of Swift,

---

[1] Jonathan Swift, 'An Answer to Several Letters Sent Me from Unknown
Hands', in *The Prose Works of Jonathan Swift*, xii (Oxford, 1955), 89.

[2] Conversation with Professor William Matthews, Department of English,
University of California, Los Angeles.

[3] *The Poems of Jonathan Swift*, ed. Harold Williams, 2nd ed. (Oxford, 1958), i.
244. Hereafter cited as Williams.

[4] John Barrett, *An Essay on the Earlier Part of the Life of Swift* (London, 1808),
pp. 46–77.

delivered the speech in the character of *Terrae Filius* ('Son of Earth') or licensed fool; university saturnalia of this kind were also permitted at Oxford and Cambridge, besides giving rise to macaronic poetry at the Italian universities.

Even if Dr. John Barrett, who first published the 'Tripos', was wrong in believing that Swift had a hand in it, the speech shows that at least one of Swift's Anglo-Irish contemporaries had a taste for the macabre and grotesque. Since this medley of lampoon and crude humour in a mixture of Latin and English is not very well known, I feel justified in quoting brief excerpts. 'The Last Will and Testament of Mrs. Mary Hewetson', sister of a don, is a most macabre production in which she wills her brains, tongue, teeth, breasts, &c., to various people who doubtless needed them.[1] The Trinity authorities objected most, however, to lampoons directed against themselves, including Richard Acton, the Vice-Provost.[2] F. Elrington Ball thought that the verses on Acton were Swift's;[3] they contain these lines:

> Actonio loudly sung by Fame:
> A wight inferior to none
> For ponderosity of bum . . .[4]

And continue in the same grotesque, Hudibrastic style. Most severely treated of all was one Bernard Doyle, a scandalous character who was eagerly seeking a Fellowship of the College at the time. The audience were treated to 'a view of his breeches', which were described as 'most worn at the codpiece, and least at the pockets'. They were infested with vermin:

> 'Tis almost incredible so many cattle should thrive on so bare a pasture. Every night he dares venture them off, he's in danger of losing them. Once when he lay without them, they crept from the garret to the street-door; and had bid him adieu for ever, but his landlady seized them by an habeas corpus, and brought them to him with a pair of tongs.[5]

Though reminiscent of a passage in *The Vision of Mac Conglinne*, this is crude stuff; few, however, would dare claim that Swift

---

[1] Barrett, pp. 54–61.

[2] He was the acting head of the College in the absence of the Provost. See Barrett, p. 15.

[3] F. Elrington Ball, *Swift's Verse* (London, 1929), pp. 8–9.

[4] Barrett, p. 73.

[5] Barrett, p. 69.

could not have written it. As Swift's friend Dr. Patrick Delany was to say long afterwards:

> Thus much is certain: that Swift never could keep his stile clear of offence, when a temptation of wit, came in his way.[1]

Swift's passion for word play, witty or not, has already been dealt with in the appropriate chapter. As for parody, Swift is like Joyce in that he can hardly write anything, particularly in prose, without verging on parody. *A Tale of a Tub* parodies learned treatises; *Gulliver's Travels* parodies the 'true relations' of adventurous and not-too-veracious travellers; *The Drapier's Letters* parody the earnest pamphleteering of public-minded tradesmen; *A Modest Proposal* parodies the schemes of 'projectors'; *The Bickerstaff Papers*, *The Last Speech and Dying Words of Ebenezer Elliston*, and 'A Meditation upon a Broomstick' were such successful imitations of, respectively, the predictions of almanac makers, the broadsides hawked at executions, and Robert Boyle's *Meditations* that editors have assured us they were taken seriously when first published or read in manuscript.[2]

Similarities between Swift and the Gaelic satirists

Before discussing the resemblances between Swiftian and Gaelic satire, I want to mention the one tenuous but direct link between Swift's circle and *The Parliament of Clan Thomas* or some of its literary progeny. A number of Swift's friends and possibly Swift himself, under the leadership of William Dunkin, wrote epigrams against one Charles Carthy, who in 1731 had the misfortune to publish a bad translation of Horace. These appear in Harold Williams's edition of Swift's *Poems* and other collected editions of Swift. Among them is the following quatrain, headed 'Irish Epigram English'd':

> While with the Fustian of thy Book
> The witty Ancient you enrobe,
> You make the graceful *Horace* look
> As pitiful as *Tom Mac Lobe*.[3]

---

[1] [Patrick Delany], *Observations upon Lord Orrery's Remarks on the Life and Writings of Dr. Jonathan Swift* (London, 1754), pp. 74–75.

[2] See Jonathan Swift, *A Tale of a Tub and Other Satires*, Everyman's Library, No. 347 (London, 1909), pp. 196, ix, for the uncritical reception of *The Bickerstaff Papers* and 'Meditation upon a Broomstick,' respectively. For the reception of *The Last Speech . . . of Ebenezer Elliston*, see *The Prose Works of Jonathan Swift*, ed. Temple Scott, vii (London, 1905), 56.   [3] Williams, ii. 670.

Although 'Tom Mac Lobe' is described in the original note as '*A notorious* Irish *Poetaster, ridicul'd by all the Ancient Wits of this Kingdom, insomuch that he became a Proverb*', he is undoubtedly Tomás Mac Lóbus, the eponymous ancestor of Clan Thomas. If the note was by the author of the epigram, he cannot have known very much about Tomás or about Irish literature. Nevertheless, this quatrain does connect Swift, however flimsily, with a whole cycle of Gaelic satire.

I must stress, too, that an academic knowledge of Gaelic was more widespread among Trinity College men of Swift's generation than is generally realized. Swift entered the College in the Provostship of Narcissus Marsh, who did not resign until 1683. Marsh himself knew Irish and employed a converted Roman Catholic priest, Paul Higgins, as a lecturer in the language. According to Professor Constantia Maxwell,

. . . both Fellows and students attended the Irish lectures to the number of eighty, and . . . following the Provost's example, made considerable progress in the language.[1]

Provost Robert Huntington (1683-92) continued Marsh's interest in Gaelic.[2] Of course the Williamite War intervened to dampen the enthusiasm of the College authorities for the language, but later Provost Benjamin Pratt (1710-17) also employed a lecturer in Irish.[3] All in all, there was more knowledge of the Irish language among Dublin Protestants in Swift's time than there had been a century before or would be a century after. The main interest in Gaelic sprang from a desire to convert the native Irish to Protestantism, but Dr. John Fergus, a Dublin physician, was a Gaelic scholar and 'patron of Irish letters' in the 1720's.[4]

Whatever the cause, Swift and the Gaelic satirists have a great deal in common. First of all they share an attitude, a sense of power and prestige. Swift, like the *fili*, expects the objects of his satire to quail and tremble before him: he describes himself in 'Cadenus and Vanessa' as 'Of half mankind the dread and hate'. When the Dean is displeased, viceroys, bishops, peers, members of parliament, sometimes even the

---

[1] Constantia Maxwell, *A History of Trinity College, Dublin, 1591–1892* (Dublin, 1946), p. 73. [2] Ibid., p. 76 n. [3] Ibid., p. 89.
[4] Thomas F. O'Rahilly, 'Irish Scholars in Dublin in the Early Eighteenth Century', *Gadelica*, i (1912–13), 156, 162.

king himself, must listen and do penance. Swift is always completely certain that he is in the right; I think the most arrogant lines he ever wrote were those denouncing a victim of his satire because the benighted man

> . . . kindled as if the whole Satire had been
> The oppression of Virtue, not wages of Sin.[1]

Along with this arrogance went a scorn of moderation that carried Swift to lengths unheard of even among the Gaelic poets, in *A Modest Proposal* and in the Fourth Part of *Gulliver*, where he denounces the whole human race as obscene animals. It is rather the immoderate fury of his personal satire, the utter disproportion of cause and effect, which reminds us of the Gaelic satirists. Take for example 'A Character, Panegyric, and Description of the Legion Club' (1736). The Irish Parliament had ventured to disagree with Swift's notion of what was due to the clergy, by opposing the tithe of agistment; his reaction was to characterize the entire parliament as a madhouse and to single out thirteen members for specially obscene and sadistic ridicule, such as we find in this passage:

> *Dick Fitz-Baker, Dick* the Player,
> Old Acquaintance, are you there?
> Dear Companions hug and kiss,
> Toast *old Glorious* in your Piss.
> Tye them Keeper in a Tether,
> Let them stare and stink together;
> Both are apt to be unruly,
> Lash them daily, lash them duly,
> Though 'tis hopeless to reclaim them,
> Scorpion Rods perhaps may tame them.[2]

To find parallels for Swift's (feigned?) intemperate rage we must seek out O'Bruadair's denunciation of the woman who refused him a glass of ale or Owen Roe O'Sullivan's curse on the woman who kept his socks as a pledge for fourpence.

Another characteristic of Swift that reminds us of the Gaelic poets is his readiness to engage in a 'flyting', even with his friends, whose feelings he sometimes hurt in the heat of the

---

[1] See 'The Yahoo's Overthrow', Williams, iii. 814–17.
[2] Williams, iii. 835–6.

contest.[1] In the excitement of satire, indeed, he could forget not only the decencies of friendship but all reverence for the sacred: a trait he shares with Brian Merriman, the anonymous author of *The Vision of Mac Conglinne*, and many another Gaelic satirist. Poems such as 'Judas' and 'On the Irish Bishops' may perhaps be justified by the argument that the Irish bishops as men did not deserve the reverence that was due to their holy office, but 'The Day of Judgement' deals irreverently with the Deity in order to make a satiric point against mankind:

> 'I to such Blockheads set my Wit!
> I damn such Fools!—Go, go, you're bit.'[2]

The influence of Swift on Gaelic satire

It is truly ironical that Swift, who regarded the native Irish and their language as barbarous, should have been posthumously incorporated into the Gaelic tradition. In the previous chapter I have discussed Richard Barret's ironical elegy, *Eoghan Cóir*, on the death of a rapacious land agent, mentioning that Barret had learned his irony from Swift. We are told of Barret that he 'did not seem to admire Burns, but he talked of Swift with rapture'.[3]

There is very good reason for believing that Barret was not the only nor the most important Gaelic satirist who admired and imitated Swift. W. B. Yeats, prompted by Dr. Robin Flower, argued that the 'court of love' framework in Brian Merriman's *The Midnight Court* was derived from Swift's 'Cadenus and Vanessa'.[4] True, the court of Venus appears only at the beginning and end of Swift's poem, whereas the entire action of Merriman's takes place at the midnight court of Aoibheal, the fairy queen; nevertheless, it is hard to see where else Merriman could have encountered the idea of a court in which each sex blames the other for the decay of love.

[1] The classic case is the offence he gave to the Rev. Thomas Sheridan by 'An Answer to the Ballyspellin Ballad'. See Williams, ii. 437–43, and also Chapter 4 above, p. 98.

[2] Williams, ii. 579. For 'Judas', &c., see Williams, iii. 801–6.

[3] Patrick Knight, *Erris in the 'Irish Highlands' and the 'Atlantic Railway'* (Dublin, 1836), pp. 120–2, quoted in Thomas F. O'Rahilly, 'A Song by Richard Barret', *Gadelica*, i (1912–13), 115.

[4] W. B. Yeats, 'Introduction', in Percy Arland Ussher, tr., *The Midnight Court and The Adventures of a Luckless Fellow* (London, 1926), pp. 5–7.

Merriman ended his life as a teacher of mathematics in Limerick and so must have had a fair education, but there is nothing to indicate that he knew anything of medieval literature in any language other than Gaelic; and nobody has yet come forward with an example of the previous occurrence of the 'court of love' motif in that language.

Piaras Béaslaí has suggested that Merriman was familiar with the poetry of Richard Savage and draws analogies between passages in the *Court* and some in Savage's 'The Wanderer' and 'The Bastard'.[1] But Béaslaí, noting the colloquial flavour of Merriman's verse, also remarks in passing that it 'compares with the work of his [Gaelic] contemporaries, as, for instance, the language of Swift's verses compares with that of Pope's'.[2] Surely Swift's colloquialism is a far likelier influence on Merriman's style than the conventional diction of Savage?

It has been said that Merriman's verse form (which he was the first to employ in Gaelic, according to Béaslaí) embodied in its paired rhymes a conscious attempt to imitate the English heroic couplet.[3] But it could as easily be considered an imitation of Swift's octosyllabic couplets, for Merriman's line, though containing more than eight syllables, has only four stresses. An Irishman familiar with English poetry would surely have a special feeling about Swift and regard the latter's verse form as peculiarly suitable for imitation in a satire. Indeed, the verse form he adopted, whatever its origin, has much to do with the originality of Merriman's one great poem. Professor T. F. O'Rahilly is explicit on this point:

> In as far as Merriman employs 'the spoken speech' it is to a considerable extent due to the metre in which he wrote; when he writes the lyric 'Mac Alla' he is much like any other contemporary.[4]

Furthermore, the first translator of the *Court*, Dennis Woulfe, who was not far removed from Merriman in either time or place (he flourished during the 1820's in Merriman's native County Clare)[5] and may have had special knowledge of

[1] Piaras Béaslaí in Bryan Merryman, *Cúirt an Mheadhon Oidhche*, ed. Riseárd Ó Foghludha (Dublin, 1912), pp. 16–17, 182–3. Hereafter cited as *Cúirt*.

[2] *Cúirt*, p. 5.

[3] I am confident that my memory has not deceived me, but the source of this statement now eludes me.

[4] Thomas F. O'Rahilly, reviewing *Cúirt*, *Gadelica*, i (1912–13), 190.

[5] *Gadelica*, i. 202.

Merriman's intention, used the octosyllabic couplet in his translation. The brief quotations from it that I have seen are often reminiscent of Swift; for example:

> Your cabin sluiced from soot and rain,
> And springing fluids that oozed amain;
> Its weed-grown roof so rudely shaped
> By hens at roost all scooped and scraped.[1]

Or perhaps better still:

> Favour not for rank or riches
> Lazy men or Moll in breeches.[2]

These facts, coupled with the opinion of so fine a Gaelic scholar as Robin Flower, are to me sufficient proof that the greatest Gaelic satire written after Swift's time owed much of its power to his example.

So perfectly did Swift fit the Gaelic tradition both as a man and as a writer that he has been incorporated into Irish folklore, certainly in the English language and possibly also in Gaelic. Besides the apocryphal stories concerning his sexual irregularities—so common in connexion with Gaelic poets also —and his witty repartee with his Irish serving man, there is at least one anecdote which circumstantially relates how the great Dean became a Roman Catholic on his deathbed by a characteristic ruse.[3]

Anglo-Irish imitators of Swift

For more than a century after the death of Swift any Anglo-Irish satire worthy of the name was deeply indebted to him. Maria Edgeworth's *Castle Rackrent* imitated his irony least slavishly and yet most successfully. Some of Thomas Moore's verse and his prose *Memoirs of Captain Rock* also deserve notice, as does John Mitchel's *Apology for the British Government in Ireland*. On the other hand, the anonymous political satire *Baratariana* (1772),[4] mainly by Sir Hercules Langrishe, Henry

---

[1] *Cúirt*, p. 122.   [2] *Cúirt*, p. 129.
[3] Patrick Kennedy, *The Banks of the Boro* (London and Dublin, 1867), pp. 211–14. See also Yeats in Ussher, p. 6 n.
[4] *Baratariana: A Select Collection of Fugitive Political Pieces: Consisting of Letters, Essays, &c. Published during the Administration of His Excellency Lord Viscount Townshend, in Ireland* (Dublin, 1772).

Grattan, and Henry Flood,[1] owes little to Swift and is a tepid piece of work. Goldsmith, who imitated Montesquieu's *Lettres Persanes* in his *Citizen of the World*, had not the temperament for satire and could hardly have imitated Swift if he had wished to: the best letters in *The Citizen of the World*, such as those dealing with the 'Man in Black', have rather the tone of familiar essays.

The irony of *Castle Rackrent* is so low in key as to be easily overlooked. Yet it is hinted at in the very first sentence, where Thady Quirk says that he has undertaken to publish his memoirs of the Rackrents 'out of friendship for the family'.[2] Thady seems never to realize that their worst enemy could hardly have given a more damning account of the Rackrents than he does. He never denounces even those whom he plainly reveals to have been grasping and cruel; as for his favourite, Sir Condy, he praises him to the skies while showing him to be a heedless fool and a drunkard. Occasionally the shadow of a doubt crosses his mind:

> Sir Kit Rackrent, my young master, left all to the agent; and though he had the spirit of a prince, and lived away to the honour of his country abroad, which I was proud to hear of, what were we the better for that at home?[3]

But later, after Sir Kit has imprisoned his wife in the castle for many years and solemnly promised each of three young ladies that she will be his second wife, Thady can say of him that 'he was never cured of his gaming tricks; but that was the only fault he had, God bless him!'[4] After Sir Kit's death, Maria Edgeworth directs the same gentle irony against his neighbours:

> No sooner was it known for certain that he was dead, than all the gentlemen within twenty miles of us came in a body, as it were, to set my lady [an heiress] at liberty, and to protest against her confinement, which they now for the first time understood was against her own consent.[5]

Nobody comes very well out of this novel, neither the Rackrents, nor Thady their loyal dupe, nor Thady's son Jason, who gets the Rackrents' estates into his hands, scandalizing Thady

---

[1] For their authorship, see William J. Fitzpatrick, '*The Sham Squire*'; and *The Informers of 1798* (Dublin and London, 1886), pp. 163–4.

[2] Maria Edgeworth, *Tales and Novels*, 18 vols. (London, 1832–3), i. 1.

[3] Ibid. i. 14–15.   [4] Ibid. i. 27.   [5] Ibid. i. 30.

by his 'ingratitude' and duplicity. Even the generous, heedless Sir Condy, last of the Rackrents, is mercilessly exposed: he 'was very ill used by the Government about a place that was promised him and never given, after his supporting them against his conscience very honourably . . .'.[1] Thady's indulgent praise of Sir Condy, even when true, diminishes his master in our eyes:

. . . he sits him down, and my son Jason hands him over the pen and ink to sign to this man's bill and t'other man's bill, all which he did without making the least objections. Indeed, to give him his due, I never *seen* a man more fair, and honest, and easy in all his dealings, from first to last, as Sir Condy, or more willing to pay every man his own as far as he was able, which is as much as any one can do.[2]

The weakness and shiftlessness of Sir Condy are exposed—in the word 'easy', for instance—with a gentle understatement which Maria Edgeworth never mastered again; perhaps she came to feel implicated in the guilt of the Irish landlords or grew too emotionally involved in the sufferings of the Irish peasantry; at any rate, a tendency to moralize replaces irony in *The Absentee*, for example.

Thomas Moore's irony suffers from a similar handicap in *Memoirs of Captain Rock* (1824). An Irish Catholic by upbringing, Moore does not identify himself with the Protestant landlords; his sympathy lies with the native Irish, but it mars the detachment necessary for irony, nevertheless.

'Captain Rock' was a generic name for the leader of any Irish group which took the law into its own hands against rapacious landlords, agents, or tithe proctors. The hero of Moore's satire claims that his real name *is* Captain Rock and that he is descended from a long family of Rocks, who have thrived on outlawry ever since the first invasion of Ireland from England in the twelfth century. The irony of the book lies in the Rocks' constant dread that England, by good government, may deprive them of their livelihood. However, they gradually become convinced that there is little danger of this happening:

As Property and Education are the best securities against discontent and violence, the Government, in its zeal for the advancement

---

[1] Ibid. i. 57.   [2] Ibid. i. 69.

of our family, took especial care that we should be as little as possible encumbered with either.[1]

Unfortunately, Moore allows himself to be led into a detailed account of all the measures of misgovernment which bring about this happy situation for the Rocks; thus irony remains in abeyance for scores of pages at a time.

Moore's viewpoint, clearly, is not that of an Irish nationalist: he writes as an English liberal who wishes to make the Irish loyal citizens of the United Kingdom by granting them civil, religious, and economic liberty. Some of his most effective irony is directed against the enforced payment of tithes by Roman Catholics to the Established (Anglican) Church of Ireland. Captain Rock imagines himself trying to explain the tithe question to a spirit from another world, as follows:

'There is a class of men among us, set apart to instruct the people in religion, and to place before their eyes examples of piety and peacefulness. In order to qualify them for this mission, and give them, in their respective neighbourhoods, that popularity which is necessary to ensure its success, the Law empowers them to seize annually a tenth part of the produce of all the cultivators, however indigent, entrusted to their care.

'As this annual depredation is seldom taken in good part, and sometimes even leads to bloodshed and rebellion, the time of the said teachers is almost exclusively occupied, in wrangling with their pupils and, occasionally, having them shot and hanged—in consequence of which, they have but little leisure left for lessons of religion, and still less for examples of moderation and Christian charity.'[2]

In this passage at least Moore has succeeded in capturing the sweetly reasonable tone of Gulliver's explanations of British and European customs to the King of Brobdingnag or his master the Houyhnhnm.

The supposed editor of the *Memoirs* is an English Protestant, to whom Captain Rock gives these final words of advice, which hover between irony and bitter truth:

'Let an Act be passed, transferring to the Roman Catholic Clergy all the Tithes that are at present paid to the Protestant Establishment; and, if *that* does not alienate the whole body of Roman

[1] [Thomas Moore], *Memoirs of Captain Rock, The Celebrated Irish Chieftain, with Some Account of His Ancestors. Written by Himself* (London, 1824), p. 141.
[2] Moore, pp. 296–8.

Catholics from their Pastors, the case is desperate, and you must be content to let Ireland remain Popish.'[1]

Some of Moore's poems on this same subject of Roman Catholic disabilities do not lag too far behind Swift's verse satire, particularly 'A Dream of Hindostan' and 'Letter IV' of *Twopenny Postbag*. The latter contains one couplet,

> Of Councils, held for men's salvation,
> Yet always ending in damnation . . .[2]

which is worthy of *Hudibras* at least, and perhaps of Swift.

John Mitchel's *Apology for the British Government in Ireland* (1860) is of course a bitter denunciation of British rule, imperfectly disguised as a defence; he hopes, he says,

> . . . to prove that the government of the British Empire is administered in Ireland with as much lenity, kindness, and indulgence as is compatible with the continued existence of that British Empire as a Power in the world.[3]

But within a page or two his real feelings break forth, whereas Swift in *A Modest Proposal* keeps his under control almost throughout; admittedly, Mitchel's pamphlet is much longer than Swift's.

It was, in fact, humanly impossible for Mitchel to be coolly ironic about a catastrophe so vast as the Great Famine of 1846-7, believing as he did that the British Government deliberately fostered the famine while pretending to relieve it:

> . . . Providence, say the English, graciously interposed at the right moment. The affair had come to a crisis: the Irish were nine millions, and were imperatively demanding their national Legislature. They had even studiously declined, in all the excitement of their agitation, to give an enlightened government the slightest excuse for letting loose troops and making a *battue* of them. What was to be done? The spirit of the Age was entirely averse to that project of Dean Swift, namely, taking nine in every ten of the young children and cooking and eating them: for England is now one of the kindest and tenderest of countries, and all the finer sensibilities

[1] Moore, pp. 375-6.

[2] *The Poetical Works of Thomas Moore*, ed. A. D. Godley (Oxford, 1915), p. 153. For 'A Dream of Hindostan', see p. 627.

[3] John Mitchel, *An Apology for the British Government in Ireland* (Dublin, 1905), p. 2.

of the heart revolt against roast baby. It was just at this juncture that the potato crop of Ireland failed; and, by great good fortune (still looking from the British point of view), Sir Robert Peel was Prime Minister of England.[1]

What weakens this passage is Mitchel's fear that his own side will misunderstand him. If he had left out parentheses like 'say the English' and 'still looking from the British point of view' and written consistently from the Machiavellian viewpoint which he attributes to England—if, in fact, he had written the whole work under an English pseudonym instead of his own name—the *Apology* could have been a satiric masterpiece.

As it is, true irony appears only in brief flashes like the following passage on the conversion of Roman Catholics:

> A few souls, now and then, in seasons of dearth, may be purchased with soup, at so many quarts per soul; and an occasional pauper in a workhouse can be induced to renounce the errors of Popery; but on the whole the progress of Anglican religion is sadly slow.[2]

Here again, a few phrases later, the tone shifts, when Mitchel turns to discuss other 'essential functions' of the Established Church; irony drops away as he states what he really believes rather than what he professes to believe:

> The Anglican Church in Ireland has these two most indispensable functions as one of the engines of British rule—to keep an effective garrison in pay, and to make two sections of the people hate one another with all their hearts. If it does not save many souls, it supports many families of the better classes. If it is not useful for instruction, for rebuke, for exhortation, it is at least fruitful in party-fights and houses wrecked over Papists' heads to the tune of the 'Protestant Boys.'[3]

It was the easier for Mitchel to make this attack because he had been brought up a Presbyterian, not an Anglican; he had no fear of 'rocking the boat', especially since he had been transported to Australia as a felon for his part in the Rising of 1848 and was writing in exile in Paris. As an apostle of nineteenth-century enlightenment, he felt that personal scurrility was beneath him; on the other hand, his personal sufferings helped to make ironic detachment next to impossible for him.

[1] Mitchel, pp. 15-16.　　　[2] Ibid., p. 54.　　　[3] Ibid., p. 57.

In examining the problems confronting Swift's nineteenth-century imitators or would-be imitators, we come to a fuller realization of the paradox inherent in his career as a satirist: on the one hand his lampoons are full of the bitterest personal feeling, or at least seem to be; on the other hand, his general satire achieves a detached tone which the average polemical writer finds it almost impossible to imitate. Perhaps we, his modern readers, mistakenly attribute too much sincerity to his lampoons; like the Gaelic satirists, he may be indulging in verbal fireworks, playing a game for all it is worth but not taking it too seriously.

A similar paradox confronts us in James Joyce, a twentieth-century imitator of Swift. For all the personal allusions in his major works, Joyce remained essentially faithful to the view of the artist expressed by Stephen Dedalus:

> The artist, like the God of the creation, remains within or behind or beyond or above his handiwork, invisible, refined out of existence, indifferent, paring his fingernails.[1]

Yet Joyce was the author of two Swiftian lampoons, 'The Holy Office' (1904)[2] and 'Gas from a Burner' (1912).[3] 'The Holy Office' in particular imitates Swift's octosyllabics with great skill, while its personal allusions, its scatology, and its fierce pride almost make one believe that the young Joyce is the Dean reincarnate. By the time *Finnegans Wake* was under way, Swift had become a Joycean *alter ego*; there is hardly a page of that book which does not contain some reference to him.[4] In 'Gas from a Burner' Joyce rends John Falconer, the Dublin printer who broke his promise to print *Dubliners*, by the favourite Swiftian device of putting words in an enemy's mouth. Falconer, in defending his treatment of Joyce and repenting the 'sin' of having accepted *Dubliners*, makes himself abjectly ludicrous.

Joyce was the last true Irish imitator of Swift, though we can still trace a hint of the latter's influence in the satirical verse of Austin Clarke and Patrick Kavanagh. The most

[1] *The Portable James Joyce*, ed. Harry Levin (New York, 1947), pp. 481–2.
[2] *The Critical Writings of James Joyce*, ed. Ellsworth Mason and Richard Ellmann (New York, 1959), pp. 149–52.
[3] Ibid., pp. 242–5.
[4] James S. Atherton, *The Books at the Wake* (New York, 1960), pp. 114–23.

successful major works of satire in twentieth-century Anglo-Irish literature, as I have already indicated, exploit a vein of fantasy in the Gaelic tradition that long antedates Swift. I cannot fully explain the decline in Swift's influence; I merely record it.

Twentieth-century Anglo-Irish satire

The five works discussed in this section have in common the fact that they call upon an older Ireland to redress the balance of the new. The juxtaposition of the two Irelands which permits the new to be judged inferior to the old is achieved by means of fantasy.

The first of these works in point of time is a little-known one-act play by Douglas Hyde, *Pleusgadh na Bulgóide; Or the Bursting of the Bubble.* This bilingual fantasy appeared just after a number of Trinity College, Dublin, dons had given evidence before the Royal Commission on University Education in Ireland. Several of them had expressed views hostile to the Irish language in rather strong terms. In particular, Dr. Robert Atkinson, Professor of Sanskrit and Comparative Philology, had remarked of Gaelic literature that

... it would be difficult to find a book in which there was not some passage so silly or so indecent as to give you a shock from which you would never recover during the rest of your life.[1]

Hyde represents, under very thinly disguised names, a distinguished group of Fellows of the College—Mahaffy, Dowden, Tyrrell, E. J. Gwynn, and Traill—denouncing the Irish language, in English of course. To them there appears the Poor Old Woman, a personification of Ireland, who pronounces this curse on them:

... the thing which in this world ye most loathe and dread shall instantly come upon you.[2]

Immediately they all in turn begin to speak fluent Gaelic; in fact, they discover that they can speak no other language. The Lord Lieutenant or Viceroy of Ireland arrives on a state visit to the College and thinks they must all be speaking Greek. He is greatly offended. Professor Atkinson, who is with him, does

[1] An Craoibhín Aoibhínn [Douglas Hyde], *Pleusgadh na Bulgóide; Or the Bursting of the Bubble* (Dublin, n.d.), p. 26 n.   [2] Hyde, pp. 8–9.

not recognize Modern Irish at first, though he is a Celtic scholar. Finally the word '*bréagadóir*' ('liar') gets across to him. He tries to communicate with the Fellows in Old and Middle Irish, without much success, but he refuses to admit that any kind of Irish is unknown to him. Instead, he glibly mistranslates the Fellows' remarks to the Lord Lieutenant, who becomes convinced that the pleading, expostulating Fellows want to kill him and beats a retreat. The Poor Old Woman then returns, denounces the Fellows in vigorous Gaelic, which of course they can now understand, and takes off the spell. 'Magaffy' wants to run after the Lord Lieutenant to explain matters to him, but the others insist that this would be in vain. With a cry of 'Oh, my God! the Bubble is burst, is it?' he collapses in their arms.

The published version of this play contains translations into Irish English of all the Gaelic speeches, so that the English-speaking reader can savour the inappropriateness of remarks like this: 'Magaffy, it cannot be that it is speaking Irish you are.'[1]

I may perhaps be overestimating this squib, but its whole conception seems quintessentially Irish. The employment of magic to reduce to absurdity the pompously opinionated recalls, for instance, *The Proceedings of the Burdensome Bardic Company*. When we remember that Douglas Hyde was the head of the Gaelic League at the time and might have been expected to feel great indignation at remarks like Atkinson's, we cannot but admire the gaiety with which he chose to annihilate his opponents. Not many Irishmen have been able to carry on controversy at this joyous level, but we have encountered a few—for instance, Peter O'Durnin.

Denis Johnston's full-length play *The Old Lady Says 'No!'* (completed 1926) is to my mind the only work by an Abbey Theatre dramatist, except Hyde's playlet, which is integrally conceived as a satire. Other plays with a satiric intent, such as O'Casey's *Cock-a-Doodle Dandy*, shift uneasily from fantasy to realism and back again, whereas Johnston's expressionist technique gives his entire play the dual focus, the half-unreal perspective, which seems essential to satire. Where Swift, employing irony, writes one thing and means another, Johnston

[1] Hyde, p. 9.

has his characters say and do things in a context which invites us to supply another meaning for their words and deeds. No doubt irony is the basic device of all true satire, as opposed to mere invective.

The basic situation in Johnston's play is simple, though imaginatively conceived: an actor playing the part of the Irish hero Robert Emmet (executed 1803) in a sentimental patriotic melodrama receives an accidental blow on the head in the opening scene. The 'play' is halted, and a doctor is called for; he diagnoses concussion. Suddenly the audience are projected into the injured actor's hallucination: he imagines that he is Robert Emmet returning to modern Dublin and finding that no one any longer understands his idealism.

The phantasmagoria that follows, in which scenes and characters dissolve into one another, dream-fashion, resembles the 'Circe' episode of Joyce's *Ulysses*: for instance, the actress who played Emmet's beloved, Sarah Curran, in the melodrama becomes the symbolic Poor Old Woman and also a Dublin flower seller who prostitutes herself after dark. Many of the lines spoken in the play are quotations from patriotic poems and speeches, just as many of the speeches in 'Circe' contain quotations and proverbial sayings.

All through the play, the unsuccessful revolutionary's hunger for an ideal is contrasted with the 'peace and prosperity' complacency of Ireland after her successful revolution. A highly comic and ironic passage is the speech made by a time-serving politician who introduces Emmet at a contemporary political rally. A longer comic scene depicts the evening spent by Emmet in the *salon* of the Minister for Arts and Crafts, where exgunmen members of the new government, bohemian artists and writers, and Lady Trimmer, a survivor of the British régime, fraternize in a hideously genteel atmosphere.[1]

After a final affirmation of idealism by Emmet, the play ends on a note of irony: the injured actor's last words before the doctor wraps him in a travelling rug and the curtain falls are 'Let my epitaph be written'. This recalls the peroration of the historical Emmet's speech from the dock before sentence of death was passed on him; as every Irish schoolboy knows, he

[1] Denis Johnston, *The Moon in the Yellow River and The Old Lady Says 'No!'* (London, 1932), pp. 211–33. For the political speech, see pp. 196–7.

said, 'When my country takes her place among the nations of the earth, then, and not till then, let my epitaph be written.'[1] But the greater part of the play has suggested that Emmet would be profoundly disappointed in his newly liberated country.

Eimar O'Duffy (1893-1935) also brings back to life a hero of the Irish past in his satirical novel *King Goshawk and the Birds*. The events of this book and its two sequels take place some time in the twenty-first century. O'Duffy envisages a continuous growth of monopoly capitalism from the 1920's onwards which has made it possible for Goshawk, the Wheat King, to buy up all the wild birds in the world and cage them to satisfy a whim of his Queen. Everyone has grown so accustomed to monopolies that only one voice is raised against King Goshawk's purchase, that of a penniless Dublin philosopher. Finding no one to support him on earth, the philosopher journeys in the spirit to the Land of Youth, where he obtains the aid of Cuchulain. Having reached the earth, Cuchulain's spirit at once borrows the body of a grocer's assistant named O'Kennedy. Behaving just as he used to in the old sagas, Cuchulain soon gets into difficulties through refusing to pay for hospitality, fighting, and asking a pretty girl to sleep with him the moment they meet. In disgust he abducts a millionaire's daughter and returns to the Land of Youth, promising to beget a son who will right some of our world's wrongs. The remainder of *King Goshawk* and all of *Asses in Clover* deal with the adventures of this son, Cuanduine, who finally frees the birds and tries vainly to teach human beings how to fight fair in the old epic manner.

O'Duffy lacked the style and constructive power necessary for the full development of his original conception. His style wavers between the epic and the commonplace, and his imagination falters; *Asses in Clover*, written after he had adopted Social Credit theories, bogs down in expositions of capitalist fallacies and monetary reform. Nevertheless, both the books mentioned contain remarkable passages of irony and satiric humour. The chapter in *King Goshawk* describing the Shaw Centenary celebrations is particularly rich in irony; Shaw is represented as an opponent of socialism, a British patriot,

[1] Ibid., pp. 267, 272. See Helen Landreth, *The Pursuit of Robert Emmet* (Dublin, 1949), p. 358.

and—on the strength of *The Admirable Bashville*—a mighty poet; his works are described as 'delightful human creations, untroubled by the cloven hoof of the propagandist', and he is declared free from 'a tendency to choose unpleasant subjects'.[1]

In *Asses in Clover* there occurs a comic scene of Rabelaisian scope: Cuanduine, in the excitement of victory, 'buzzes' Dublin with his magic airplane Poliorketes; the slipstream of its propeller not only gathers up all the millennial filth of 'dear, dirty Dublin' and sweeps it away but also strips the citizens naked, leaving them mightily ashamed.[2]

The Spacious Adventures of the Man in the Street, in which O'Duffy recounts the adventures of the clerk O'Kennedy's spirit while Cuchulain is using his body, possesses greater unity, though less originality, than the other two books; it reminds one more of *Gulliver's Travels*, *Utopia*, or *Erewhon* than they do. O'Kennedy borrows a body on the planet Rathé, where the people of Bulnid, though completely free in their sexual activities, are full of inhibitions in their approach to food. They practise 'monophagy', choosing a single food for which they have an affinity and continuing to eat it all their lives; O'Duffy works out the analogy in thought-provoking detail.[3] Other aspects of Bulnidian life are less originally conceived: for instance, a familiar type of utopian communism is practised, though this is in direct contradiction to the Bulnidians' religion, which preaches sordid greed.

Elsewhere on Rathé, O'Kennedy finds less endearing peoples than the Bulnidians. The Harpaxeans, for instance, remove the brains of their slaves and sometimes graft them into the heads of their favourite dogs. In a Swiftian chapter entitled 'Astonishing Opinions of a Lucky Dog', O'Kennedy meets one of these humanized animals, 'Mr.' Towzer, who has been given his freedom and has set up in business as a ratcatcher. Being neither man nor dog, Towzer experiences all the miseries of the *parvenu*. His children, farther up the social scale than he, treat him with contempt, as do all humans, while he himself will have nothing to do with dogs.[4]

[1] Eimar O'Duffy, *King Goshawk and the Birds* (London, 1926), pp. 249–55.
[2] Eimar O'Duffy, *Asses in Clover* (London, 1933), p. 214.
[3] Eimar O'Duffy, *The Spacious Adventures of the Man in the Street* (London, 1928), pp. 116–35.
[4] Ibid., chap. xli.

With the help of the Harpaxeans, O'Kennedy tries to conquer the Bulnidians and impose capitalism upon them. Luckily he is defeated; trial and execution follow. After interviews with several gods and the Devil, his spirit rejoins his earthly body. One god's remarks effectively sum up O'Duffy's ethical position, while at the same time recalling Swift's 'Day of Judgement':

'Do you think', said the god, 'that Omnipotence has nothing better to do than to bribe you into making the best of yourself and terrify you out of doing yourself injury? O, Aloysius, at your pride the stars laugh.'[1]

O'Duffy's ambition outstripped his achievement, but at least he proved that an Irishman of native stock could, like Swift in *Gulliver's Travels*, encompass the whole world in his satiric vision. Most Irish satire has been provincial in its scope, and indeed much of O'Duffy's has a purely local reference, though I have not stressed this aspect of his trilogy. Nevertheless, O'Duffy has judged the entire modern world by the standard of certain traditional Irish values, found it guilty, and punished it with his laughter. Joyce too has taken the world for his province, in *Finnegans Wake*; I cannot regard that work as a satire, however: a satirist rejects all or part of life, whereas Joyce, though more keenly aware of life's essential absurdity than anyone else in human history, accepts the world in all its imperfection; he has no wish to change or transcend it.

The future of Irish satire

It has often been said that the bards were the journalists of Gaelic society; recent Anglo-Irish poets have felt a traditional obligation to comment, often satirically, on current events. The law of libel, as already indicated, has restrained them from publishing lampoons, but this chapter would be incomplete without some reference to the brief, generalized satirical poems by Yeats and others which have annotated Ireland's controversies—political, religious, or literary—in the past half-century. All readers of Yeats are familiar with such poems as 'September 1913' or 'To a Shade', and with his epigrams on self-appointed censors of the Abbey Theatre. They may not, however, be aware that his role as commentator has been

[1] Ibid., p. 395.

assumed by, for instance, Austin Clarke and Patrick Kavanagh. Very little that is worthy of satire takes place in modern Ireland without receiving its tribute in the form of a cryptic, allusive poem, impregnable against libel suits but perfectly well understood. Such poems usually appear on the Saturday book page of the *Irish Times* newspaper. Most require too much annotation to be quoted here, but one or two are to be found in Kavanagh's volume *A Soul for Sale*,[1] and Clarke has recently published in limited edition two small volumes, *Ancient Lights* and *Too Great a Vine*, both subtitled 'Poems and Satires'.[2] The second volume supplies notes on the occasions of some of the poems. Here is the sestet of a sonnet on the plan to re-enact the trial of Robert Emmet in the original court; the scheme was later abandoned:

> See British greed and tyranny defied
> Once more by that freethinker in the dock
> And sigh because his epitaph remains
> Unwritten. Cheer revolution by the clock
> And lastly—badge and holy medal guide
> Your cars home, hooting through our dirtiest lanes.[3]

This poem mocks complacency rather in the mood of Denis Johnston's play; the notes indicate that high prices were to be charged for seats at the mock trial, while the poem, among its other ironies, stresses that the courthouse is located in a slum neighbourhood.

As for the future of Irish satire, I think one can safely say that the end of such a long tradition is not yet in sight. A thorough knowledge of Gaelic is coming more and more to be taken for granted among Irish intellectuals, however reluctant the man in the street may be to learn the language. It will be very surprising if this growing knowledge, which has inspired a revival of Gaelic poetry, does not lead eventually to the rebirth of Gaelic satire. So far as I know, Brian O'Nolan's *An Béal Bocht* (*The Poor Mouth*), a parody of such popular peasant autobiographies as Maurice O'Sullivan's *Twenty Years*

---

[1] Patrick Kavanagh, *A Soul for Sale* (London, 1947), pp. 28–30. See also Patrick Kavanagh, 'The Paddiad', *Horizon*, xx (1949), 80–85.

[2] Austin Clarke, *Ancient Lights* (Templeogue, Co. Dublin, 1955); Austin Clarke, *Too Great a Vine* (Templeogue, Co. Dublin, 1957).

[3] Clarke, *Too Great a Vine*, p. 10.

A-Growing and Tomás Ó Crohan's *The Islandman*, is the only recent satirical work to be printed in Gaelic, though no doubt oral and manuscript verse satire still flourishes. But satire is so deeply rooted in the Gaelic tradition that one cannot imagine the revival of Gaelic literature continuing much longer without the appearance in print of a veritable school of satirists. The timid conformism and reluctance to criticize of modern mass culture can hardly exert much pressure on a literature which now even more than in the past is the preserve of an intellectual *élite*.

8

James Joyce and the Irish Tradition
of Parody

The nature of Joycean parody

PUCK MULLIGAN footed featly, trilling:

> *I hardly hear the purlieu cry*
> *Or a Tommy talk as I pass one by*
> *Before my thoughts begin to run*
> *On F. M'Curdy Atkinson,*
> *The same that had the wooden leg* . . . .[1]

Here we have the Irish tradition of parody represented in full career, travestying the lines of a great poet almost as soon as they are published. The time is supposedly 1904, the place the National Library of Ireland; 'Baile and Aillinn', the poem parodied, formed part of *In the Seven Woods*, which Yeats published in 1903. Buck Mulligan's parody follows the brief prologue to the poem line by line:

> *I hardly hear the curlew cry,*
> *Nor the grey rush when the wind is high,*
> *Before my thoughts begin to run*
> *On the heir of Uladh, Buan's son,*
> *Baile, who had the honey mouth* . . . .[2]

Oliver St. John Gogarty, universally recognized as the original of Buck Mulligan, may not in fact have parodied this particular poem, but friends of Yeats did regularly produce travesties of his work for his and their amusement.[3] There is a reference to this practice in his published correspondence. A letter of 5 November, 1922, written while the Irish Civil War was still raging, describes a dinner given in his honour at the Dublin Arts Club:

[1] *Ulysses* (Hamburg, 1935), p. 223.
[2] *The Variorum Edition of the Poems of W. B. Yeats* (New York, 1957), p. 189.
[3] Conversations with the late Mrs. Kathleen Cruise O'Brien (*née* Sheehy).

At 10.15 . . . somebody threw a bomb outside in the street and the parodist, who was in the middle of a parody of my 'Innisfree', did not pause nor did his voice hesitate.[1]

Joyce depicts Dublin as so saturated in parody that Stephen Dedalus, who rather despises Mulligan's mockery, allows more than one snatch of parody to intrude upon his own reverie.

Before going any farther, I should like to sketch a definition of parody and to indicate some of the ways in which Joyce uses this device in *Ulysses*. Joyce's work prior to *Ulysses* appears to me to contain a great deal of pastiche, such as the poem recited in 'Ivy Day in the Committee Room' or the juvenile poems by Stephen in *A Portrait*, but almost no parody.

Buck Mulligan's lines, however, constitute parody in the strictest sense, for they bear a very close metrical, verbal, and syntactical resemblance to their original. Parody is always traced to the Greek rhapsodists, who often interspersed their recitals of Homer with

little poems composed of almost the same lines as those they had recited, whose meaning they twisted in order to express something else calculated to amuse the audience.[2]

Octave Delepierre, whose excellent book on parody I have just quoted, underlines this expressing of 'something else' as essential to parody:

It is . . . the substitution of a new subject which separates parody from the burlesque or the comic.[3]

As anybody who reads the Yeats lines and their parody to the end can see, not only have the personages been changed, but a passage exalting platonic love has been twisted so as to refer to onanism.

Most definitions of parody agree that it need not confine itself to the imitation of a specific passage or even of a specific work. Prose parodies frequently limit themselves to the imitation of an author's characteristic *style*; such are the parodies of English prose style through the centuries in the hospital ('Oxen of the Sun') episode of *Ulysses*; some of these even parody the general style of a period rather than that of a particular author.

[1] *The Letters of W. B. Yeats*, ed. Allan Wade (New York, 1955), p. 692.
[2] Octave Delepierre, *La Parodie chez les Grecs, chez les Romains, et chez les modernes* (London, 1870), p. 8 n. My translation.   [3] Ibid., p. 10.

We may go farther still and speak of parodying an entire literary or sub-literary genre: Gerty MacDowell's reverie in the 'Nausicaa' episode imitates what used to be called the *'Peg's Paper* style' in Ireland, after an English publication once popular among servant girls. The newspaper headlines in the 'Aeolus' episode may also be described as parodies. In the 'Cyclops' or pub episode we find parody of such genres as nineteenth-century translations of the Gaelic sagas; accounts of spiritualist séances; newspaper reports (of an execution, a Gaelic Athletic Association meeting, a parliamentary debate, a wedding); an almost apocalyptic description of a religious procession, with copious illustrations from the Latin liturgy, and a hilarious excerpt from a Gaelic League journal, purporting to deal with the dog Garryowen's ability to recite Gaelic verse. The supposed translation of 'the canine original' runs as follows:

> The curse of my curses
> Seven days every day
> And seven dry Thursdays
> On you, Barney Kiernan,
> Has no sup of water
> To cool my courage,
> And my guts red roaring
> After Lowry's lights.[1]

This parody has so many possible applications that one wavers between the original verse of Synge and the translations of Douglas Hyde, or between Yeats and Lady Gregory in certain phases, before finally deciding that the entire Anglo-Irish Literary Revival is their true victim.

Before leaving *Ulysses* we must take note of the type of parody implicit in the book's title. I say 'parody' advisedly, for the subject of *Ulysses* is no longer that of the *Odyssey*. Even if Bloom were called Odysseus and all the other characters were allotted their Homeric names, I do not think we could describe *Ulysses* as a burlesque. In true burlesque Bloom would have to draw the bow of Odysseus while speaking with the accents of Dublin. He would have to undergo shipwreck and all kinds of other physical hardships, or at least some semblance of them. The 'tedious brief scene' of Pyramus and Thisbe acted by

[1] *Ulysses*, p. 324.

Bottom and his friends is a good example of the genre. An older Irish contemporary of Joyce's begins a characteristic piece of burlesque thus:

'Essex,' said Queen Elizabeth, as the two of them sat at breakwhist in the back parlour of Buckingham Palace; 'Essex, me haro, I've got a job that I think would suit you. Do you know where Ireland is?'

'I'm no great fist at jography,' says his Lordship, 'but I know the place you mane. Population, three million; exports, emigrants.'[1]

On the other hand, *Ulysses* is not a stylistic parody of Homer, as are the *Batrachomyomachia* and *The Rape of the Lock*. The chief formal elements of the *Odyssey* parodied in *Ulysses* are the over-all rhythms of search for the father, wandering, and return home, emphasized by the division of the book into three unequal parts, indicated by Roman numerals.

No doubt one could say that the personages of the *Odyssey* are parodied, though 'caricatured' would be a more precise term. The plots of individual episodes—plot, of course, constitutes a formal element—are travestied also. It would hardly be stretching the meaning of 'parody' too far to describe *Ulysses* as a thematic and structural parody of the *Odyssey*. This type of parody has at least one precedent in Irish literature: *The Vision of Mac Conglinne*, which I shall discuss later, presents many parallels with the life of Christ, though it makes no recognizable attempt to imitate the language of the Gospels.

It may be objected that *Ulysses* is not a true parody, since it does not expose the work of Homer to even the mildest sort of ridicule, though it belittles modern life by comparison with the heroic past. I disagree. In the light of *Finnegans Wake* we can safely read into *Ulysses* the implication that Homer's heroes were not quite so heroic as he painted them, and that Penelope, like Molly Bloom, was no better than she should be. Hugh Kenner, in his *Dublin's Joyce*, reproduces Joyce's own table of the Homeric correspondences in *Ulysses*.[2] Twice, Joyce seems to show a knowledge of Bacon's *The Wisdom of the Ancients*: first, when he equates Proteus with Primal Matter; second, when he has Scylla ('The Rock') symbolize Aristotle and

---

[1] *Prose, Poems and Parodies of Percy French*, ed. Mrs. De Burgh Daly (Dublin, 1953), p. 174.

[2] Hugh Kenner, *Dublin's Joyce* (Bloomington, Indiana, 1956), pp. 226-7.

Charybdis ('The Whirlpool') symbolize Plato. Bacon writes of 'the Rocks of Distinctions and the Gulfs of Universalities; which two are famous for the Wrack both of Wits and Arts'.[1] If Joyce did know Bacon's work, he cannot have missed this surprising account of the origin of Pan:

... others attribute unto him a far different beginning, affirming him to be the common Offspring of *Penelope's* Suitors, upon a Suspicion that every one of them had to do with her . . . .[2]

Those who are not convinced should at least consider the possibility that the past as well as the present is being held up to ridicule in *Ulysses*.

Examples of Gaelic parody

I shall have more to say later about the ways in which Joyce uses parody to focus the past upon the present and vice versa. First, however, I want to justify the reference in the title of this chapter to an Irish *tradition* of parody. It will be necessary to examine in some detail certain Gaelic works already mentioned in earlier chapters which must be unfamiliar to most readers of Joyce, even though they have been translated into English. I must also discuss briefly several rather more familiar Anglo-Irish parodists, some of whom may have had a direct influence on Joyce.

The Vision of Mac Conglinne seems to be the oldest as well as the best major work of parody in Gaelic. Professor Myles Dillon finds no reason to disagree with the judgement expressed by Kuno Meyer and Wilhelm Wollner in 1892—namely, that the *Vision* 'was composed in the twelfth century . . . the work of a wandering scholar with a grudge against the church . . .'.[3]

The *Vision* tells of a clerical student named Aniér Mac Conglinne who has abandoned his studies for poetry and become a *scholaris vagans*. Having received the most meagre hospitality at the Abbey of Cork, he recites a satire on the monks. The abbot sentences him to be crucified, but during the night before his execution Mac Conglinne has a vision of a land so abounding with food that everything—boats, houses, clothing—is made of it. When the abbot hears of this vision,

---

[1] Francis Bacon, *The Essays . . . with the Wisdom of the Ancients*, ed. S. W. Singer (London, 1857), p. 340. For Proteus see pp. 291–3.   [2] Bacon, p. 262.

[3] Myles Dillon, *Early Irish Literature* (Chicago, 1948), p. 143.

he decides that the poet may be able to cure Cathal, king of Munster, of a hunger demon that makes him perpetually ravenous.

After various preliminaries, Mac Conglinne arranges to have the king bound firmly to the wall of the palace. He then prepares a delicious meal and passes tasty morsels before the king's mouth while describing last night's vision of gluttony. Finally the demon leaps out of the king's mouth to get at the food. Mac Conglinne traps him under an overturned cauldron and has the palace evacuated and burned to the ground. The king rewards Mac Conglinne, who triumphs over the monks.

In the words of the late Dr. Robin Flower:

The tale . . . is one long parody of the literary methods used by the clerical scholars. At every turn we recognize a motive or a phrase from the theological, the historical, and the grammatical literature. A full commentary on the Vision from this point of view would be little short of a history of the development of literary forms in Ireland. And it is not only the literary tricks of the monks that are held up to mockery. The writer makes sport of the most sacred things, not sparing even the Sacraments and Christ's crucifixion. He jests at relics, at tithes, at ascetic practices, at amulets, at the sermons and private devotions of the monks . . . .[1]

We must regret that Dr. Flower never found time to provide such a 'full commentary' himself. I can, however, substantiate some of his statements. For instance, the beginning of this riotous tale solemnly adheres to a traditional formula:

The four things to be asked of every composition must be asked of this composition, viz., place, and person, and time, and cause of invention.[2]

The ending, too, is a conventional one for saints' lives or other edifying narratives:

There are thirty chief virtues attending this tale, and a few of them are enough for an example.

The married couple to whom it is related the first night shall not separate without an heir. . . .

The new house, in which it is the first tale told, no corpse shall be taken out of it. . . .[3]

---

[1] Robin Flower, *The Irish Tradition* (Oxford, 1947), p. 76.

[2] Kuno Meyer, ed. and tr., *Aislinge Meic Conglinne* (London, 1892), p. 2. The translation only is reprinted in *Ancient Irish Tales*, ed. Tom Peete Cross and Clark Harris Slover (New York, 1936), pp. 551–87.   [3] *Aislinge*, pp. 110–12.

Many of Mac Conglinne's adventures seem devised intentionally to burlesque the life of Christ. He is unjustly convicted, scourged, condemned to be crucified, tied to a pillar-stone instead of a pillar. (In the later version of the tale found in Trinity College, Dublin, MS. H. 3.18, King Cathal plays the role of Pilate; he 'said he would not crucify a bard, but the clerics might do it themselves, for it was they that knew the wrong he had done'.[1]) Aniér himself makes the blasphemous comparison, saying, '. . . we will go in humility, as our Master, Jesus Christ, went to His Passion'.[2] He carries his own cross to the place of execution. When he is finally triumphant, he is permitted to sit always at the king's right hand and is granted the right of intercession—all but one-third of it, which is reserved to the men of Ireland.

Within its loose framework the *Vision* includes several very specific parodies of literary and liturgical forms, all harping on the food theme. In one, Aniér traces the genealogy of Abbot Manchín up to Adam, as the genealogy of Christ is traced in the third chapter of St. Luke's Gospel:

'Bless us, O cleric, famous pillar of learning,
    Son of honey-bag, son of juice, son of lard . . .'

and so on for twenty lines more, up to

'Son of bone-nourishing nut-fruit, son of Abel,
    son of Adam.'[3]

Elsewhere we find what seems to be a parody of a *lorica* or 'breastplate prayer' for protection, several of which survive from the early Celtic Church:

'Off with thee now to the suets and cheeses,' said the phantom.
'I will certainly go,' said MacConglinne, 'and do you put a gospel around me.'
'It shall be given,' said the phantom, 'even a gospel of four-cornered even dry cheese, and I will put my own paternoster around thee, and neither greed nor hunger can visit him around whom it is put.' And he said:
'May smooth juicy bacon protect thee, O MacConglinne! . . .
May hard yellow-skinned cream protect thee, O MacConglinne!

---

[1] *Aislinge*, p. 149.   [2] Ibid., p. 26.   [3] Ibid., pp. 32–34.

May the cauldron full of pottage protect thee, O MacConglinne!
'May the pan full of pottage protect thee, O MacConglinne!'[1]

In similar vein, Austin Clarke, a living Irish poet, makes the
king say an act of *nu*trition instead of *con*trition in his verse play,
The Son of Learning, based on the *Vision*.[2]

This kind of blasphemous parody has of course the utmost
relevance to Joyce's work, but it was commonplace during
the Middle Ages; blasphemy has little charm except in ages
of faith, just as we relish most those parodies which ridicule
the authors we most admire. The most sacred portions of the
Catholic liturgy were the most frequently parodied, so that the
Council of Trèves felt obliged to pass the following decree:

> *Item, praecipimus ut omnes sacerdotes non permittant Trutannos et alios
> vagos scholares, aut Goliardos cantare versus super Sanctus et Agnus Dei,
> in missis, &c.*[3]

No doubt it was frequently disobeyed. Delepierre mentions
the great number of parodies of the Mass which still survive,
and he quotes a typical one in honour of Bacchus from Harleian
MS. 913:

INCIPIT MISSA DE POTATORIBUS

> *Introibo ad altare Bacchi. R. Ad eum qui
> laetificat cor hominis.*

It continues in the same spirit down to

> *. . . per dominum nostrum reum Bacchum, qui bibit et
> poculat, per omnia pocula poculorum.*[4]

Joyce might well have written the last phrase if he had thought
of it. Two of the changes that he rings on *secula seculorum* in
Finnegans Wake—'*Insomnia, somnia somniorum*' (p. 193) and 'from
circular circulatio' (p. 427)—can be allowed to stand for all
the thousands of such blasphemous parodies in the book.
Protestants may take note, for instance, of two parodies of the
Lord's Prayer, on pages 530-1 and 536.[5]

[1] *Aislinge*, pp. 80–82.
[2] *The Collected Poems of Austin Clarke* (London, 1936), p. 195.
[3] Delepierre, p. 54 n.
[4] Ibid., pp. 39–40.
[5] *Finnegans Wake* (New York, 1947). All later quotations are from this edition,
but incorporate Joyce's own corrections, as given on pp. 629–43 of the same edition.

Since the *goliardi* were such notorious parodists, they may well have forged more than one saint's life. Professor R. A. S. Macalister says flatly that the 'Life of Findchua of Bri-Gobann' in the *Book of Lismore*, a codex of the late fifteenth century, is a goliardic parody.[1] Father John Ryan, S.J., makes a less sweeping statement. Referring to the hospitality given to visiting monks in early Christian Ireland, he writes:

> So common was this feature that it was burlesqued by the imaginative writer of St. Findchua's life. When this abbot was informed that Ronán the Fair, a holy elder of Fir Breg, was on the way to visit him with some companions, he is reported to have exclaimed: 'Let a vessel of ale, enough to intoxicate fifty, and food enough for a hundred be given them, and if they deem that insufficient, add more!'[2]

Such a piece of exaggeration would not prove anything by itself, since even the account of Findchua's suckling a boy at his right breast is hardly out of keeping with the other saints' lives in the *Book of Lismore*. But the saint is represented as taking part in seven battles and giving way constantly to the sin of anger; on one occasion his head gets so hot that it burns his tutor's cowl; his lay neighbours describe him as a 'slaughterous warrior'. In one battle he behaves more like a Celtic war god than a Christian saint:

> Then the cleric's nature rises against them, so that sparks of blazing fire burst forth out of his teeth. And that fire burnt up the shafts of the spears, and the wrists and forearms of the marauders . . .[3]

It is comforting to learn that at the end of his days Findchua made a pilgrimage to Rome: '. . . for he was repentant of the battles which he had fought and the deeds which he had done for friendship and for love of brotherhood'.[4]

If the 'Life of Findchua' is a parody, it missed its mark, for it was obviously taken seriously by the compilers of the *Book of Lismore*. Nobody who has even the most superficial knowledge of the Gaelic saints' lives will wonder why. Typically, the earliest version of a saint's life is written in Latin and is a sober

---

[1] *The Book of Mac Carthaigh Riabhach* (Dublin, 1950), p. xvii.
[2] John Ryan, *Irish Monasticism* (London, 1931), p. 326.
[3] *Lives of Saints from the Book of Lismore*, ed. and tr. Whitley Stokes (Oxford, 1890), p. 236.   [4] Ibid., p. 243.

enough document. Later come the Gaelic versions, in which the Latin life is either ignored or overlaid with a tissue of pagan folklore.[1]

It will cheer many people to learn that the *goliardi* did not have all the laughers on their side. As Robin Flower has shown, lay learning regained its independence in Ireland about the twelfth century, when the hereditary bardic families once more achieved prominence under the patronage of the native, and even of the Anglo-Norman, aristocracy. Naturally the bards incurred the jealousy of their clerical rivals.[2] It is probably to this rivalry that we owe the uproarious parody and burlesque of earlier druidic pedantry which we find in *Imtheacht na Tromdháimhe* (or *Tromdámh Guaire*) which was edited and translated from the *Book of Lismore* almost a century ago by Professor Owen Connellan. He translated the title as *The Proceedings of the Great Bardic Institution*, but Dr. Flower gives a more accurate version, *The Proceedings of the Burdensome Bardic Company*. This satire studded with parodies and burlesques seems to consist of four different stories; the hero—or rather, victim—of the first is a *fili* named Dallán Forguill, who belongs to the late sixth or early seventh century.[3]

The three remaining stories deal with Dallán Forguill's successor as chief of the poets of Ireland, Seanchán Torpéist. The first of these, in which he and his huge company (*dámh*) of poets, students, servants, and womenfolk make extravagant demands upon the hospitality of King Guaire, seems to be the main source of *The King's Threshold*, a tragedy in which Yeats ignores the tale's satiric aspect and takes the side of the poet against the king.

In the next story Seanchán satirizes the mice that steal his food and the cats who should have killed the mice. A giant cat carries him off, and he is saved only by the intervention of St. Ciarán of Clonmacnoise. Seanchán does not show the least gratitude to the saint, 'for', says he, 'I would rather that Guaire would be satirized than that I should live and he not satirized'.[4]

---

[1] See R. A. Stewart Macalister, *The Secret Languages of Ireland* (Cambridge, 1937), pp. 64, 67.

[2] See Flower, pp. 67–93.

[3] See Chapter 5 above, p. 107.

[4] *Transactions of the Ossianic Society* V (Dublin, 1860), 87.

The last story recounts a battle of wits between Seanchán and Marbhán the hermit, who has already helped Guaire to meet the harsh demands of the bards. Marbhán, champion of Christian learning—and something of an old wizard into the bargain—completely outwits the bards by forcing them to admit that they do not know *Táin Bó Cualnge*, the greatest of the Gaelic sagas. In order to learn it they finally have to summon the hero Fergus from the dead.

Dallán Forguill's mission in the first part of the satire is to obtain the magic shield of the King of Oriel for his own patron, Aedh Fionn (Hugh the Fair), King of Brefni. First he tries to win it by compliments; the poem he addresses to the King of Oriel must be either a parody or a burlesque:

'That is a good poem,' says the king, 'whoever could understand it.' 'That is true for you,' says Dallán, 'and whosoever composes a poetic remonstrance, it is he himself who ought to explain it . . .'[1]

Inevitably, by the time he has finished we wish he would explain his explanation. Having failed to obtain what he wants by flattery, Dallán tries satire; the king again replies politely:

'We must confess . . . that we do not know whether that is better or worse than the first poem you composed.'[2]

The bard then proceeds to gloss his own invective. His satire, being unjust, recoils on his own head, in accordance with the laws laid down by the saints of Ireland, and he dies three days later.

The satires of Seanchán against mice and cats, which cause ten mice to fall dead before him, but merely anger the giant cat Irusan, are true parodies, since the scathing verses usually directed against humans—and widely credited with the power to cause disfigurement or even death—are here directed against insignificant victims. The outrageous demands or wishes expressed by Seanchán and his companions are obvious parodies, being long, almost meaningless, and seemingly impossible of fulfilment until Marbhán comes to the rescue.

In the final story Marbhán obtains his choice of whatever music he wishes because he can show his relationship to the arts:

'. . . the grandmother of my servant's wife was descended from poets.'

[1] Ossianic Soc. V. 15.   [2] Ibid., p. 27.

'You shall obtain your choice of the arts, though very remote is your connection with them,' said [Seanchán]. . . .[1]

From such examples as the *Vision of Mac Conglinne* and the *Proceedings of the Burdensome Bardic Company* we can learn what kind of social and cultural situation it is that gives rise to major works of parody, such as *Don Quixote* or the attacks of Aristophanes upon Euripides and Socrates. Mere intellectual rivalry is not enough; an outmoded literary tradition or one that has yet to establish itself must be seen as the symbol of a rival social group, whether it be a class or a political party. The lay intellectuals—*goliardi* or bards—lampoon their clerical rivals for social power and prestige; the clerics return the compliment.

We find the same efflorescence of parody, and an even greater bitterness, in the attacks on the 'Cockney School' of poetry in early nineteenth-century England. Mistrust of and contempt for a new kind of poetry were reinforced by class and political prejudices in the minds of writers for the *Quarterly Review*, *Blackwood's*, and, later, *Fraser's*. The same complex of feelings had produced the parodies of *The Anti-Jacobin* a little earlier.

Joyce's astonishing outburst of parody results from his fighting a war on two fronts at once. On the one hand, he is fighting the old battle of the wandering scholar against the clergy, who must inevitably tend to dominate intellectual life in a Catholic country. On the other hand, he is fighting the battle of philosophy and the humanities as he had learned them from his Jesuit teachers against the science and pseudo-science that capture the allegiance of an untutored man of good will like Leopold Bloom and encourage his native vulgarity. Such an intellectual position as Joyce's may not be entirely self-consistent, but it's a grand place from which to start a fight.

Anglo-Irish parody

I have no wish to attempt anything like a full history of Anglo-Irish parody, which is indistinguishable from English parody whenever its victims are the great English poets. William Maginn's best parody, 'Don Juan Unread', based on Wordsworth's 'Yarrow Unvisited', may stand for all such work. I should like, however, to mention one remarkable squib of Maginn's on which he lavished all his humour and learning,

[1] Ibid., p. 91.

the '"Luctus" on the Death of Sir Daniel Donnelly, Late Champion of Ireland' which appeared in *Blackwood's* for May 1820. This symposium of mourning for an Irish prizefighter fills thirty-five pages in Maginn's collected works and includes commemorative poems allegedly by Byron, Wordsworth, and others; a Greek elegy; a Latin one; a Hebrew dirge, supposedly by 'Jackie' Barrett, the eccentric Fellow of Trinity College, Dublin, accompanied by a characteristic letter; and fulsome poems and speeches said to be the work of leading citizens in Maginn's native Cork.[1] Here and elsewhere in Maginn's work we find anticipations of Father Francis Mahony's audacious and sometimes libellous pranks in his *Reliques of Father Prout*, a series which appeared in *Fraser's* under Maginn's editorship. I prefer Mahony to Maginn; though perhaps not so versatile, he draws on a far richer personality.

Mention of 'Father Prout' brings us to a vein of parody which is peculiarly Anglo-Irish. Gaelic as a spoken language was dying out in Ireland as the eighteenth century faded into the nineteenth, but the traditional Irish tunes did not die. New English words were fitted to them, which often bore no relation to the Gaelic. Usually these words were supplied by Anglo-Irishmen—including Goldsmith, it is said—but sometimes they were the work of folk poets. One such ballad, 'Castlehyde', by an itinerant heir of the bards from County Cork whose name has not come down to us, inspired a famous parody, 'The Groves of Blarney', which in its turn was imitated and parodied *ad nauseam*.

The poet of 'Castlehyde' admittedly knew more Gaelic than he did English, but those who scoffed at him failed to realize that he was attempting to render the assonantal patterns of Gaelic poetry in English. What seem to be ludicrously bad shots at rhyme are really assonances; in accumulating these, the poet has undoubtedly strained the English language severely. Here is my favourite excerpt:

> The grand im*prove*ments
> They would a*muse* you,
> The *trees* are *droop*ing
> With *fruit* all *kind*;

[1] *Miscellaneous Writings of the late Doctor Maginn*, ed. Shelton Mackenzie (New York, 1855), ii. 47–82. For 'Don Juan Unread' see i. 179.

The *bees* per*fum*ing
The *fields* with *mu*sic,
Which *yields* more *beau*ty
To Castle*hyde*.[1]

'The Groves of Blarney', by Richard Millikin of Cork, while it won its author's bet that he could write something more ridiculous than 'Castlehyde', displays little of the skilled vowel harmony of its original. I shall quote here not Millikin's authentic text, but the one given by 'Father Prout' in 'A Plea for Pilgrimages', his tongue-in-cheek account of the pilgrimage of Sir Walter Scott to the Blarney Stone in 1825. I give an excerpt from what Mahony claimed was the Greek original, an incredibly accurate rendering, as I hope my literal translation will show. He also offered a French version which avoids all the absurdities of the English and a Latin version which is not up to the usual high standard of Mahony's Latinity. There is even an alleged rendering into Gaelic of one stanza. Mahony later produced an Italian version also.

THE GROVES OF BLARNEY	῾Η ῞Υλη Βλαρνικη
I	α
The Groves of Blarney,	Της Βλαρνιας αἱ ὑλαι
They look so charming,	Φερισται, καλλιφυλλαι,
Down by the purlings	῾Οπου σιγῃ ρεουσι
Of sweet silent brooks,	Πηγαι ψιθυριζουσαι·
All decked by posies	῾Εκοντα γεννηθεντα
That spontaneous grow there,	῾Ομως τε φυτευθεντα
Planted in order	Μεσσοις εν αγκονεσσιν
In the rocky nooks.	Εστ' ανθε' πετρωδεσσιν.[2]

[Literal translation of the Greek: 'Of the Blarney the woods, best, with beautiful leaves, where silently flow springs murmuring; spontaneously generated and likewise planted in the middle dells are flowers.' The last word in the Greek means 'rocky' and agrees with the word for 'dells' in the previous line. A prose translation could hardly be more faithful to the original than Mahony's rhymed one is.]

[1] Kathleen Hoagland, ed., *1000 Years of Irish Poetry* (New York, 1947), p. 255. I have divided the lines and used italics to emphasize the assonances.

[2] *The Works of Father Prout*, ed. Charles Kent (London, 1881), pp. 34–35. Greek accents omitted in original.

Mahony wrote at least two imitations of 'The Groves of Blarney' in English; one is entitled 'The Attractions of a Fashionable Irish Watering-Place' and sings the praises of a little seaside village near Cork, 'The town of Passage'.[1] Much more famous, however, is 'The Shandon Bells'. This *jeu d'esprit* has somehow stumbled into *The Oxford Book of English Verse* and thence to a terrific New Critical drubbing at the hands of Messrs. Brooks and Warren,[2] thus answering Pope's rhetorical question, 'Who breaks a butterfly upon a wheel?'

In truth 'The Shandon Bells' is but a pastiche of a parody; the occasion for its first appearance throws a light on the perverse wit of Francis Mahony. In one of the 'Prout Papers' he presented what he alleged to be the French, Latin, and Greek originals of poems by Thomas Moore—who, being a Whig, was a favourite target of Maginn and Mahony. These 'originals' were written by Mahony himself with the help of a former pupil, Frank Stack Murphy, who appears as 'an obscure Greek poet, called Στακκος Μορφιδης'. The article ended with Father Prout's account of how he had sung his own 'The Shandon Bells' to Moore—verses which the latter soon plagiarized in 'Those Evening Bells', one of the songs in his *National Airs*.[3]

I have dwelt rather long on Mahony because, like Joyce, he received his entire formal education from the Jesuits. Any remote chance Mahony still had of being ordained a Jesuit priest disappeared when he was forced to resign from the post of Master of Rhetoric at Clongowes Wood College, Joyce's first alma mater, partly as the result of a drunken spree with his students; some of the blame for this escapade rests with the father of one of them.[4]

Mahony's long residence and death on the Continent and his skill in polylingual puns also remind us of Joyce. I cannot prove that Joyce knew of Mahony's connexion with Clongowes, but he is mentioned at least once in *Finnegans Wake*: 'The prouts who will invent a writing there ultimately is the poeta, still more learned, who discovered the raiding there originally'

---

[1]   *The Works of Father Prout*, p. 257.
[2]   Cleanth Brooks, Jr., and Robert Penn Warren, *Understanding Poetry* (New York, 1946), pp. 220–4.
[3]   *The Works of Father Prout*, pp. 83–103.
[4]   Ibid., pp. ix–xiv.

(p. 482). One could not be sure that Father Prout, as well as Marcel Proust and the Latin dissyllable *prout*, was among those present, were it not that the same paragraph contains a reference to 'the bells of scandal'.

Both Maginn and Edward Vaughan Kenealy—a linguist, but hardly a wit, who translated 'Castlehyde' into Greek—were graduates of Trinity College, Dublin, where the undergraduate weekly magazine, *T.C.D.*, is still known for its parodies, as *Hermathena*, the college's learned journal, is for its Greek and Latin renderings of English verse. Robert Yelverton Tyrrell, a Fellow of the College and one of the great Latin and Greek scholars of his day, carried on the Maginn tradition admirably. Shortly after being elected to Fellowship in 1868 he founded a magazine named *Kottabos*, which became world-famous for its parodies and Greek and Latin verse as well as for the original English poetry of Oscar Wilde and others. The best of the work in its scarce volumes was reprinted in an anthology, *Echoes from Kottabos*.[1] Tyrrell's own 'Herodotus in Dublin (*The original Greek is added when it is deemed necessary*)' was a favourite parody, as was R. F. Littledale's 'The Oxford Solar Myth'. The latter, which put forward the view that Max Müller, the philologist and dabbler in comparative mythology, was the sun, had the distinction of being translated into German! The link between Tyrrell and Joyce was of course Gogarty, who was at one time a friend of both.

Imitations from the (Percy) French

Finally we come to a Trinity graduate whose work as a parodist and author of popular songs was peculiarly dear to James Joyce, as to many other Irishmen of his generation. William Percy French (1854-1922), better known as Percy French, was distinguished for his banjo playing rather than his classical learning while at college. His greatest achievement there was the writing of 'Abdullah Bulbul Ameer', now better known to American undergraduates than to Irish ones. A London publisher pirated and copyrighted the song, so that French never earned a penny by it nor even had the satisfaction of being acknowledged as its author.

After futile attempts to settle down as a civil engineer, French

[1] Ed. R. Y. Tyrrell and Sir Edward Sullivan, Bart. (London, 1906).

became first a humorous journalist, then a travelling entertainer
singing his own comic songs, giving his own recitations, and
doing clever lightning cartoons.[1] This Anglo-Irish successor
to the medieval gleemen wrote a number of songs to original or
traditional Irish tunes, some of which have become so popular
that they are often mistaken for anonymous folksongs. 'The
Mountains of Mourne', 'Phil the Fluter's Ball', and 'Come Back
Paddy Reilly (to Ballyjamesduff)' are probably the best-known.

'Phil the Fluter's Ball' bulks almost as large in *Finnegans
Wake* as the ballad which gave the book its title. As a matter of
fact, the paragraph on p. 6 of *Finnegans Wake* in which the
wake of the hod-carrier Tim Finnegan is first described contains at least two detailed allusions to 'Phil the Fluter's Ball'.
First we read, 'And the all gianed in with the shoutmost
shoviality', which corresponds to the line in the fourth verse of
the song, 'Then all joined in wid the greatest joviality . . .'.
Later comes, 'Tee the tootal of the fluid hang the twoddle
of the fuddled, O!' which parodies the opening of the chorus,
'With the toot of the flute, And the twiddle of the fiddle,
O . . .'.[2] Even in the previous paragraph on p. 6 there is
what may be described as an allusion to French's song. Tim
when drunk is called 'Phill'—'. . . wan warning Phill filt
tippling full'. Wherever one finds a further allusion to 'Phil
the Fluter', a reference to the hod-carrier's wake is usually not
far away. Not counting those on p. 6, I have found at least
sixteen allusions to French's ballad in *Finnegans Wake*.[3]

I can find no allusion to 'The Mountains of Mourne'—
which does not prove that there is none—but on p. 485 we
read these words: 'Come back, baddy wrily, to Bullydame-
stough! Cum him, buddy rowly, with me!' The following other
songs by French are alluded to: 'Mick's Hotel (by the Salt
Say Water)', p. 50; 'Phishlin Phil McHugh', p. 50; 'Shlathery's
Mounted Fut', pp. 137, 181, 405; 'Are Ye Right There,
Michael?' pp. 66, 296; 'Abdullah Bulbul Ameer,' p. 355; and
'Drumcolliher', pp. 60, 176, 540.

The 'Drumcolliher' references on p. 540 require special

[1] *Chronicles and Poems of Percy French*, ed. Mrs. De Burgh Daly (Dublin, 1922),
contains a great deal of biographical detail about French, some in his own words.

[2] Sheet music. 'Copyright 1937 by Keith Prowse & Co., Ltd. Published by
arrangement with Messrs. Pigott & Co., Ltd., Dublin.'

[3] Pp. 12, 58, 63, 230, 240, 277-8, 297, 318-19, 335, 341, 351, 363, 444, 491.

explanation. The song tells of a typical one-horse (and one-store) town:

> There's only one house in Drumcolliher,
> For hardware and bacon and tea . . . .[1]

None the less, the native of Drumcolliher is proud of it and wouldn't live anywhere else. Hence the travel agent's slogans in four languages on p. 540 of *Finnegans Wake*. The last of these, however, strikes a sinister note: '*Vedi Drumcollogher e poi Moonis.*' You will say that it is merely a variation on 'See Naples and die.' No doubt—but note the spelling of 'Drumcollogher'. There is a real town of that name in County Limerick; in 1926 forty-eight people were burned to death there in a cinema fire.[2]

In accordance with Joycean punctilio, Percy French is mentioned twice by name in *Finnegans Wake*, once in the first footnote on p. 296 as 'Parsee ffrench', and again on p. 495 in the phrase 'skirriless ballets in Parsee Franch . . .'. Percy French indeed wrote many ballads, but none of them was scurrilous; the nearest this kindly man ever came to satire was in verses entitled 'The Queen's After-Dinner Speech', as supposedly reported by a waiter at the Viceregal Lodge during Queen Victoria's state visit to Ireland in 1900. The references to Maud Gonne and W. B. Yeats should be better known than they are:

> 'That Maud Gonne,' sez she,
> 'Dhressin' in black,' sez she,
> 'To welcome me back,' sez she;
> 'Though I don't care,' sez she,
> 'What they wear,' sez she,
> 'An' all that gammon,' sez she,
> 'About me bringin' famine,' sez she.
> 'Now Maud 'ill write,' sez she,
> 'That I brought the blight,' sez she,
> 'Or altered the saysons,' sez she,
> 'For some private raysins,' sez she,
> 'An' I think there's a slate,' sez she,
> 'Off Willie Yeats,' sez she.
> 'He should be at home,' sez she,
> 'French polishin' a pome,' sez she,

[1] Sheet music. 'Copyright 1940 in the U.S.A. by Pigott & Co.'
[2] *Irish Independent* (Dublin), Golden Jubilee Edition (3 Jan. 1955), p. 39.

'An' not writin' letters,' sez she,
'About his betters,' sez she,
'Paradin' me crimes,' sez she,
'In the "Irish Times",' sez she.[1]

This verse form, if I may so dignify it, has a long history in Anglo-Irish humorous writing. French's lines appear to be an imitation of 'Looey Philip and Her Grayshus Majesty', by M. J. Barry of Cork, a squib which presumably dates from 1848.[2] Barry's verses stem ultimately from the 'Dialogue Between Tom Flinter and His Man', quoted in Sir Jonah Barrington's *Personal Sketches of His Own Times* (otherwise known as his *Recollections*):

Dick! said he.
What? said he.
Fetch me my hat, says he;
For I will go, says he,
To Timahoe, says he . . . .[3]

This, in turn, may be modelled on a Gaelic humorous poem; I have come across one which repeated the verb of saying in similar fashion, but if I noted the source at the time, I have since lost the reference. I could prove that Joyce knew Barrington's book, but I feel sure that it is French's verses he is parodying on pp. 519-20 of *Finnegans Wake*: 'He is doing a walk, says she, in the feelmick's park, says he, like a tarrable Turk, says she . . . .'

In the 'Proteus' episode of *Ulysses* Stephen's meditations include his own parody of some lines by Percy French:

The aunt thinks you killed your mother. That's why she won't.

Then here's a health to Mulligan's aunt
And I'll tell you the reason why.
She always kept things decent in
The Hannigan famileye.[4]

The original is entitled 'Mathew Hanigan's Aunt'; the first four lines of the chorus are almost identical with those above, except where 'Mulligan' is substituted for 'Hanigan.'[5]

[1] *Prose, Poems and Parodies of Percy French*, p. 56.
[2] Daniel Casey, ed., *Cork Lyrics* (Cork, 1857), pp. 148–52.
[3] *Recollections of Jonah Barrington*, with an introduction by George Birmingham (Dublin, n.d.), p. 93.   [4] *Ulysses*, p. 46.
[5] *Prose, Poems and Parodies of Percy French*, p. 155.

Joyce's motives for parodying a parodist

French himself was no mean parodist; note particularly his renderings of nursery rhymes in the styles of various nineteenth-century English poets. These can be found in *Prose, Poems and Parodies of Percy French*, a volume still regularly reprinted in Ireland.[1] It is curious to see Joyce, the arch-parodist, so frequently parodying a fellow-parodist. What were his motives? A satisfactory answer to that question would tell us a great deal about his choice and treatment of sources for *Finnegans Wake*.

In the first place, we must remember that Joyce was still working in the Flaubert tradition, which places a premium on historical accuracy. Humphrey Chimpden Earwicker, the dreamer of *Finnegans Wake*, recapitulates the history of the human race in his Jungian dreams, but he is also a dweller in a particular time and place. He is an Irish middle-class Protestant, aged fifty-odd in or about 1939; so was my late father, who was able to give me many of the words of 'Drumcolliher' before I obtained a copy of the sheet music. It would be surprising if H. C. E.'s free association of ideas in dreaming did *not* contain reminiscences of songs by Percy French, as well as of Moore's *Irish Melodies* and the *Irish Country Songs* collected by Herbert Hughes in this century.[2]

To reinforce my argument on this point, I must stress the fact that Joyce introduces a number of very precise contemporary touches into the bar-room scene of *Finnegans Wake* (pp. 309-82). When the customers pay for their drinks, they do so in the handsome Irish coinage introduced in 1928:[3] 'he scooped the hens, hounds and horses biddy by bunny, with an arc of his covethand . . .' (p. 321). The 'bunny' on the threepenny piece is more correctly termed a 'hare' on p. 313. On p. 324 the radio announcer prefaces an S.O.S. ('lessonless') message with the words 'Rowdiose wodhalooing'. The allusions to the noise in the bar and the Battle of Waterloo are clear enough, but only those who have heard an Irish announcer say '*Radio Átha Luain*' ('Radio Athlone') will

[1] Pp. 84–98. See also pp. 65–83 and 121–5.
[2] *James Joyce: sa vie, son œuvre, son rayonnement*, ed. Bernard Gheerbrant (Paris, 1949). An exhibition catalogue; see Nos. 120, 122.
[3] See *The Letters of W. B. Yeats*, p. 749.

recognize the primary reference; this is an authentic period touch, as announcers now say '*Radio Éireann*' ('Radio Ireland'). On p. 325 we have radio commercials, not all of them authentic. I am not sure that Arthur Guinness, Sons and Company ('Art thou gainous sense uncompetite!') or Anne Lynch's Teas ('Anna Lynchya Pourable!') advertised on the Irish radio before 1939, the year in which *Finnegans Wake* was published, but I do remember that the Irish Hospitals Sweepstakes advertised regularly ('Don't forget. I wish auspicable thieves-dayte for the stork dyrby.'). As for references to De Valera, such as 'Devine's Previdence' on the same page, Andrew Cass has collected a number of them and presented his case for the identification of 'Shaun' with De Valera in two brilliant articles.[1]

In the second place, French's songs would naturally form part of the equipment of the ideal reader of *Finnegans Wake* —one who, like Joyce himself, knew both the microcosm and the macrocosm, both twentieth-century Ireland and the wider human world in time and space to which that Ireland, often reluctantly, belongs. The more familiar the underlying jingle, the more extravagantly can Joyce counterpoint his puns against it without the experienced reader's losing the melodic line altogether. Look at the distortions suffered by the three-word phrase 'Phil the Fluter' without its becoming totally unrecognizable; I have arranged them in the order of their difficulty, not that of their occurrence in the text:

> Phil fluther (p. 444)
> fillthefluthered (p. 63)
> foil the fluter (p. 230)
> foil the flouter (p. 363)
> fill the flatter (p. 335)
> feel the Flucher (p. 58)
> Flinn the Flinter (p. 240)
> Puhl the Punkah (p. 297)
> Tham the Thatcher (p. 318)
> Pied de Poudre (p. 12)

The longer the recognizable quotation parodied, the greater the opportunity it offers for verbal arabesques. Here are some

[1] 'Sprakin Sea Djoytsch', *Irish Times*, 26 Apr. 1947, p. 6; 'Childe Horrid's Pilgrimace', *Envoy*, v (1951), 19–30.

variations on the passage from the chorus of 'Phil the Fluter'
which I quoted above:

> for the total of your flouts is not fit to fan
> his fettle, O! (p. 58)
> to the tickle of his tube and the twobble of
> his fable, O .... (p. 319)
> *with the sickle of a scygthe but the humour of*
> *a hummer, O ....* (p. 341)
> To the tumble of the toss tot the trouble
> of the swaddled, O. (p. 444)

To go back for a moment to 'Pied de Poudre'—why am I
confident that this is a reference to 'Phil the Fluter'? Let me
quote part of the context:

... hopping round his middle like kippers on a griddle, O, as he
lays dormont from the macroborg of Holdhard to the microbirg of
Pied de Poudre.

The citizens of Dublin are hopping round the middle of the
sleeping giant—who is Finn MacCool, H. C. E., Finnegan, and
the city of Dublin, among other things. The giant's head is
Howth Head ('Holdhard'), while his feet lie at the Powder
Magazine in Phoenix Park ('Pied de Poudre'). Now, 'hopping
round his middle like kippers on a griddle, O' is almost a
direct quotation from the chorus of 'Phil the Fluter's Ball',
where the words are 'Hopping in the middle like a herrin' on
a griddle, O!'

Furthermore, if one reads 'Pied de Poudre' with a Dublin
pronunciation instead of a Parisian one, it sounds much closer
to 'Phil the Fluter'. It cannot be too often stressed that, as
Joyce's own recording shows, the basic language of *Finnegans
Wake* is English with a Dublin accent. The quickest way to
understand almost any passage is to read it *aloud* as if it were
English. If a passage in roman type seems to be entirely in a
foreign language, then the reader must be particularly on guard
against a hoax. The reference to 'that once grand old elrington
bawl' on pp. 55-56, coupled with the parody of Swift's epis-
tolary style which occupies most of p. 413, suggests that Joyce
was familiar with F. Elrington Ball's edition of Swift's *Correspondence*. If so, he must have known the language which Swift
and the Rev. Thomas Sheridan called *Latino-Anglicus*. It looks

like Latin, but turns out to be English. Sheridan began his first letter in the new language with the words 'De armis ter de an', which mean nothing more than 'Dear Mr. Dean.'[1] So when we find, on p. 91 of *Finnegans Wake*, what seems at first sight a passage of Modern Irish, '. . . mhuith peisth mhuise as fearra bheura muirre hriosmas,' we must beware. The rule, 'Read aloud as English', does not apply here, but when given a Gaelic pronunciation the words sound very like 'with best wishes for a very merry Christmas'.

In the third place, the songs of Percy French, besides forming part of the culture of H. C. E. and the ideal reader of *Finnegans Wake*, also helped to make up the culture of Joyce himself. He could not have parodied them if he had not known them. I deliberately use the word 'culture' in its anthropological sense. In recapitulating the history of mankind through the ages Joyce was fully aware that he must represent 'culture' in the most inclusive sense of that word. Man's religion, politics, art, science, and technology are all parts of his culture—but so are his dirty jokes, his children's games, and the songs pounded into his head by gleemen or crooners. Everything was grist that came to Joyce's mill; much of it did not come spontaneously, but had to be sought for by Joyce and his band of unpaid researchers; other material, including most of the popular culture he used, was already stored in his memory. We can be sure of this last point, because Joyce's parodies of the Percy French songs often reflect a version which varies considerably from the printed text.

Like every other reader of *Finnegans Wake*, I am deeply indebted to Messrs. Campbell and Robinson's *Skeleton Key*.[2] They will, I hope, pardon me for regretting that, in their analysis of Joyce's references, they show so much knowledge of Sanskrit and so little of 'stage Irish', so much of the Egyptian *Book of the Dead* and so little of the Irish book of the living.

A philosophy of parody

Having explained, at least tentatively, why Joyce parodied so much trivial verse, I must go on to ask a more fundamental

---

[1] *The Correspondence of Jonathan Swift, D.D.*, ed. F. Elrington Ball, v (London, 1913), 73. And see above, Chapter 4, pp. 97–98.

[2] Joseph Campbell and Henry Morton Robinson, *A Skeleton Key to Finnegans Wake* (New York, 1944).

question: *why parody at all?* I have suggested above that much of the parody in *Ulysses* had a satiric intention, but I cannot detect the same animus in most of *Finnegans Wake*. A majority of the critics I have read agree that the latter is by far the mellower book, yet parody is far more integral to its structure than to that of *Ulysses*. If Joyce wished to fuse past and present into a single work of literature, why did he not quote the great and trivial phrases of the past without parody, as Ezra Pound has done in his *Cantos*? One answer, of course, is that Joyce was not Pound. Another might be that the Irish mind is innately destructive; though appallingly loosely phrased and impossible to prove, this answer has the merit of being difficult to refute. Even the philosophic systems of Berkeley and Erigena contain an undeniable element of nihilism. However, I do not think we need discuss this second answer, as the view of history which Joyce was putting forward almost inevitably finds expression in parody.

If I were to attempt a philosophy of parody, I might produce merely a parody of philosophy; instead, let me look for help from the philosophers. A reading of Susanne K. Langer's chapter on 'The Comic Rhythm' in *Feeling and Form* suggests that the sense of human continuity which Joyce sought to express is basically comic; the moment history is represented as imitating itself, parody is only a step away. The following quotation forms the kernel of Mrs. Langer's argument:

What justifies the term 'Comedy' is not that the ancient ritual procession, the Comus, honouring the god of that name, was the source of this great art form—for comedy has arisen in many parts of the world, where the Greek god with his particular worship was unknown—but that the Comus was a fertility rite, and the god it celebrated a fertility god, a symbol of perpetual rebirth, eternal life.[1]

'Eternal life' here of course means eternal life on earth.

Support for the view that there is something inherently comic in the repeat performances of history comes to us from an unexpected quarter:

Hegel remarks somewhere that all great, world-historical facts

[1] Susanne K. Langer, *Feeling and Form* (New York, 1953), p. 331. Compare Francis Macdonald Cornford, *The Origin of Attic Comedy* (Cambridge, 1934), and Albert Cook, *The Dark Voyage and the Golden Mean* (Cambridge, Mass., 1949).

and personages occur, as it were, twice. He has forgotten to add: the first time as tragedy, the second as farce . . . . The tradition of all the dead generations weighs like a nightmare on the brain of the living.

Who wrote that? Can it have been Joyce himself, who made Stephen Dedalus say, 'History is a nightmare from which I am trying to awake'? Is not *Finnegans Wake* the nightmare in question, weighed down with the tradition of all the dead generations?

Let us read on:

The tradition of all the dead generations weighs like a nightmare on the brain of the living. And just when they seem engaged in revolutionising themselves and things, in creating something entirely new, precisely in such epochs of revolutionary crisis they anxiously conjure up the spirits of the past to their service and borrow from them names, battle slogans and costumes . . . . Thus Luther donned the mask of the Apostle Paul, the Revolution of 1789 to 1814 draped itself alternately as the Roman Republic and the Roman Empire, and the Revolution of 1848 knew nothing better to do than to parody, in turn, 1789 and the revolutionary tradition of 1793 to 1795.[1]

Joyce would have disagreed with Marx on only one score: he did not believe that men could revolutionize themselves or create something entirely new. Just at the point in *Finnegans Wake* where the cycle of history turns and a new age begins, we read:

Yet is no body present here which was not there before. Only is order othered. Nought is nulled. *Fuitfiat!* (p. 613)

Fuitfiat we may interpret as 'It was. Let it be.' Or 'Let what was be.' It is, of course, a parody—of God's creating words in Genesis: *Fiat lux* ('Let there be light').

Nevertheless, few people would be likely to see the comic possibilities inherent in a cyclic theory of history; most of us would regard the implied futility of human life as pathetic rather than comic. Joyce, however, had watched his own countrymen 'conjure up the spirits of the past to their service', in Marx's words. Sometimes the results had struck him as hilarious,

[1] Karl Marx, *The Eighteenth Brumaire of Louis Bonaparte* (Moscow, 1934), p. 13.

at other times as nauseating. There is a tone of bitterness underlying his parody of the various manifestations of the Gaelic Revival in the 'Cyclops' episode of *Ulysses* which suggests that he regarded the whole movement as fundamentally anti-intellectual. A similar view was expressed in his early attack on the Irish theatre movement, 'The Day of the Rabblement', and we find it in *Stephen Hero* and *A Portrait* too. No doubt he was partly right. Still, one who had distilled an aesthetic from the teachings of Aristotle and Aquinas ought to have better understood the motives of those who genuinely sought the future in the Gaelic past, as he sought it in the European past.

On the other hand, the image of the Gaelic past offered for the young Joyce's admiration was probably not one with which he could very easily identify himself. What sympathy could he feel for those bloodthirsty, unreflecting warriors and kings? With impatient, intellectually arrogant saints like 'fiery Columbanus'[1] he had more affinity, at least in his youth. Such symbols of non-conformity as Bricriu, the mocker of the Ulster Cycle, and Conan the Bald, who plays the same role in the Finn Cycle, seem to have remained unknown to him—at least I cannot trace any allusions to them in his books. Though he was so much more in the true bardic tradition than many minor figures of the Anglo-Irish Literary Revival, I doubt whether he ever became fully aware of this fact. I have no evidence that he knew *The Vision of Mac Conglinne*, for instance. Most of his knowledge of the Gaelic past seems to come from secondary sources, often of the most unscholarly kind. This was partly deliberate policy, of course; Earwicker's dream had to contain the sort of history that is made up half of folklore, half of inaccurate recollections of elementary-school history lessons. *Finnegans Wake* is in part a parody of text-book history, not unlike Sellar and Yeatman's *1066 and All That*.[2]

What remained of Joyce's reference library after his death was pathetically inadequate. Several of its Irish items were compiled for secondary or even primary schools: Dinneen's

---

[1] *Ulysses*, p. 46.
[2] Walter Carruthers Sellar and Robert Julian Yeatman, *1066 and All That* (London, 1930).

Smaller Irish-English Dictionary; Fournier D'Albe's *English-Irish Dictionary and Phrase-Book;* P. W. Joyce's *Illustrated History of Ireland.* There is nothing that could be termed a first-hand source.[1]

Is it possible for a writer to work in a tradition without being fully aware of it? I believe that it is, and I have tried to prove that Joyce was such a writer. However poor his Irish library and his Gaelic scholarship may have been, they were sufficient for the purposes of one who was, like so many of his countrymen before and after him, a 'bawd of parodies'.[2]

---

[1] *James Joyce, sa vie, son œuvre, son rayonnement,* Nos. 366, 376, 391.
[2] *Finnegans Wake,* p. 296.

9

The Archaism of Anglo-Irish
Comic Literature

Continuity and its limitations

LOOKING back over the preceding chapters to review the
evidence for the continuity of the Irish comic tradition,
I have become increasingly aware that my problem is
not too little continuity but too much. Artistically speaking,
the weakness of more than one of the chapters is that they show
little or no development—because their subject matter shows
little or none. In the chapter on fantastic humour, for instance,
we find the same motifs persisting after more than a thousand
years, though it is perhaps true that they are now treated
symbolically more often than literally. The chapters on satire
show more development, but it is destined to prove abortive:
on the one hand, attempts to escape from the prison of the
lampoon into broader fields of satire have had little permanent
effect upon Gaelic literature, while Anglo-Irish satire is con-
strained to avoid lampoon only through fear of the law of
libel; on the other hand, the new element of sustained irony
introduced by Swift soon atrophied, so that recent Anglo-Irish
satire has turned back to the devices of fantastic humour.
Similarly, although Beckett finds new possibilities in macabre
and grotesque humour through his emphasis on impotence and
apathy rather than potency and ferocity, Joyce's wit and even
his word play often seem inferior in subtlety to those of the
poets of *Dánta Grádha*. As for parody, that late-developing,
sophisticated genre early reaches a peak in the *Vision of Mac
Conglinne* that is later equalled but never surpassed, by Joyce or
any other writer.

In other words, the virtues of archaism are counterbalanced
by grave defects: by imitating the archaism and conservatism
of Gaelic literature, Anglo-Irish comic writers have imposed

serious limitations on their work's originality and capacity for growth. Ironically, world critical opinion has admired twentieth-century Irish writing specifically for its freshness, unaware that this quality was derived in large part from the imitation of literary sources unfamiliar to the world at large. Anglo-Irish writers had fallen deliberately so far behind the times that when the wheel of fashion turned they suddenly found themselves ahead. Sooner or later, however, each new enthusiast for the novelty of Anglo-Irish literature, tragic or comic, exhausts the repertoire and finds the same old motifs and devices repeating themselves. At last he learns that Irish writers, instead of being magically exempt from the conventions and repetitiousness which beset writers of other nations, are if anything more than usually subject to these limitations because of working in an old-established and homogeneous tradition.

On the other hand, one must in all fairness recognize the originality of Beckett and Swift, whose continuity with the Gaelic tradition I have been at great pains to demonstrate. In neither case was this continuity the result of conscious imitation, except for the few hints Swift may have borrowed for *Gulliver's Travels*, already discussed in Chapter 2.

A sceptical reader might well ask how a writer can show continuity with a tradition of whose very existence he is hardly aware, or imitate models which he has never seen. My answer would run as follows: the oral culture of any area is far richer and more complex than its literary culture, especially where two languages and two cultures interact, as they do in Ireland; many unrecognized elements remain in suspension in such an oral culture, waiting for the right temperament to act as a reagent and cause them to precipitate; when these elements are precipitated in literature, we are amazed, yet they were present in the culture all along and may have revealed themselves several times before under favourable conditions. This explanation has the merit of attributing cultural phenomena to cultural causes, though we do not as yet understand the laws of this literary chemistry. Any rival explanation, it seems to me, is vitiated by having to dismiss as irrelevant the fact that Beckett and Swift were born, reared, and educated in Ireland. To take this attitude is to reject all the findings of contemporary psychology, anthropology, and sociology, which stress early environment as tremendously important to and in many cases determinative of later development.

The originality of Synge, O'Casey, and O'Connor

Happily, an awareness of the Gaelic tradition, which Beckett and Swift lacked, does not inevitably destroy a writer's originality. Synge I have barely mentioned so far because, in spite of his knowledge of Gaelic, he stands almost entirely outside the Gaelic literary tradition. All his four comedies are, in a sense, satires upon rural Ireland, but by comparing these with *The Parliament of Clan Thomas* and its progeny we can easily see where the novelty lies in Synge's work. Unlike the class-conscious Gaelic poets and satirists, Synge sympathizes with the underdog and the outcast, be he tramp or tinker, parricide or blind beggar. It is the respectable citizen who is exposed to ridicule in what William Empson would call the 'mock-pastoral' genre represented by *In the Shadow of the Glen*, *The Tinker's Wedding*, *The Playboy of the Western World*, and *The Well of the Saints*. As Albert Cook has so brilliantly demonstrated in *The Dark Voyage and the Golden Mean*, most comic writing, the world over, takes the opposite position, siding with 'normal' people and established society against the neurotic, the criminal, and the social outcast. As long as Gaelic society remained intact, the professional poets were at the centre of it and upheld its norms in their satire; only after Gaelic society has collapsed and new social norms have been imposed by the English invaders do we find an occasional writer like *An Mangaire Súgach* adopting the role of the *poète maudit*, and even then he does not speak for outcasts as a group but only as a special pleader for himself. At the end of each of Synge's comedies, however, although the solid citizens are left in command of the stage, our hearts go with the outcasts. In his greatest comedy, *The Playboy*, the triumph of the outcasts is stressed with peculiar care: first of all old Mahon says, '. . . my son and myself will be going our own way, and we'll have great times from this out telling stories of the villainy of Mayo, and the fools is here'; then his son Christy, the Playboy, crows, 'I'll go romancing through a romping lifetime from this hour to the dawning of the judgement day'; finally, after the Mahons have departed, the respectable Pegeen bursts out in a wail of 'Oh my grief, I've lost him surely. I've lost the only Playboy of the Western World.' Yeats's victorious tramp in *The Pot of Broth* gave the first hint, but it was Synge's four comedies which definitively added a new genre to Anglo-Irish literature.

O'Casey, at least in his early plays, is fully as original as Synge—and partly for the same reason, in that he sides with the underdog. A further novelty is the fact that this underdog has to cope with a modern urban society, not an archaic rural one. O'Casey's slum dwellers are involved with political, social, and economic forces which they do not understand and from which, even if they did understand them, they could extract no profit. In *The Shadow of a Gunman*, *Juno and the Paycock*, and *The Plough and the Stars* the audience's indignation and some of its laughter are directed against society, but O'Casey knows the common man too intimately to idealize him, so that we laugh *at* as well as *with* his outcasts. 'Captain' Boyle in *Juno and the Paycock* is an uproariously comic character precisely because of his faults and his blithe unconsciousness of them—the closest approximation to Falstaff in contemporary literature—though O'Casey takes great care not to let him forfeit our sympathy entirely: it is comic that the old reprobate should be righteously indignant about his unmarried daughter's pregnancy; however, a scene in which father and daughter actually confronted one another would make Boyle's hypocrisy intolerable, so the playwright avoids it. There is hardly a character in the three early plays for whom O'Casey feels either unalloyed admiration or single-minded contempt—the two commonest attitudes in Gaelic poetry. Even the admirable Juno appears ridiculous once or twice because of her ignorance. O'Casey's decline as a comic dramatist dates from the period when he ceases to have a divided mind about most of his characters. Compare, for instance, two *personae* of O'Casey himself: the poltroon-poet Donal Davoren in *The Shadow of a Gunman* and the All-Irish boy Ayamon in *Red Roses for Me*, a much later play.

Frank O'Connor, much of whose humour is conventional enough, has produced a small group of short stories which form a unique comic subspecies, somewhat akin to those genres or sub-genres created by Synge and O'Casey. In these tales, abstractions like law and religion, sin and crime are opposed to the concrete behaviour of country people, who act and judge in accordance with tribal, familial, or personal values rather than those of the impersonal church or state. Typical is 'The Majesty of the Law', in which a police sergeant appears to be paying a social call; actually he has a warrant for the committal to prison of the old man he is visiting, a fact which he mentions as a seeming afterthought; it is quite clear that neither policeman nor 'criminal' feels that the assault committed by the old man was in any sense a crime. Furthermore, the old man is going to jail, instead of paying a fine, solely to humiliate his accuser:

'. . . I'll punish him. I'll lie on bare boards for him. I'll suffer for him, sergeant, so that neither he nor any of his children after him will be able to raise their heads for the shame of it.'

Thus the ends of impersonal modern justice are frustrated by an older code, which reverses the roles of punisher and punished. Again, part of the comic effect of this story depends on our sympathizing with the supposed underdog. While O'Connor is not working in an archaic mode here, he is, like Synge, exploiting the attitudes of an archaic society. The old man's method of reprisal is reminiscent of the Early Irish custom of fasting against someone who has done one an injustice. If archaism unmistakably lurks beneath the surface in Synge and O'Connor, we may perhaps detect it in O'Casey too as his underdogs try to maintain older, simpler values against the modern world.

The vigour of Anglo-Irish literature

For all the limitations which it imposes, archaism must be acknowledged as chiefly responsible for the vigour not only of Anglo-Irish comic literature but of Anglo-Irish literature as a whole. Whereas the writers of other Western countries have lately striven to re-establish contact with primitive modes of thought and feeling through the study of mythology, anthropology, and psychoanalysis, the Anglo-Irish writer has the past always at his elbow—in cold storage, so to speak—preserved in the Gaelic language and literature, in bilingual folklore, in Gaelic modes of thought and feeling and speech which have become part of the rural Anglo-Irish dialects.

Colleagues and students frequently ask me, in jest or in earnest, why the greatest figures in twentieth-century 'English' literature are Irishmen, meaning usually Joyce and Yeats. I can suggest at least four reasons to those who are in earnest. Their Irish background gave (or at any rate offered) Joyce and Yeats these four priceless gifts: contact with a living folklore and thus with myth; contact with a living folk speech; a traditional sense of the professional, almost sacred prestige of poetry and learning; a traditional sense of the supreme importance of technique to a writer, coupled with the realization that technique must be learnt, by imitation, study, and practice.

These four gifts correspond to a fourfold division which can be made in the body of this book: humour springs from folklore, magic, and myth; wit and word play permeate folk speech; satire is inseparable from the traditional prestige of the poet; while parody grows naturally out of the Gaelic poet's obsession with technique.

It is easy to see the importance of this fourfold influence for Yeats, since he consciously and articulately set out to obtain at least three of the four gifts from his Irish heritage; I don't think he ever knew enough Gaelic to realize fully what technicians the Gaelic poets were, but Irish folklore, Irish folk speech, and the exalted status of the poet in Gaelic society were three of his constant preoccupations.

The case of Joyce is more interesting than that of Yeats because the younger man virtually began his literary career by denouncing the Yeatsian ideals of the Irish Literary Revival in his polemic 'The Day of the Rabblement'. Protesting that 'it is strange to see the artist making terms with the rabblement' by writing folk plays, he went on to characterize the Irish as 'the most belated race in Europe':

A nation which never advanced so far as a miracle-play affords no literary model to the artist, and he must look abroad.

He failed to see then that being 'belated' might prove an asset to the Irish writer. A preoccupation with technique and a sense of the prestige of the poet were already his, but he probably attributed these to his reading of the *Symbolistes* and of Ibsen rather than to his knowledge of Mangan's translations from the Gaelic poets.

Nevertheless, as *Dubliners* and later works were to reveal, Joyce had a source of folk speech at hand in his own family.

His father, John Stanislaus Joyce, had been brought up in the small city of Cork, where the open countryside was within walking distance in any direction; John Joyce possessed 'the gift of the gab' and his speech was larded with vivid phrases, often ultimately Gaelic in origin. After his father's death, Joyce said in a letter:

> Hundreds of pages and scores of characters in my books came from him. His dry (or rather wet) wit . . . convulsed me often with laughter.

Richard Ellmann's biography of Joyce, which identifies a number of characters modelled on the father, enables us to discover many of those hundreds of pages and to form from them a vivid picture of the old rascal's speech. When he learned that James's mistress was named Barnacle, he remarked with characteristic punning wit, 'She'll never leave him.'

Nora Barnacle herself, with her Galway speech, was another important oral source for Joyce, particularly when he was creating the monologues of Molly Bloom and Anna Livia Plurabelle. But long before that stage Joyce had quoted her in a letter to his brother Stanislaus as his authority for rural Anglo-Irish speech:

> . . . no old toothless Irishman would say 'Divil an elephant,' he would say 'Divil elephant.' Nora says 'Divil up I'll get till you come back.'

Though some of Joyce's characters are country-bred, the speech of even his most typically Dublin characters reveals a rich substratum of rural usage: from the pages of *Ulysses* alone one could compile a list of Gaelicisms which would perhaps outnumber those in the entire works of Yeats.

To Irish myth Joyce came last, but in *Finnegans Wake* he made ample use of the Finn Cycle in particular, besides referring to a number of figures in the other cycles, as Adaline Glasheen's *A Census of Finnegans Wake* conveniently documents. The trickster god Manannán, whom one would naturally expect to find, has been overlooked by Mrs. Glasheen, but he is referred to in the word 'moananoaning', which describes the sound of the sea at the end of the *Wake*. Obviously the individual references are less important than the new, almost Yeatsian, attitude to Irish myth and folklore which is implicit throughout

Joyce's last book. Like the myths and folklore of other peoples, they were used by Joyce as keys to dreams and to prehistory because they preserved the mental processes of primitive levels of consciousness and primitive eras of culture; but because the dream of human history which is *Finnegans Wake* was dreamed in Ireland, Irish keys possessed a peculiar value for Joyce. Having deliberately rejected archaism in his youth, he just as deliberately adopted it in his maturity. The consequent upsurge of the play-spirit took all history, philosophy, and religion for its playground.

Many other writers of the Irish Literary Revival sought one or more of the four gifts as deliberately as Yeats had; in particular, several Anglo-Irish poets of a post-Yeatsian generation—Austin Clarke, F. R. Higgins, and Robert Farren among them—became so fascinated with Gaelic poetic technique as to be in danger of sacrificing all the other characteristics of poetry to their cult of a rigid metric. From its beginnings the Literary Revival was a consciously archaistic movement, as any cultural 'revival' must be to justify its name, but we have already seen that some archaic tendencies were present in Anglo-Irish literature from the time of Swift. In the last analysis these tendencies always constituted a source of strength.

The scope of the play-spirit

As I have already suggested in my opening chapter, the archaic nature of Irish life as well as of Irish literature fostered Johan Huizinga's play-spirit in a way that a more modern civilization could not have done. This fact was of tremendous value to a number of Anglo-Irishmen who had no patience with self-conscious archaism but, on the contrary, hastened to modernize, or at least Anglicize, themselves as quickly as possible. The secret of Anglo-Irish success in stage comedy, particularly comedy of manners, lay with the play-spirit: young men who had grown up in Ireland could not take the English fashionable world entirely seriously; viewing it as a game, they so presented it upon the stage. Wilde carried this tendency to its farthest limit in the pure playfulness of *The Importance of Being Earnest*, while at the same time treating all preconceived ideas of the nature of drama as his playthings—a feat duplicated by another Anglo-Irishman, Samuel Beckett, in *Waiting for Godot*. Some have wondered whether Sterne's few Irish years had any bearing upon his similar treatment of preconceived notions about the novel in *Tristram Shandy*. As for Berkeley, whose epoch-making books had been written before he ever set foot outside Ireland, it is impossible not to feel that he approached philosophy as if it were a game, doing to it what Wilde did to the drama and Sterne to the novel.

No writer has more consistently exemplified the play-spirit throughout a long lifetime's work than the Anglo-Irish Bernard Shaw. Some critics insist that he ruined a potential masterpiece of tragedy, *Saint Joan*, by the playful 'Epilogue' which he appended to it; I cannot agree, for I think it gives his drama a new perspective. Shaw always insisted that play could be serious and warned his critics against confusing seriousness with solemnity; 'every jest', he wrote, 'is an earnest in the womb of time'. In so far as his play-spirit manifested itself in anti-climax, he was aware of its Irish origin, attributing it to his father's example in various anecdotes, of which the following, from *Sixteen Self Sketches*, is the best:

When I was a child, he [Shaw's father] gave me my first dip in the sea in Killiney Bay. He prefaced it by a very serious exhortation on the importance of learning to swim, culminating in these words 'When I was a boy of only fourteen, my knowledge of swimming enabled me to save your Uncle Robert's life.' Then, seeing that I was deeply impressed, he stooped, and added confidentially in my ear 'and, to tell you the truth, I was never so sorry for anything in my life afterwards.' He then plunged into the ocean, enjoyed a thoroughly refreshing swim, and chuckled all the way home.

The same kind of destructive anticlimax gives point to innumerable scenes in Shaw's plays. A talent for it in the preceding generation can hardly have been peculiar to Shaw's undistinguished father, since the classic example of this trait in Irish history dates back to the fifteenth century. When Henry VII accused Garret More Fitzgerald, the Great Earl of Kildare, of burning the cathedral of Cashel, 'By Jesus,' replied the earl, 'I would never have done it but I thought the Bishop was in it!' A regard for law and morality, for his own prestige, or even for his life itself could not prevent the great Anglo-Norman noble, patron of Gaelic poets, from having his subversive joke. Luckily Henry VII admired his insouciance: when the indignant Bishop of Meath said, 'All Ireland cannot rule this man', the king answered, 'Then he shall rule all Ireland.' Though the earl might perhaps be reckoned an Anglo-Irishman, this talent for ridicule and anticlimax belongs to Irishmen of every heritage without distinction. To be certain of this, we need only recall that Gaelic literature revels in exposing to ridicule its greatest heroes: not merely the pagans Finn and Cuchulain, but the Blessed Saint Patrick himself.

Conclusion

I believe I can fairly claim that this book has accomplished its purpose: it has demonstrated that there *is* an Irish comic tradition, one which can be traced from the very beginnings of Gaelic literature and be shown to flourish in the Anglo-Irish literature of our own day. I would go even farther and say that contemporary Anglo-Irish literature cannot be fully understood and appreciated without some knowledge of that tradition. If the reader of this book does not find that his appreciation of Joyce and Beckett, Yeats and Synge, Shaw and O'Casey has been enriched and his understanding of them deepened, then I have failed in part of my self-imposed task.

But I hope I have accomplished something more, something that was no part of my conscious intention when I embarked upon this book, something that has significance not only for Irish literature but for world literature as a whole. In this Age of Anthropology, where the ideas of Vico have come into their own, so that it is impossible to discuss almost any subject without introducing the notions of magic, ritual, and myth, everything which touches on the archaic and the primitive has become invested with an aura of solemnity. The modern Western intellectual, who has usually cut himself off from the myths and rituals of Judaism and Christianity, whence our Western culture has drawn and continues to draw so much of its symbolism, is smitten with superstitious awe at the slightest hint of an earlier, more primitive symbolism. Taking *The Golden Bough* for his Bible, he prostrates himself before fertility symbols wherever they may be found—and he finds them everywhere. All that is primitive or archaic, he believes, can grant him that contact with the great elemental forces which he so poignantly feels that he has lost through the spread of urban industrial civilization.

And all these great elemental forces are to him so solemn, so serious: its origin in phallic ritual does not make Greek comedy funnier or more obscene but rather sacred, earnest, *respectable*. The macabre humour and comedy of manners, the parody and dialect mimicry to be found in Eliot's *The Waste Land* are ignored in favour of the underlying fertility myth. Joyce's propensity to treat sex as a joke has led many readers either to consider D. H. Lawrence a greater artist or to ignore Joyce's humour and obscenity in order to claim for him too the role of a Laurentian prophet.

Think for a moment about the title of this book: did it not at first strike you as a contradiction in terms? The word 'tradition' has gathered round it so many solemn connotations that it seems blasphemous to apply the epithet 'comic' to it. The tragic tradition, the epic tradition, the lyric tradition, these concepts we can easily understand, but the *comic* tradition . . . ?

I have referred to Johan Huizinga a number of times in the course of this book because his *Homo Ludens* seems the one dissenting voice in a solemn chorus. Even in myth and ritual he sees the play element at work—though he reminds us that play can be serious. To him, the savage is not entirely a Rousseauist but views his own rituals with a half-scepticism that is sometimes Voltairian. I had been working on this book for years before I read *Homo Ludens*, so that Huizinga nourished views I already held rather than implanting them in me. Huizinga proves to my satisfaction that all literature, tragedy included, shows the operation of the play-spirit, but it is obviously much easier to see this spirit at work in comedy.

To say that the Anglo-Irish Literary Revival was an archaistic and primitivistic movement is the tritest of literary judgements. The point has been made over and over again by the revivalists themselves. No critic or historian can discuss the Revival without mentioning the tragic power, the mysticism, the sense of elemental forces, the simplicity, the beauty, the dignity conferred on Anglo-Irish literature by this movement toward the primitive and the archaic. Equally, nobody has been able to explain why the first undeniable masterpiece produced by the Revival, *The Playboy of the Western World*, should negate most of the literary virtues I have just enumerated. The obvious answer is that a sincere, unprejudiced approach to the primitive and the archaic discovered in them other characteristics besides those comprehended in Rousseau's picture of the Noble Savage. On the whole, as we look back, it is the comic and satiric aspect of the Revival that has worn best—in the drama, in the novel and short story, even in poetry. To say this is, from my point of view, not to deny the archaism of the Literary Revival but to proclaim it.

In world literature we may everywhere expect to find a similar state of affairs. In some literatures the comic tradition may not be so long or so continuous as it is in Irish literature, but we can be sure that a folk tradition of humour, wit, and satire stretches back far beyond the commencement of any given literary tradition. Likewise, any archaizing movement is apt to beget a comic revival; if it fails to do so, the genuineness of its search for the archaic should fall under suspicion. The prevalence of grotesque and macabre humour in modern art and literature is an index of the sincerity of twentieth-century primitivism.

The Irish comic tradition, then, is not something peripheral, not an interesting bypath for the literary dilettante. On the contrary, one may even claim its right to be considered the central tradition of Irish literature. In other literatures whose archaism is not so pronounced, the centrality of the comic tradition may be more open to dispute, but even there the comic heritage cannot be dismissed as insignificant. In an era which tends to value the Dionysian more than the Apollonian, it is worth remembering that Greek comedy as well as Greek tragedy is associated with the ritual of Dionysus. As Freud well knew, the Id manifests itself in comic as well as tragic modes. Myth, ritual, the unconscious, all our modern sacred cows, can be detected and studied in the comic if we trouble to look for them. Even the gods are comic; if 'they kill us for their sport', we, like Homer, can win a sort of victory by laughing at them in our turn. As I have said before, no aspect of life is too sacred to escape the mockery of Irish laughter. By the fullest exercise of this great human gift the Irish have remained true to one of the deepest impulses of all mankind.

Index

The numerals indicating pages which contain bibliographical information (usually in the footnotes) are printed in bold-face type.